M000207113

PRAISE FOR
THE CORPORATENEUR PLAN

A brilliant masterpiece—a seminal piece of work. Rohl and Danziger provide a clear, step-by-step path to entrepreneurial success. It's specially designed for midcareer professionals who, for reasons laid out in the book, desire to create and run their own business. Appropriately named "Corporateneurs," they start their new journey with knowledge already learned, but need to fill the gaps to launch a new business. And, for the increasing number of young people, eager to create their own dream career, this book is a must-read as well. If a "how to" book could be a page-turner, this is it.

—ROBIN LEWIS

CEO of The Robin Report, professor at the Graduate School of Professional Studies at the Fashion Institute of Technology, and co-author of The New Rules of Retail

Don't miss *The Corporateneur Plan*. It's your opportunity to at once gain clarity and hold the road map to your next professional journey into entrepreneurship. Combining powerful stories, important research, and handy anecdotes, this book will help you achieve new clarity in starting a business. But there's more: authors Rohl and Danziger also deliver the tools and rules you'll need if/when you leave the corporate mothership and work without a net as a business owner. At first, you'll see *The Corporateneur Plan* as a powerful chronicle of the current disruptive forces impacting both the workplace and marketplace. And then it will become a personal GPS to the address of your new professional quest.

—JIM BLASINGAME

"The Small Business Advocate" and award-winning Main Street thought-leader, columnist, futurist, and author of The 3rd Ingredient *and* The Age of the Customer

The Corporateneur Plan is a personally curated list of research, books, and tools for entrepreneurs. I became an entrepreneur after twenty years with Starbucks and five years as CEO of Lululemon, and I found a lot of kinship with the values, discipline, structure, and tools laid out in *The Corporateneur Plan*. The benefit of being a "Corporateneur" is that we set out to fulfill a mission with the skills to build a strong business model and organization. The danger is not managing risks and only focusing on growth or the purpose of the product, not how it relates to business models and customers. Ken's lessons provide a clear warning to those ex-corporate leaders who may over-hire, sign up expensive consultants and contracts, and overload their SG&A because that is how they are used to working. It takes a lot of grit and humility to go back to doing whatever is needed, including having no assistants, traveling economy, and doing spreadsheets and books one minute and then presentations to raise capital the next. You have to earn your staff and perks as you grow revenue. This book will set you on the right path.

—CHRISTINE DAY

Founding partner of the House of LR&C with Russell and Ciara Wilson

THE
CORPORATENEUR
PLAN

THE
CORPORATENEUR
PLAN

YOUR ROADMAP FROM
MIDCAREER PROFESSIONAL
TO **ENTREPRENEUR**

KEN ROHL & PAMELA N. DANZIGER
WITH GREG ROHL

 *Advantage* | Books

Copyright © 2023 by Ken Rohl, Pamela N. Danziger, and Greg Rohl.

All rights reserved. No part of this book may be used or reproduced in any manner whatsoever without prior written consent of the author, except as provided by the United States of America copyright law.

Published by Advantage Books, Charleston, South Carolina.
An imprint of Advantage Media.

ADVANTAGE is a registered trademark, and the Advantage colophon is a trademark of Advantage Media Group, Inc.

Printed in the United States of America.

10 9 8 7 6 5 4 3 2 1

ISBN: 978-1-64225-835-6 (Paperback)
ISBN: 978-1-64225-834-9 (eBook)

LCCN: 2023905110

Cover design by Matthew Morse.
Layout design by Analisa Smith.

This publication is designed to provide accurate and authoritative information in regard to the subject matter covered. It is sold with the understanding that the publisher is not engaged in rendering legal, accounting, or other professional services. If legal advice or other expert assistance is required, the services of a competent professional person should be sought.

Advantage Books is an imprint of Advantage Media Group. Advantage Media helps busy entrepreneurs, CEOs, and leaders write and publish a book to grow their business and become the authority in their field. Advantage authors comprise an exclusive community of industry professionals, idea-makers, and thought leaders. For more information go to **advantagemedia.com**.

CONTENTS

KEN'S ACKNOWLEDGMENTS

This book was inspired by my son Greg Rohl, who in 2020 trademarked his consulting company "The Rohl Model." I complimented him on the play of our family name representing the "rules of the road" that we followed as we evolved our entrepreneurial adventure. He explained that the business's value proposition was rooted in the forty years of proven processes my lifetime of learning, teaching, leading, and building relationships with employees, customers, suppliers, and the myriad of associations that, combined, contributed to my successes. Ergo, why don't you chronicle your business life story? Sixty-four handwritten pages later we had the nexus of something that we felt may be a help to others who, like me, were stepping out of a corporate career to start a business of their own.

Greg then reached out to Pam Danziger, a recognized expert of luxury, an established business writer, and a book author, who had collaborated with our company on an influencer program years earlier. She reviewed our "research" (some 40,000 words of recollections, transcribed interviews, essays, and presentation notes), listened to our vision, and ultimately agreed to partner with us. So began an eighteen-month collaboration, Pam's research perspective creating context for my remembrances of upbringing, corporate evolution, and finally the launching of an entrepreneurial venture. I am truly grateful for the experience, skill, creativity and commitment she has invested in this endeavor.

Having acknowledged thanks to the co-authors of this narrative, there are so many others without whom this book would not have been possible.

To my parents Bernice & Louis Rohl, I can only say your steadfast emphasis on the "Golden Rule" was a sacred foundation without which nothing else would have been possible. A grateful and respectful salute to Sandy Kuhl Rohl, who for twenty-five years partnered, supported and sacrificed as we grew our family in a corporate world of multiple cities, homes, social and cultural challenges. And to my sister, Nancy, and her husband, Edward Napoleon, whose personal and professional lives so often mirrored ours through the years. Their support and council has been invaluable.

1983 marked the end of that corporate life, and the beginning of an entrepreneurial adventure, with all the attendant risks and rewards for myself and a small startup crew consisting of wife Amber-Helene, her daughter Valinda, and my son Lou, headquartered in the second bedroom of our house in Irvine, California.

Amber was a constant source of inspiration, moral support and unselfish dedication to my dream. I am forever grateful for her partnering at trade show events, on European customer incentive trips, and most importantly her sense of luxury and how to present it to the architectural and interior design communities.

My incredibly talented sons Mark, Lou, and Greg performed their executive responsibilities with dedication and professionalism as we scaled the Corporateneur process. No amount of thanks can adequately measure their contribution to our success.

And throughout the years, our company had the great fortune to employ hundreds of amazing people. I am so thankful to each of them for bringing their spirit, talents, and hard work to our business. I particularly want to acknowledge individuals who I call "the changemakers." Employees, Sales Representatives, Consultants, Suppliers, and Customers who were instrumental in helping our company evolve and grow, some through yeomanlike dedication, others by challenging my thinking at critical moments, and some who stepped out of a transactional relationship into something more like family. Tom Duino, Al Rykus, Stan & Paula Gaskins, Paul Satkin, Sherry Qualls, Jake Smith, Skip Johnson, Richard Beddome, Ezio Albertoni, Wolfgang Wolk, Bertrand LeJemtel, Jonas Weiner, Hank Darlington, and Sam Rose – hail to you all for your wonderful combination of emotional and professional talents that made all the difference through each chapter of our story.

A final thumbs up to the angels that guided me through the canyons of corporate America, the team members who partnered in my career successes, the mentors who provided the platform for me to "teach what I had to learn," and the world of customers, designers, consumers, manufacturers, Southern California friends, UCI influences, and Barclay Theater artists that help me shape relevancy in this life.

PAM'S ACKNOWLEDGMENTS

My greatest thanks go to Ken and Greg Rohl, who gave me the honor to tell Ken's story and, through the process, taught me much about business, management, and leadership.

I also thank the entire Advantage Books team, who made the publication of this book a breeze, and most especially the editorial staff, who gave us what every author craves: confidence that they have a worthy story to tell and that they told it well.

And final thanks go to my husband Greg, who boosted me when my energy and brain span languished.

—PAM DANZIGER

Founder, Unity Marketing

Principal, The American Marketing Group

Senior Contributor, Forbes.com

GREG'S ACKNOWLEDGMENTS

T hank you to my father Ken for the lifetime of wisdom and opportunity and for allowing me to "executive produce" this project; Pam Danziger for her dedication and skills as a writer and researcher; the Advantage Publishing team for bringing our vision into reality; my wife Mishel for her love and encouragement; and every person I have had the good fortune to work with and learn from along the way.

STARTING PLAN

BY KEN ROHL

For years I traveled on behalf of enterprise
A loyal recruit of the corporate world.
My calendar was marked by meetings and deadlines
and on occasion, a brief respite all too short,
for some sort of break with family and friends.
Then like so many, the gnawing began at first, just
an uneasiness of purpose,
Later it became defined.
There must be more…there must be time.
There must be ways to live each day with some
measurement other than ratios, market shares and bottom lines.

Today I sit by the ocean and reflect.
No planes to catch, no meetings to chair.
No care-taking of third generation business fortunes.

Now, let's make sure these new pursuits bring an essence to life
beyond just changes, or some new master of my fate.

INTRODUCTION

"I have only newspaper accounts of the Air Balloons, to which I do not know what credence to give; as the tales related of them are marvelous, and lead us to expect that, in a little time, [people] will come flying thro' the air, instead of ploughing the ocean to get to America."

—GEORGE WASHINGTON, 1784

F rom its beginning, the United States of America has been a country of dreamers, people escaping the tyranny of kings and rigid hierarchical social structures to forge a better life free of those constraints. It's the definition of the American Dream: "The ideal that every citizen of the United States should have an equal opportunity to achieve success and prosperity through hard work, determination, and initiative," as defined by the *Oxford English Dictionary*.

The dreams that drove the first settlers and every newcomer since to these shores are much the same as those that drive people to start their own businesses. Not surprisingly, entrepreneurship is part of our shared cultural DNA. When asked "What makes America great?" economics professor Lee Ohanian answered in one word: "Entrepreneurship."

Assuming that's true, then America is headed for even greater greatness in the years ahead. In 2021 more than five million new companies were formed, following a record 4.4 million start-ups in 2020. To put those numbers in perspective, consider that an average of 2.9 million new business applications were filed each year from 2010 to 2019. And during only the first six months of 2022, the number of new business start-ups has nearly reached the past decade's yearly average, with more than 2.5 million applications filed, according to census data.

And signs are that the number of new entrepreneurial enterprises is not going to slow but grow in 2022. That's because of what's been called the "Great Resignation." Employees are quitting their jobs in unprecedented numbers since the COVID-19 pandemic. Many of them are joining the ranks of the new American entrepreneurial dreamers, as the *Wall Street Journal* reported, "Workers quit jobs in droves to become their own bosses." They are discovering their "inner entrepreneur" as they seek more flexibility and an "escape from corporate bureaucracy."

Ian Cook, vice president of people analytics at Visier, writing in *Harvard Business Review*, reported the most significant increase in corporate resignations is among midcareer professionals between thirty and forty-five years old. Their numbers rose by 20 percent from 2020 to 2021. Resignations were also elevated among those aged forty-five to sixty years but not as much as the thirty- to forty-five-year-olds.

Emboldened by low unemployment and the plethora of help-wanted notices, some midcareer professionals are walking off one job right into another. But others are choosing a different path. Some are going solo and joining the gig economy—nearly 9.5 million

Americans are self-employed unincorporated workers, the highest since 2008.

Others, like the record number of new businesses registered in 2021 show, have a vision to start a real business.

"TAKE THIS JOB AND SHOVE IT!"

The disruption caused by the pandemic can't take all the credit for the current entrepreneurial boom, but it certainly paved the way. Quarantined at home, we all had more time to reflect on our life goals and ambitions. Many have found their current careers and employers wanting.

Further, forced to work from home while corporate offices were closed, midcareer professionals discovered they liked the flexibility. They could accomplish more in less time without all the office distractions. And since time is money, not having to spend time commuting to the office was an even bigger plus.

Some enterprising folks put those found hours into gig work using services like Upwork to take on freelance assignments. And success there can become a professional's springboard out of the corporation into self-employment.

Upwork reports some 20 percent of people working remotely during the pandemic planned to leave their full-time jobs for freelancing. And a survey by Digital.com found 32 percent of Americans are quitting their jobs to start a business.

LEAVING THE CORPORATION BEHIND

It's not without risks to leave corporate careers behind and leap into entrepreneurship, but for an increasing number, the rewards are worth it. People pursuing entrepreneurship want:

- More control, greater autonomy. Being your own boss—in control of one's work and time—is a compelling motivation to pursue an entrepreneurial journey. While an entrepreneur still has people to answer to—whether clients, customers, or investors—self-employment is a way to get out from under a boss's thumb and do your own thing. Being your own boss gives you more control over who you work for and with, what you do, and when you do it.

- More meaning. Everyone wants their life to mean something, and since the typical American adult spends more time working than doing anything else besides sleeping, their work must be meaningful too. Writing in *MIT Sloan Management Review*, professor Catherine Baily and senior lecturer Adrian Madden define meaningful work as "when an individual perceives an authentic connection between work and a broader transcendent life purpose beyond the self." Research has shown that the meaning behind the work is more motivating than any other aspect of work, including pay and rewards, opportunities for promotion, or working conditions. For each individual, their meaning is different, but for the entrepreneur, it usually is found by matching one's interests, innate capabilities, and talents to one's passions to create something that others need and will pay for.

- Pursuing purpose. Meaning and purpose are closely intertwined; however, meaning is deeply personal and inwardly focused.

Purpose is how one's personal meaning is expressed outward into society. Purpose is about making a difference in the world. Finding purpose may make some individuals give up high-paying corporate jobs to pursue work in the nonprofit sector. For others, it motivates them to build a purposeful business. A McKinsey study found that the uncertainties caused by the pandemic have turned people's attention toward more purposeful work. And those who find it are better for it, with those who say they are "living their purpose" at work reporting five times greater levels of well-being compared with those who are not.

- Grow wealth. Achieving greater financial means and the social status that goes with it is another motivator to start a business, though it is probably the weakest reason to do so. The statistics don't favor start-up businesses. Some 20 percent don't make it into their second year, yet few people get wealthy working for someone else. And if you build a successful business, the business itself becomes a valuable asset. Don't count on becoming as fabulously wealthy as Elon Musk, Jeff Bezos, or Bill Gates, but they all started out where you are today—with a dream of starting a business.

If you feel these factors pulling you to leave your old work life behind and venture out on your own, then this book is for you. *The Corporateneur Plan* will come alongside you with hard-earned wisdom and practical guidance from Ken Rohl.

Ken has been where you've been. After successfully climbing the corporate ladder for the first half of his career, at age fifty, he founded a business in the spare bedroom of his home, grew it to become a globally recognized brand, then thirty-three years later, sold it to a *Fortune* 500 industry leader.

Ken wasn't the first *corporateneur*, nor did he coin the term. CX Series podcast host Terrence Fox gets that credit, defining it as an "executive who combines the business acumen and decision-making abilities of an entrepreneur with the best attributes of a corporate manager." But Ken has lived it, studied it, and taught it, and now he is sharing his insider secrets with you

He will provide the game plan to direct you through the planning phase of a new business, help you manage its growing pains, and power you over the inevitable speed bumps. His insights will equip you with the personal and business tools you'll need to step out on your own and turn your dreams of starting a business into a reality.

MEET KEN ROHL

Let me introduce you to Ken Rohl, a kitchen-and-bath-industry legend, yet not well known outside of it. But if you've remodeled a kitchen or bath in the past thirty years, many of the trends and products you considered—if not selected—were because of, or at least influenced by, Ken's work and the company he built. Take the fireclay farmhouse sink, which is *Fixer Upper* star Joanna Gaines's signature kitchen-design element.

Everything but the Kitchen Sink

"My kitchen—it's the heart of the home for me. I love the farmhouse sink, and I love looking out the window at the animals and cows while I work," says Joanna Gaines.

You'd have to be living under a rock if you don't at least have a passing acquaintance with Joanna Gaines and her distinctive farmhouse-country chic style. Working alongside her husband, Chip, since they married in 2003, they've built a $20 million empire, Magnolia, out of Waco, Texas.

The couple shot to fame in 2013 with their *Fixer Upper* show on HGTV. Using that as their launchpad, their business has grown to include a broadcast network with Discovery (which owns HGTV), real estate, books, restaurants, retail shops, e-commerce websites, and licensing deals with Target and Anthropologie.

This made-for-prime-time couple is a study in yin-yang, brains-and-brawn contrasts. Chip provides comic relief and literally does the heavy lifting. He delights in "demo day" when he takes a sledgehammer to a fixer home to get it ready for Joanna to do the upper part of the show with her transformational design magic.

Kitchens are her particular passion. Invariably, they feature shiplap siding and a signature farmhouse sink, like the one she has in her own home. Its apron-front design was a complete departure from the typical American undermount sink when Rohl introduced the farmhouse sink to the US market in the early 1990s.

Without Joanna's design sensibility and television show, fireclay farmhouse sinks wouldn't be the "thing" that they are today, and without Ken Rohl, she'd probably never have discovered her signature kitchen-design statement.

THE ROHL MODEL FOR CORPORATENEURSHIP

You might say Ken became a "big fish in a small pond," but that is far from the complete picture. With his sixty-five years of experience, including over a quarter century in corporate America working across many different industries, he has honed a business model—what we call the *Rohl Model*—to identify white space in a crowded market and

17

to introduce groundbreaking innovation that others inevitably follow. Effectively, he aims to make a small pond bigger.

On the question of taking market share, he says, "It is much better to grow the pie than to try to make your slice bigger." It's a credo he lives by that has won him acclaim among his peers—he was inducted into the Kitchen and Bath Association Hall of Fame in 2008—and respect from all who have the pleasure to know him.

He grew the pie in the kitchen-and-bath industry by elevating the design, quality, and performance of the *water appliance*—all the products related to water-delivery needs of "the total home," including kitchen, bath, bar, patio, and laundry. He effectively raised the bar for an industry trapped in a commoditized space. He elevated kitchen-and-bath products to a premium, highly differentiated space.

Ken started with what is a now a ubiquitous product—the pullout kitchen faucet. But at the time, it was the harbinger of European innovation entering the US plumbing-and-fixtures market and, along with European cabinetry and appliances, redefined the modern American kitchen. It was a product that his then corporate employer decided not to back. It was deemed too new, too different, and too expensive to compete in the American market. Ken knew differently, and the rest is history.

KEN'S STORY IS UNIQUE

One of the personal qualities that distinguishes Ken among the people who've known and worked with him is his generosity. That is why Ken has undertaken this book—*The Corporateneur Plan*. Its purpose is to help other people caught midcareer feeling unfulfilled, stifled, and underappreciated in their corporate jobs to reboot and gain more personal fulfillment and potentially greater financial rewards.

And since exiting the company he founded, he has devoted himself to mentoring young entrepreneurs in industries as diverse as healthcare, wine, fashion, gifts, home services, and hospitality. So aspiring entrepreneurs who don't want to bother working for a corporation but want an entrepreneurial head start can find valuable insights here too. It will provide the corporate know-how and wisdom from Ken's experience to help them create a sustainable, growing business from the ground up.

Being a good listener is another distinguishing quality of Ken's. He is always willing to listen to new ideas and give his perspective. But he never pontificates or shoots from the hip. Rather, he will search his internal database for similar situations he may have faced and frame his answer in the form of a story. You'll find many of those throughout this book.

Besides being a consummate storyteller—and we all know the power of story in business—Ken is a master of crafting catchphrases to seal his pearls of wisdom into memory. Called "Ken-isms" by those who've worked with him, his ability to turn profound insights into memorable slogans is a skill he picked up along the way, working with advertising agencies and marketing executives. And those Ken-isms—which you will find sprinkled through *The Corporateneur Plan* as "Life Lessons Learned"—will help you turn his insights into action in your future business.

One of his most quoted is "Make a plan. Work the plan." Al Rykus, who worked with Ken for ten years before becoming a corporateneur in his own entrepreneurial venture, explains:

> When I would get ready to do something, one of the things he always said was "Make a Plan. Work the Plan." It was a discipline he learned in corporate America. Everything is about the business and the corporate goals and objectives.

You've got to commit yourself to a plan and then follow it down the path to see the results because something—lots of things—will always come up to sway you to move in another direction. Otherwise, you'll never be able to measure results.

At the same time, Al reflects that American-style corporate discipline can too easily turn into rigidity that can crush an entrepreneurial enterprise: "That's what Ken found stifling in corporate America.

"In corporate America, it's all about the business, and it doesn't account for the personal and emotional element which is critical when running your own company," Al continues. "So when we would 'make a plan' at Rohl, everyone it impacted had to be involved in the decision-making. If we couldn't get the buy-in up front, I saw Ken pull back any number of times and start again. You've got to get the right plan in order for everybody to work the plan. That involves personal relationships."

Making a plan and working the plan is a maxim Ken learned early and has followed not just in his career but in every aspect of his life.

 ## *Ken's Life Lesson Learned* ────

MAKE A PLAN. WORK THE PLAN

I only met Malcolm Forbes once, and we talked about ballooning—a hobby we both shared. I'd admired him for a lifetime. He held values of self-determination and business achievement I shared, and he believed in trying harder to make yourself better. We balloon people are a small but passionate group—there are only about six thousand licensed hot-air balloonists in the country—that share those same values. We are a community of achievers.

I got into ballooning in 1972. My neighbor, a United Airlines pilot, invited me to attend a presentation by Raven Industries. Learning how to master the effects of low-level winds like they have at O'Hare drew him to ballooning, something he felt they don't teach pilots enough about.

I was interested because I thought ballooning might be a nice complement to my sailing hobby. Both are dependent on the vagaries of the wind. It also fit my lifestyle. I could balloon in the early morning and late afternoon and sail late mornings and early afternoons.

So after some very persuasive marketing—and a couple of martinis—he and I became the owners of a $10,000 Raven 55 aluminum-frame gondola and a green-and-white balloon envelope. We christened it La Mere Gran Verte—the Big Green Mama.

Back then, $10,000 was a lot of money, so we decided to start a chapter S corporation and sell shares to commercialize our venture by giving balloon rides and making the balloon available for commercial events. We had a lot of other commercial pilots in our neighborhood, so a couple of them came along for the "ride," but even one neighborhood housewife bought in, thinking it would be fun.

Becoming a hot-air balloon pilot fulfilled my lifelong dream of flying. In college, I was in the Air Force ROTC and had my sights set on a military career flying. But that got sidelined when I learned there were more pilots than planes in the Air Force back then.

We all had to get licensed to fly, which included going into free fall from ten thousand feet, then relighting the propane and safely landing. That maneuver isn't for the faint of heart.

Getting ready for a balloon flight requires a ground crew and chase vehicle ready for action. We'd usually take off from our Tower Lake neighborhood in the early morning when the wind is lighter and more predictable. Besides prepping the gondola and propane tanks and filling the balloon envelope, you must check with the local weather service to estimate your flight path and landing choices.

But that is always speculative because you can only make assumptions about wind shifts. Ultimately you never really know where you're going to land, but you're hoping it will be in a cornfield or open farmland. It's tradition to give the landowner whose property we've invaded a bottle of champagne, and hopefully, but not always, it becomes a joyful celebration with the landowner and our passengers.

Even when you plan your balloon trip as carefully as possible, there are still many things that can crop up that aren't in the plan. You've got to be on alert for all kinds of hazards, like high-tension wires, golf courses, private estates, barbed-wire fences, lakes, and even the occasional bog. You have to account for lift, or lack thereof, from heat coming off the ground. And then the winds may not blow as expected.

One of the last flights I piloted almost turned into a nightmare. I was with one of my partners, who'd had a bad flight recently. Just like when you fall off a horse, we figured you need to get right back on it. So that is what we decided to do together.

Everything looked in order before the flight, but after we took off, the wind changed. Instead of blowing us toward the farmland west of Chicago as planned, we were heading right toward the city and Lake Michigan. I tried to find places to land, but below were only industrial parks, railroad yards, highways, and high-tension electrical towers.

At the last minute, I finally found some land where we could put down before hitting Lake Michigan. After that experience, we decided we'd already used up one too many of our nine lives and knew it was time to quit. So after seven years, we sold the balloon for less than we paid, but it was an adventure well worth it.

I learned a lot from my time flying. I learned about taking responsibility for yourself and others who depend on your skill and experience. I gained a new understanding of risk, and it was a confidence builder. I learned how to stay calm when facing potential dangers and the unknown. And most especially, I got a new understanding about the consequences of making bad decisions.

These were lessons I took into managing my own business. As diligently and carefully as you plan, you've always got to be ready for contingencies. When the unexpected pops up, you have to rely on experience, common sense, and intuition to persevere through it and come out on the other side. Even so, things may not turn out according to plan, but they'd be inevitably worse with little or no plan.

There is nothing like the joy and freedom you feel when hot-air ballooning; it's like being a bird. That's the experience we want to feel as we lift off out of our current corporate career into our own entrepreneurial adventure. But to be successful, it takes rigorous planning and careful assessment of our strengths and weaknesses. You need to play to those strengths and compensate for the weaknesses. Then you are ready to fly.

On the pages that follow, you'll find a guide to make your plan for your entrepreneurial journey. Ken and I will come along beside you to show how to make the most of life experiences, including time spent working for others, and use this to create a sustainable, productive, and profitable business to support yourself, your family, and, if you decide, potential employees.

Be prepared because that journey may be more challenging and take longer than you expect, but with diligence and hard work, it will be exhilarating, joyful, and more rewarding than any professional endeavor you can imagine.

The Corporateneur Plan is first and foremost a business book, but it unapologetically and intentionally has a personal-development and self-help aspect too. Most business books are focused on building, managing, and getting return on capital invested in the business.

For the entrepreneur, one's human capital—their skills, experience, knowledge, energy, inspiration, passion, and personal qualities—is far more important than financial capital. The financial capital piece will fall into place when the right human capital is invested in the most productive ways. But for the entrepreneur, all the financial capital in the world can't overcome a shortfall in human capital.

In the following chapters, we will share how learning from one's corporate experience—organization, process, strategy, and discipline—can be the key to success in an entrepreneurial venture as long as other qualities are added into the mix, such as humanity, innovation, flexibility, and intuition.

So with Ken as our expert guide who's been there and done it all—and me, a market researcher and writer who's followed an entrepreneurial path for thirty years, after ten years in corporate America—we set off on an exciting adventure together. Get ready for liftoff.

HOW TO USE THIS BOOK

"Nothing stays the same and nothing changes. What is old today will be new tomorrow. What is new today will be forgotten tomorrow," wrote Harley King, author and poet.

You might ask, What can a guy who was born before World War II teach me about building and running a business today? And our answer is simple: that's why you need to learn from Ken. "Business is business, now and then," he says.

Ken has experienced it all: economic ups and downs; massive cultural and consumer market shifts, as one generation makes way for another, along with the resulting generational wealth transfers.

Ken also can overcome a critical shortfall businesses currently face: the talent gap caused when mature managers leave the workforce and take their skills, knowledge, and experience with them. Next-generation managers are left to repeat the same mistakes that those who came before them made.

Moving from a structured corporate environment into the unstructured world of entrepreneurship presents talent-gap challenges all its own. Ken can fill that gap.

And over the years, he has been passing along the Rohl Model for business building by mentoring the next generation of aspiring entrepreneurs, such as Jenni Martin, a PGA-certified golf instructor who now runs a golf-training business.

"I can't tell you how much I benefited from all the lessons Ken taught me about business and myself. The real breakthrough was him teaching me how to manage my time and resources by playing to my strengths in order to overcome my weaknesses," she says.

"He also showed me a structured way to segment my target market so that I leaned into clients with long-term potential and didn't get distracted by potential clients who would deplete me and had much lower potential. That was a real game changer for me," she adds.

This isn't a book where you'll learn the latest and greatest marketing tricks and business-building tactics. Rather, it will pass along rock-solid, proven strategies the corporateneur can use to start, run, and build a sustainable business. And a critically important part of that is self-reflection: identifying your innate strengths and playing to them.

That's why each chapter will end with a bullet list of Ken's most important takeaways and a checklist for you to complete to prepare you for your corporateneurial adventure.

PART ONE
Ken's Story

Working Capital

*"My definition of a philosopher is of a man up in a balloon,
with his friends and family holding the ropes which confine
him to earth and keep trying to haul him down."*

—LOUISA MAY ALCOTT

Money—it's top-of-mind for any aspiring entrepreneur. No matter how much you've put aside or how confident you are about reaching your sales goals, you'll never feel that you have enough money. And without a doubt, it's scary to step out into the unknown, leaving the security and comfort of a job and career and putting your standard of living at risk.

When it comes to planning a new business start-up, the rule of thumb is that you should double what you think you'll need to get your company off the ground and halve your expected revenues in year one—that is, you should overestimate the amount of money you'll need and underestimate your takings in the first year and maybe the year after. So in terms of a SWOT analysis—strengths, weaknesses, opportunities, and threats—running out of money is top on the threats list for a new business start-up.

But threats are only that: the *possibility* that something might happen, not the certainty of it. In a weird twist of human nature, we are programmed to *overestimate* the threats and *underestimate* our strengths in a typical SWOT analysis. In psychology, it's called the *negativity bias*, and for the entrepreneur, it throws an emotional monkey wrench into what should be a rational business decision-making process.

We overemphasize the negative possibilities in decision-making and underplay the potential positive outcomes. As a result, people are more likely to act to prevent a potential loss than to pursue a path to achieve potential gain. Thus, they revert to their inbred status quo bias—to keep things as they are—by choosing not to make potentially risky decisions.

But aspiring entrepreneurs can't be held hostage by their innate psychology. Anyone can develop ways to overcome it. As the saying goes, "No risk, no reward." So instead of getting caught up in a risk-avoiding cycle of fear around the potential of losing money or running short, focus instead on the strengths you bring to the table and the potential opportunities that lie ahead.

MAXIMIZING SOFT CAPITAL

It all comes down to how you use and allocate your strengths, which go far beyond just financial or economic capital. The *hard* financial and economic capital is fungible. Any potential weaknesses there can be shored up by your *soft capital*, which is plentiful. And what's even more powerful about your soft capital, as opposed to the hard kind, is that it never goes away but is only strengthened over time.

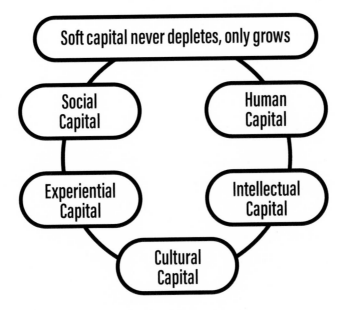

There are essentially five types of ever-replenishing soft capital:

- Human capital is the combination of your life experiences, skills, and creativity and your physical, mental, and emotional well-being.

- Intellectual capital is developed through education, training, and hands-on experience, and it equips you with critical-thinking, problem-solving aptitude and the ability to innovate.

- Cultural capital helps you forge wider connections across different groups of people with common interests, backgrounds, and behaviors.

- Experiential capital is gained through firsthand experience working on projects, investigating new ideas, learning new skills, and achieving goals.

- Social capital broadens your base through personal connections made throughout your network of associates, colleagues, family, and friends. Your network connections influence you, and you influence them.

Taken together, the strengths of the corporateneur's soft capital outweigh any shortfall in financial or economic capital. And unlike financial capital, you don't have to go to a bank or venture capitalist to get more. There's no limit to your soft capital potential.

Ken Rohl was rich in soft capital when he started his company at forty-seven years old after twenty-five-plus years in corporate America. Hard capital was in short supply, but he overcame that by leveraging his human, intellectual, cultural, experiential, and social capital and applying it to what the business needed to grow: sales and profits.

"My accountant said that I started the business with $1,000 in the bank and never spent a penny of it," Ken quips. "And that's because we planned carefully and used our time most efficiently to make sales and keep the cash flowing. I put everything into growing the business."

 # Ken's Life Lesson Learned

You Can Only Control Two Things: Your Time and Resources

When first starting a business, even before, you worry about all kinds of things that are entirely beyond your control. That's a total waste of the two most valuable things you have going for you: your time and your personal resource. That's the capital you must conserve and use wisely.

And since these are also the only two things you can control in business, whether as a one-person operation or a big corporation, you must allocate that capital for the maximum return on investment.

Back in the spare bedroom where I started the business, it was a full-on family enterprise with me, my wife Amber, my stepdaughter Valinda, and Lou, my middle son who joined the company right after graduating from the University of Illinois. Thank God for Lou being there because he saved the company in those early days, but more on that later.

Starting out, we only had one product—the pullout kitchen faucet—which we imported from a company in Switzerland called KWC. It was a new design in the US market, so people had to see it to understand it. Plus, we were selling a $250 product into a commodity market used to paying $50 for any old tap that turns the water on and off. We were effectively selling a Rolls-Royce into a market used to buying Chevys.

My mission in those early days was to fill the trunk of my car with our fancy kitchen faucets on Monday morning and not return home until the trunk was empty. I must have put on over one hundred thousand miles that first year crisscrossing California to develop a dealer network.

I learned early on not to waste time on the road. I didn't call on the largest kitchen-and-bath dealers where we'd get lost in a crowd. I needed specialty dealers who could help me reach a high-end target market. Our dealers were what you'd call *influencers* today, though we didn't use that term back then.

We selected our early influencers because they would be advocates for our products to customers ready for the Rolls-Royce of faucets. Our first dealers may have been small, but they were mighty and became critical partners in our long-term success.

Like *The Little Engine That Could*—a book my mother repeatedly read to me as a child—my time on the road proved the success of our process and product, and our business was growing, mile by mile. Eventually, our home-office operations were working so smoothly that Lou was deployed overseas to KWC's home office in Switzerland. He was our Trojan horse there—to learn the ropes, support the import/export side of the business, and to gather intelligence we could use back here.

I could see a bright future ahead for the company; then it nearly crumbled before my eyes after I got a panicked call from Lou. "You better get over here now," he said. "There's been a management shake-up, and talk is they are going to pull the plug on our US distribution and give it to the son of KWC's founder."

Lou learned that KWC had brought in a professional CEO who was displacing the KWC owner's family in the corporate hierarchy. The CEO taking US distribution from us and giving it to the owner's son would be a nice bone to throw.

A KWC corporate board meeting was planned for the following Monday, so I hopped on a plane to make my case to the board of directors, half of whom spoke very little English and all of whom knew next to nothing about the US market, most especially the owner's son who'd lived his whole life in Switzerland.

Clearly, if the board gave the son US distribution, it would be an emotional decision. I was determined to persuade them to make the right, rational business decision and stay with us.

I went into the meeting with one prop—a map of the United States. During a thirty-minute presentation, I took the KWC board on a virtual tour across the US, explaining all the different sales and marketing nuances of our country, the time zone challenges, distribution channels, and most importantly, our relationships with key dealers.

I laid out all the reasons why they should continue working with us, then pressed for an immediate answer by announcing that I had a plane to catch and wasn't going to leave without a decision. The time I waited outside the boardroom turned out to be the most critical minutes I spent for our business. In less than half an hour, they called me back into the room and gave me complete authority for the US.

TIME IS MONEY

We've all heard the cliché "time is money," but I never knew how true it was until those early days in my own business, from the hours spent driving up and down the California coast to those minutes that felt like hours sitting outside the KWC boardroom.

As an entrepreneur, how and where you spend your time matters most. Every minute of your time amounts to either money lost or gained. Don't waste your time doing things that won't get you closer to your goal, and make sure your time is spent only on the high-potential activities and most-influential customers that will have the biggest payoff.

You must plan each day so that the activities you engage in are maximized for the greatest return on your irreplaceable time investment. Once your time is gone, it's gone, unlike money that will come and go. Yes, it is important always to practice good financial management—but even more so to develop good habits in time management.

> **Once your time is gone, it's gone, unlike money that will come and go.**

And by managing your most valuable asset well—your time—you will also be leveraging your soft capital to help grow the hard kind. I did that by spending time developing a network of the best potential dealers to showcase our product and fostering true partnerships with them.

The goodwill we built with our customers in those early days allowed me to convince them to pay our invoices in thirty days, giving them an extra discount if they paid their invoices early. At the same time, I convinced KWC I needed 180 days to pay my bills, so I was able to leverage my payables against my receivables—"borrow from Peter to pay Paul."

That's how I kept that first $1,000 nest egg invested in my company in the bank. I focused my time on not only making sales but generating cash flow to keep moving forward.

And most of all, you can't afford to spend time on the unproductive distraction of worry. That depletes your soft capital rather than builds it.

Make your plan, and work your plan inch by inch, step by step, and mile by mile. The "I think I can, I think I can" spirit of the *Little Engine That Could* will take you far in building your business.

You know the arc of Ken's career. He worked in corporate America for twenty-five-plus years and grew personally and professionally each step along the way. "I was on a typical 'corporateer' path during those years—advancing in each job, taking on greater responsibilities, and learning different parts of business in different industries. That structured corporate approach happily gave me a solid foundation that I applied to my own business later," he says.

Then approaching fifty years old, he started his own business. With no time to waste, Ken built it into a $75 million company with seventy employees plus fifty independent sales reps, then sold it to a *Fortune* 500 industry leader to fill a void in their product line.

"I was finally able to combine my corporate experience and stretch it with my entrepreneurial side to create a balance between an organized, corporate approach and a disruptive one in my own business. I became a corporateneur," he explains.

After his business got established and he transitioned from CEO to chairman of the board, Ken began to devote time to mentoring aspiring entrepreneurs at the University of California, Irvine, Graduate School of Business. That relationship continues to this day and is part of his commitment to pay forward his knowledge and experience.

"Only in this country could I have accomplished the things I've accomplished. And those of us who are successful have a responsibility to make a difference for the next generation. Giving back must work into your life plan," he admonishes.

STARTING OUT

The journey of a thousand miles begins with one step.

—LAO TZU

Ken is a member of the Silent Generation, born April 20, 1935, in Chicago during the Great Depression. Seared into his memory are the milestones that shaped the trajectory of this country over the last eighty-plus years.

"I remember sitting at a gas station on a Sunday afternoon with my dad when we heard President Roosevelt announce over the radio that we were going to war after the attack on Pearl Harbor. I was all of six years old," he shares. "Then, when I was fourteen, I went to Camp Minnehaha in West Virginia. Two of our counselors were in college and active in the Marine Reserves. Just a year later, both had been killed in the Korean War."

Ken grew up in a hardscrabble Irish neighborhood on the south side of Chicago. As a young man, he had a strong work ethic instilled by his Catholic upbringing and modeled by his father and mother. "My mother especially had a huge influence on me. Because we lived in a tough Irish neighborhood, she suggested I take up boxing," he explains.

"And as the middle child among eight, including five brothers, she admonished me always to throw the first punch. To prove it, she'd take a quasi-fighting stance when she gave me advice or when I needed correction, which was more than I would have liked," he recalls.

Soon after World War II ended, his father, who worked in product planning and metallurgy with Carnegie Illinois Steel, was transferred to Pittsburgh, Pennsylvania, after a merger with US Steel. That got Ken started in the steel industry, working summer jobs in the steel mills when he was only sixteen years old. "I liked having my own money," he says.

"I thought the streets of Chicago were tough but discovered working in the steel mills was even tougher," he continues. "There were a lot of boys my age and even older working there, too, but I was the son of an executive, not a blue-collar steelworker like they were. On day one, I had to prove my 'metal' by duking it out with a couple of them in a boxcar during lunch. My mom taught me well."

Settling into a suburban Pittsburgh high school, Ken reflects on the early influence of a vice-principal who took him under his wing. "Particularly when I started believing that I didn't need a college education to succeed," he says. "Between my mother and the vice-principal, I was persuaded otherwise and went on to graduate from Denison University with a liberal arts degree."

EARLY ENTREPRENEURIAL VENTURE

Always a go-getter, Ken wanted to supplement his college funds and started a business selling monogrammed sweatshirts to his university's fraternity and sorority houses. He employed fraternity brothers and sisters to sell the sweatshirts by offering them one free sweatshirt for every ten they sold.

Success on his Denison University campus led him to expand that enterprise across five college campuses within a fifty-mile radius.

"My initial sales strategy was proven, but I realized it needed more volume to grow, so I broadened my reach to other campuses. I had a process that worked with a marketable product that I could take on the road," Ken explains.

By the time he graduated, he had realized $8,000 in income (about $77,000 in current dollars) and learned that success in any business depended upon filling a need or desire that people would pay for—in this case, a student's desire to wear their fraternity or sorority logo. He also learned that having a great product was not enough. You had to surround that product with a compelling story to make the sale.

"Success in life is a formula of ongoing experiments which over time create a benchmark of success. This sets the stage for managing through the various detours on life's voyage," Ken explains. "Maintaining that established goal in mind becomes your personal North Star, and keeping it in sight enables you to always find a way back if you get off track."

STEPPING UP THE CORPORATE LADDER

Upon college graduation in 1957, he took a job with US Steel, where he was enrolled in a thirteen-month executive-management training program. That gave him a virtual MBA on the job. His first son, Mark, was born during this time.

Then in 1959, he was moved to Chicago to work in customer service, where he was responsible for multimillion-dollar accounts like BorgWarner and Ford. "I wondered why, as a twenty-four-year-old, they would throw such major accounts to a young buck like me. My boss was a no-nonsense World War II vet who'd given life-and-death orders to soldiers under his command. He didn't have patience for such a silly question. 'You'll either sink or swim, Rohl. Now, get back to your desk,' he barked at me."

Ken's boss wasn't one to coddle an elite management trainee. He expected Ken to find the answers and solve problems on the spot through intuition and simple common sense. And his first responsibility was to keep the clients happy.

It was all part of the company's established training process: to throw management trainees into the deep end with big accounts to see if they would sink or swim. "I decided to swim," Ken says.

"Back in those days, US Steel had a well-developed executive-training program, and the first stop for a trainee like me was customer service. It turned out to be the most impactful stepping stone in my corporate career," Ken reflects.

"It gave me an early understanding of customer priorities, needs, concerns, and frustrations. I developed empathy for the person on the other end of the phone. My word was my promise to the customer. Sometimes I had to move mountains to keep those promises. It was a lesson I carried forward throughout my corporate career, and it ultimately turned out to be critical for success in my own business," he shares.

After less than a year proving himself in customer service, Ken was called to St. Louis for a sales position where he provided steel for the Air Force Cadet Chapel in Colorado Springs and the iconic St. Louis Arch. That was also where the family settled in, and his second son, Lou, was born.

"My wife and I thought St. Louis would be a great city to raise a family and that we would spend the rest of our lives there. But at that time, companies didn't like you to get too comfortable in one place. So after three years, I got a call to move to Birmingham, Alabama. It was 1963 and deep in the Jim Crow South," he shares. "The evils of

Jim Crow were everywhere—separate lines in liquor stores, bathroom facilities, buses, and society in general. It was an uncomfortable reality for someone who regularly frequented Pittsburgh's Black jazz clubs in the late '50s."

The Birmingham assignment was both a cultural and professional shock to his system. At only twenty-seven years old, he and a similarly young engineer were given the responsibility to build a brand-new factory from the ground up and to line up customers for a new type of prepainted steel it would produce. They had a multimillion-dollar budget and two years to accomplish the project.

After successfully completing that assignment, he was brought back to Pittsburgh headquarters in 1966, where his third son, Greg, was born. It was a major promotion to product manager for tubular and sheet steel products, which brought in a sizeable chunk of US Steel's business. "I was in my early thirties, and here I was given a management job with a four-window office and huge responsibilities. I felt I had a meteoric rise," he reflects.

NO TIME TO GET TOO COMFORTABLE

Yet Ken couldn't settle comfortably into his new executive position. Not long after arriving back in Pittsburgh, US Steel was hit with new environmental regulations to reduce industrial pollution and started reallocating resources away from marketing. "It was the beginning of the end for the US steel industry," he reflects.

"In an ironic twist, the regulations, intended to clean up American rivers, lakes, and air, ended up causing the steel industry to 'off-shore' production to developing countries, where environmental regulations did not constrain plants and processes," Ken explains. "It opened the door to foreign steel and effectively brought an entire US industry to a full stop, with plants closed and workers laid off across the country."

That effectively closed the door for Ken in the steel industry. But he took with him the extensive experience from the formidable responsibilities he was given at such an early stage in his career and a deep well of confidence to be ready to tackle the next challenge.

NEW JOB, NEW INDUSTRY

That challenge came through connections he'd made in the steel industry. In 1968 he joined DeSoto Chemical in Des Plaines, Illinois, a diversified company producing industrial paints, coatings, and other products.

His initial job was as marketing and product director, a position similar in scope to the position he held at US Steel, only managing the introduction of an innovative product line of industrial paints that were guaranteed to last twenty years. The rest of the industry was built on products that lasted five years.

"It was much like the US Steel Birmingham job where I was responsible for building a team from the ground up and taking an innovative new product to market," he says. "While the new paint was three times more expensive than typical paints in the market, it had four times longer life. We turned it into a brand that offered meaningful value to our customers, including architecture specifiers, manufacturers of pre-engineered steel buildings, and other exterior metal components."

In that role, he managed a team of five specialists, and unlike at US Steel where he was more sales-focused, the DeSoto job got him involved with marketing too. His span of control included product development, merchandising, trade show management, pricing, expense control, and revenue and relationship building.

"We were selling a commodity product—paint—at a higher price. The best way to stand out was to elevate the perceived value and imagery of the product," Ken explains. "We brought a consumer-product mindset and storytelling to marketing a commoditized industrial product. We created buzz in the industry with that new approach."

His success there effectively put him out of a job because DeSoto decided to integrate the new product line into the company's commercial line of products with staffing in place to handle it. "I was only out of a job briefly. The chairman called me and presented a new challenge totally out of my wheelhouse. He wanted me to take the position of vice president of sales and marketing for DeSoto's United Wallcovering division."

Back in the '70s, wallcoverings were a hot commodity, but the DeSoto wallcovering business had gone flat. It was hampered by same old thinking as the market shifted from traditional wallpaper to next-generation vinyl and more durable products.

Acting as a change agent again, Ken took the industry-standard one-size-fits-all wallpaper book featuring the company's entire product line. He broke it apart to create multiple style books based on customer-use cases, especially books for the kitchen and bath where vinyl was the best choice.

"It was a first in the industry and my first experience in retail. Our new consumer-focused marketing approach revitalized the business. It was so successful that after just twenty-four months, our division was sold to a competitor, which was good for the company but bad for my career," Ken relates.

EXPANDING HIS REACH

In taking over DeSoto's wallcovering business, Ken moved from an industrial market, where he had deep roots, into the uncharted territory of the consumer market. He had to build relationships and credibility with distributors who carried multiple lines from competitors. So he became an influencer in order to be able to influence the industry's influencers (i.e., the distributors).

He differentiated his product line by telling stories in the new, themed wallcovering books featuring specific product applications in different room settings. And the books included pictures of people in their homes, another industry first. It moved the whole industry forward with DeSoto as the leader.

"In a highly competitive and tightly controlled market, like wallcoverings were in the 1970s, it was important to grow the whole wallcovering 'pie,' not carve up the same pie into smaller and smaller slices," he says. "I looked at my competitors not as somebody I wanted to take market share from but as partners to help expand and grow the pie. With that approach, there would be more than enough to make us all happy."

Ken helped grow the wallcovering pie by expanding his and his company's visibility in the industry association. He became an industry leader and prime influencer by advocating for the industry and working across company lines.

NEXT CHALLENGE

DeSoto wanted to keep Ken on after the sale of the wallcovering business, but through a connection, Ken heard about an opening at the vice presidential level with St. Charles Manufacturing closer to his home. Taking the job would mean eliminating an hour commute both ways, giving him more time for family and his hot-air ballooning passion. An introduction was made, and he was having dinner with the company owner and his son within a week.

Even before ordering dinner, they offered Ken a job as an "advisory" vice president. They wanted him to spend the first six months getting acquainted with the industry, absorbing the company's culture, and learning the ins and outs of its commercial and residential businesses.

"They said, 'You're new to the industry, so we are going to give you six months to get acclimatized before giving you the reins,'" Ken relates. "That prompted me to push my menu across the table, and thank them for the dinner invitation, and say, 'There is no point in going any further because if I can't have accountability, responsibility, and authority from day one, it isn't a good fit for me.' Taken aback, they agreed to my conditions."

Founded in 1935, St. Charles was a legacy high-end kitchen cabinetry company that gained status as the preferred brand for iconic architects like Frank Lloyd Wright and Mies van der Rohe. But after its early glory days, the company had fallen on hard times as cabinetry materials evolved and consumer tastes changed.

When Ken joined the company in 1972, it was a large corporation spanning manufacturing and retail/wholesale businesses through eleven company showrooms and numerous independent dealers. But the company had lost $500,000 the previous year, a loss it could ill afford. His job was to right the ship and get it sailing in the right direction.

"It was the age-old story of continuing to use the same old sales strategies with an aging team of uninspiring leaders," Ken reflects. At all of thirty-seven years old, he was the young blood the company needed to bring new ideas to a business serving commercial and residential customers here and abroad.

The first challenge he faced after coming on board was an incentive trip to London for the company's dealers and their wives. "That boondoggle was budgeted for $250,000—about half of what the company lost the previous year. I asked why we should reward the same people who caused us to lose so much the past year," he says. But because the company had long-standing relationships with its dealers and their wives, the company didn't want to take back a perk it had promised.

With the company caught between a rock and a hard place—it simply could not afford the London trip—Ken decided to visit each dealer and explain the business necessity to cancel London and instead hold the meeting in Chicago. He fell on his sword by taking full responsibility for making the decision.

His initial visits to dealers in Duluth, Cincinnati, Milwaukee, and Cedar Rapids weren't going as well as planned, and ahead in Omaha, he had a meeting with one of the most influential dealers. Anticipating the challenge, Ken decided to pull out all the stops.

"I had to set the dealer off-balance, so I asked the VP of sales who was traveling with me to get a flight attendant to have a wheelchair waiting for me at the gate," he shares. "I called an 'audible' and explained that an old football injury had flared up and I couldn't walk to the terminal. Well, it could have been true, and my traveling partner, a very button-down type, bought it.

"So I entered the Omaha airport, to meet the dealer, in a wheelchair with as pained a look on my face as I could muster," Ken continues. "That disarmed him and defused the situation. The meeting proceeded much more cordially than might have been the case."

While the dealers were disappointed they weren't going to London—and their wives even more so—they all understood the reason and arrived in Chicago to work together and help turn the business around. But Ken was determined to make the meeting as memorable and productive as possible and not leave them with a sour taste for St. Charles.

So he had a consolation prize in store for them. Since they lost out on the trip to London, Ken surprised them instead with a virtual around-the-world trip by taking them to different international restaurants each evening. It was Chicago Chinatown on Monday, Germantown on Tuesday, Little Italy on Wednesday, and wrapping up Thursday at an Irish pub for a pint of Guinness.

Ken cleverly repositioned something that could have been ho-hum—just another four-day sales meeting in Chicago—into an exciting adventure to experience the different world cultures available in the city.

"Dealer morale was preserved, and they got an example of how to be creative in solving business problems with out-of-the-box solutions," Ken explains. "And we did it all for $75,000—a huge savings for the company."

TIMES UP

Ken continued to work his transformation magic at St. Charles for the next seven years, until 1978 when the company was sold to Whirlpool. Shortly after that, he was offered a senior vice president position at a stainless-steel sink manufacturer also headquartered in Chicago, Elkay Manufacturing. He was to replace an executive who'd been with the company for thirty-five years.

"On paper, it was a promotion and what I thought was a good opportunity. Elkay was stalled and needed innovation and new ways of thinking," Ken reflects. "But I found it wasn't a good fit for me. The company wasn't ready for the changes I thought were necessary, so we amicably parted ways."

While his work with Elkay was a personal disappointment, it turned out to be time well spent. It was where he discovered the European pullout kitchen faucet that Elkay passed over. Ken knew in his gut that the US market was ready for it and took it with him to start his company.

Elkay hadn't been ready to take the risk. Ken understood the potential risks, too, but he saw many more opportunities ahead. So Ken closed the chapter on his corporate career and became a corporateneur in 1983. He figured he had learned as much as he could working for somebody else. It was time to put that learning to the test with the pullout faucet he knew would be a hit.

 # Ken's Key Takeaways

- Don't let the all-too-human negativity bias get in your way.

- Leverage your nondepletable and ever-growing soft capital—your human, intellectual, cultural, experiential, and social capital—against any potential shortfall in hard capital.

- Control what you can control—your time and resources—and prepare and plan for those eventualities you can't.

YOUR CORPORATENEUR ROAD MAP

1. Make a list of your soft capital assets, including your human, intellectual, cultural, experiential, and social capital. Which is your strongest? Which is your weakest? How can you maximize your strongest soft capital assets and overcome or shore up your weakest? For example, you might need more formal education or coursework to strengthen intellectual capital or need to join more groups in order to meet more people and build social capital.

2. Looking across your career, what skills, talents, and personal capabilities did you rely upon repeatedly to accomplish goals, contribute to the organization, and take on new responsibilities?

3. Prepare your "corporateneur résumé." Put yourself in the role of an imaginary business owner, and write a résumé to get the CEO job. Be objective, but don't skimp on all the soft capital assets you would bring to your new CEO job.

4. Familiarize yourself with the SWOT process: assessing your Strengths, Weaknesses, Opportunities, and Threats. For each area, be as specific as possible. Next, determine the causes of each quality. Finally, create an action plan to address your findings.

CHAPTER 2

Getting in Gear

"The odds must be against anybody being able to fly around the world in a balloon on the first attempt. All of us who are attempting to go around the world in balloons are effectively flying in experimental craft."

—RICHARD BRANSON

When it comes down to it, mere survival is the ultimate measure of an entrepreneur's success. Most entrepreneurs want to achieve a lot more than that, but far more entrepreneurs fail than survive. For example, according to the Bureau of Labor Statistics, only about one-third of companies with employees make it to their tenth anniversary. And business survival rates are even lower for solo entrepreneurs.

Despite the bad odds, that isn't stopping Americans from starting businesses. Overall, just under 20 percent of the US adult workforce is at an early entrepreneurial stage, and another 10 percent or so are established company owners, according to the Global Entrepreneurship Monitor (GEM). That adds up to some forty million Americans participating in the entrepreneurial economy.

In addition, the GEM also found that an exceptionally high percentage of Americans—about 55 percent—have started a business at some point in their lives, and 26 percent have started two or more companies. The entrepreneurial spirit runs deep in this country.

AGE, NOT PERSONALITY

In the US, younger people aged eighteen to thirty-four are more likely to start their own businesses. That's because younger people have fewer strings holding them back. They've spent less time getting a career on track. They don't have as much to lose if a new business venture goes sideways. And because they are younger, they feel they can go back and take the corporate route if they fail.

While younger people are more inclined to test their entrepreneurial mettle, older people aged thirty-five to sixty-four have a higher likelihood of future success. Their advantages are significant, given their greater life experiences. Over their careers, they've acquired the skills needed to run a business, including greater awareness of market opportunities and easier access to capital and other resources required to get a business off the ground.

Despite having more to lose if their new venture fails, mature corporateneurs, like Ken, are inclined to see the rewards of starting a business as greater than the risks. And their risk is generally more significant compared to younger entrepreneurs with less to lose. In other words, failure is not an option. That's the corporateneur advantage.

Age aside, it is widely believed that entrepreneurs are somehow different than other people, that there is an entrepreneurial personality type. Numerous studies have tried to define the entrepreneurial personality, including the Myers-Briggs Type Indicator that measures four personality variables on a scale:

- Extraversion (E) and Introversion (I)

- Sensing (S) and Intuition (N)

- Thinking (T) and Feeling (F)

- Judging (J) and Perceiving (P)

Yet a study conducted by Myers-Briggs also found no correlation between the various personality types and their likelihood for success as an entrepreneur.

Independently, Colorado Mesa University business professor Timothy Hatten also found this to be true. "The conclusion of 30 years of research indicates that there are no personality characteristics that predict who will be a successful entrepreneur," he wrote.

ENTREPRENEURS HAVE DISTINCT COGNITIVE PROCESSES, FACTORS, AND STYLES

With psychologists roadblocked in finding an entrepreneurial personality, they looked to cognitive psychology to distinguish entrepreneurs from their nonentrepreneurial colleagues. In the simplest terms, cognitive psychology studies the way people acquire and process information.

Using computers as an analogy, psychologists explain that both people and computers take input and process it in a certain way to generate output. In the case of the entrepreneur, the output is a business, and the key cognitive characteristic of an entrepreneur is the unique way they process the input.

For example, a study by Leslie E. Palich and D. Ray Bagby, both professors of entrepreneurship at Baylor University, found entrepreneurs and nonentrepreneurs have an equal propensity to take risks. Where they differ is in how they think about and process the risk. Entrepreneurs tend to focus on the upside—what's to be gained—to a much greater extent than nonentrepreneurs, who weigh the risks more heavily.

Entrepreneurs process risk differently because of a cognitive factor called *self-efficacy*—or the belief in one's ability to achieve a level of performance that will produce a desired outcome. Entrepreneurs have a higher level of self-efficacy, which leads them to perceive risks and opportunities differently and to feel more competent to overcome obstacles to achieving their goals. Higher levels of self-efficacy tend to distinguish entrepreneurs from corporate managers who are content working in a less risk-filled environment.

> **Higher levels of self-efficacy tend to distinguish entrepreneurs from corporate managers who are content working in a less risk-filled environment.**

Research has also shown that one's self-efficacy isn't set in stone but can be developed, like one's human, intellectual, cultural, experiential, and social capital. It's the "I think I can, I think I can" mantra of the *Little Engine That Could*. That kind of positive thinking raises one's self-efficacy.

Schemas, or simplified scripts that link unconnected information to identify opportunities, are another cognitive process that enables entrepreneurs to process information differently. For example, experts in any field process information differently than novices because experts have knowledge structures, or scripts, in their area of expertise. Those scripts allow them to perform better than nonexperts who don't have those knowledge structures to call upon.

Ken Rohl is just such an expert in business and has a wealth of embedded scripts or "Ken-isms" to call upon. These Ken-ism scripts also exemplify another distinguishing cognitive characteristic of entrepreneurs called *heuristics* in psychological terms.

Heuristics is a concept first introduced by Herbert Simon, a Nobel Prize–winning economist and cognitive psychologist. A *heuristic* is defined as a "mental shortcut" that allows people to solve problems and make judgments quickly and efficiently. These are rule-of-thumb strategies that successful entrepreneurs have in abundance. They have learned shortcuts that allow them to make decisions without adequate information. It's the psychological equivalent of muscle memory. They've developed problem-solving abilities by repeatedly solving problems.

BEWARE COGNITIVE BIASES

As much as heuristics can help entrepreneurs, they can also lead to cognitive biases that cause judgment errors. Some of the biases entrepreneurs are prone to include

- *confirmation bias*, the tendency to listen more often to information that confirms one's existing beliefs;

- *anchoring bias*, which is the tendency to be overly influenced by the first piece of information gathered;

- *optimism bias*, the tendency to overestimate the likelihood of success while underestimating the probability of failure; and

- *self-serving bias*, where one assumes personal credit for things that turn out well and puts the blame elsewhere when things go badly.

In the case of cognitive biases, forewarned is forearmed. That's why it's important for entrepreneurs to recruit one person, and preferably more, as a sounding board to help sort through the facts and advise on decision-making so they don't fall victim to one or more of these biases.

HOW YOU ROLL

One's cognitive style, as distinct from one's personality, also plays a critical role in the entrepreneur. Cognitive style is the way people perceive the outside environment and how they process, organize, and use information gathered from the environment to guide their actions.

For example, some people are naturally drawn to a *knowing style* that is analytical and characterized by a reliance on facts and data. Corporate managers tend to favor a knowing cognitive style.

Others are more intuitive in nature and reflect a *creative style*. They are conceptual thinkers who enjoy experimentation and do not like rules and procedures. They thrive in confronting uncertainties and working in unstructured environments.

One tends to think of entrepreneurs as exemplifying the creative style, but that is an example of confirmation bias. Yes, entrepreneurs must exhibit a creative cognitive style, but to be successful, they also need a good dose of the knowing cognitive style.

Characteristic of successful entrepreneurs is that they integrate both the analytic (knowing) and intuitive (creative) cognitive styles. Or, as Ken would say, the corporateneur develops their knowing cognitive style in the corporate environment. And they combine that with their creative style to succeed in an entrepreneurial venture. These two cognitive styles are the ying-yang or the art and science that make for a successful corporateneur.

HOW THESE COGNITIVE PROCESSES PLAY OUT

With cognitive psychology as her foundation, Saras Sarasvathy, the University of Virginia's Darden Professor of Business Administration, explains how entrepreneurs use their unique cognitive styles and processes to become high-performing entrepreneurs. Named as one of the "Top 18 Entrepreneurship Professors" by *Fortune Small Business* magazine, Professor Sarasvathy identified the concept of *effectuation* to illustrate their unique processes in creating a business.

She identifies two different cognitive thinking processes: causal and effectual reasoning. Causal reasoning, as she explains, starts with a "predetermined goal and a given set of means and seeks to identify the optimal—fastest, cheapest, most efficient, etc.—alternative to achieve the given goals."

For example, a cook thinks causally when they determine what dish they want to cook, buy the necessary ingredients, and then follow a recipe to prepare it. The goal is predetermined, and the steps to accomplish it are defined.

Business schools primarily teach the classic causation model. Like a recipe, it is a similar step-by-step process, beginning with market identification and the specific need the new product or service will address. Then it works backward to determine a business plan and marketing strategy.

The effectual thinking process turns the traditional causal process taught in business schools on its head and starts in an entirely different place. It begins with a given set of means (the ingredients available in the kitchen) and lets the result emerge from them (the dish to be served).

The effectual process is creative, requiring imagination, spontaneity, risk-taking, and salesmanship. Causal reasoning may also involve

57

creativity, such as reasoning through alternative ways to achieve a specific goal. But the causal process always focuses on the ultimate goal. The effectual process focuses on the means with the goals evolving from it.

Professor Sarasvathy explains, "Causal thinkers are like great generals seeking to conquer fertile lands. Effectual thinkers are like explorers setting out on voyages into uncharted waters."

While she notes that the best entrepreneurs use both the causal and effectual modes of thinking, they tend to prefer the effectual process, which is why they often fail to transition well into later stages of business where more causal reasoning is required. It's also the reason why so many successful entrepreneurs become serial entrepreneurs. They are naturally set for the creative effectual approach.

MEANS BEFORE THE ENDS

"All entrepreneurs begin with three categories of means: (1) who they are—their traits, tastes, and abilities; (2) what they know—their education, training expertise, and experience; and (3) whom they know—their social and professional networks. Using these means, entrepreneurs begin to imagine and implement possible effects that can be created with them," Professor Sarasvathy observes.

Whereas the causal process starts with careful planning followed by execution, the effectual process begins with execution based upon the means.

"Most often, they [effectual thinkers] start very small with the means that are closest at hand, and move almost directly into action without elaborate planning," she continues. "Through their actions, the effectual entrepreneurs' set of means and consequently the set of possible effects change and get reconfigured. Eventually, certain of the emerging effects coalesce into clearly achievable and desirable goals."

RICHARD BRANSON, THE QUINTESSENTIAL EFFECTUAL ENTREPRENEUR

Professor Sarasvathy refers to Richard Branson as an example of how an effectual thinker builds a business. Branson started out publishing a magazine when he was only sixteen. Then at twenty years old, he began a mail-order record business, followed by opening a chain of record stores called Virgin Records.

Then an accident occurred that changed the course of his life entirely. He became stranded along with hundreds of other passengers in a small Caribbean island airport when their plane was canceled. Taking an effectual-problem-solver's approach, he got on the phone and chartered a plane, dividing the cost with the other passengers, which turned out to be far less than what the original commercial airline charged.

Thus, the concept for Virgin Airlines was born. He tested the idea by calling Boeing to borrow planes they weren't using. He figured if he could successfully fill those planes, he could make a bigger deal with Boeing. But if it didn't work, then he could send the planes back to Boeing with little money lost. The rest is history.

Yes, Branson had a plan, but his initial plan was to test his vision to get a new commercial airline off the ground. So he first focused on executing a test plan—"Make a plan. Work the plan," as Ken would say.

He didn't start with the ultimate goal of creating an airline company, requiring a business plan that worked back from the goal.

Virgin Airlines would likely never have been born if he had started that way.

Instead, he worked forward, with a plan for a modest trial run requiring minimal capital investment. He learned through that test how to manage the bumps and overcome the hurdles. The ultimate business plan for Virgin Airlines evolved as it progressed. Small successes led to bigger successes and then on to major success.

Ken followed a similar effectual process as Richard Branson. He didn't set out with the goal of building a $75 million leader in the luxury kitchen-and-bath business, which would be acquired by a *Fortune* 500 company.

He started with a simple pullout faucet that he was convinced would be successful in the US market. He presented it to his then employer, Elkay, who passed on it. Only then did he put the gears in motion to start a business.

The means—his conviction that the pullout faucet would be a home run in the US market and his extensive reach into the kitchen-and-bath industry—came first. Then he put the plan together to create a company and test the concept by taking it on the road.

And as success followed success and his means grew, he transitioned into a more causal way of thinking, all the while remaining effectually vigilant for new opportunities.

CREATE YOUR FUTURE

Ken created his and his company's future by leaning into the effectual thinking process. "If you control certain things in the present, you can create the future. That is thinking effectually," Professor Sarasvathy explains. "Entrepreneurs believe in a yet-to-be-made future that can substantially be shaped by human action, and they realize that to the extent that this human action can control the future, they need not expend energies trying to predict it."

Cognitive psychology aside, Ken will tell you it all comes down to being poised for action and following a process to create a successful future for your business.

Gartner defines a business process as the way organizations "coordinate the behavior of people, systems, information and things to produce business outcomes in support of a business strategy. Processes can be structured and repeatable, or unstructured and variable."

But from Ken's point of view, an unstructured, variable process is no process at all. The key to the success of a business process is that it be structured and repeatable. When unforeseen circumstances arise, as they always will, you confront the challenge directly in front of you and repeat the process from that point.

It becomes a virtuous circle, only now you've got better information to work from—when what you thought would work but didn't work so well, or when new and unexpected opportunities present themselves. Then you can move forward from the means to the end with a new plan.

 ## *Ken's Life Lesson Learned*

Processes and Promises

Process is one of those words that is both a noun and a verb, like *a run* and *to run* or a *challenge* and *to challenge*. In a sentence, the noun is descriptive, what does or gets the action. The verb—the action—is where a sentence's power lies, and that's why writing teachers drill their students in using active voice.

A sentence that focuses on who or what is doing the action is more engaging to the reader than one that focuses on who or what is being acted upon. So "Tommy kissed Sally" and "The cat chased the mouse" (active voice) are more powerful sentences than "Sally was kissed by Tommy" or "The mouse was chased by the cat" (passive voice).

Active voice sentences move a story forward, while passive voice sentences just sit there. Likewise, in business, the power of process (the noun) is how the individual and his or her business processes (verb) all business activities.

To wit, it's not *the* process but *doing* the process that moves a business forward. And the entrepreneur is responsible for defining the process and building systems that can effectuate the process. It's what President and General Dwight D. Eisenhower alluded to when he said, "Plans are nothing. Planning is everything."

For me, it's all about working the plan, and as a company founder, it was my job to ensure everyone in the company was working our plan. Developing the plan is a creative endeavor requiring vision and imagination. Working the plan takes *discipline*—another word that is both noun and verb. And as you proceed to do the process, it often results in continued creativity to revise it as new information—the results—come in.

Looking back over my corporate career, I always took an effectual cognitive approach to my jobs, as Professor Sarasvathy describes, though I often worked with or under causally directed managers.

The corporate environment demanded discipline but also rewarded me for creatively developing new processes and procedures to more effectively and efficiently perform my job and achieve corporate goals. That set me up to climb the corporate ladder, taking on more responsibilities and span of control. It eventually led to creating my own company when the corporate world could no longer contain my vision and ambition.

That's where you are today. So how do you make the transition? Throughout my corporate career, I learned valuable lessons from the processes I put into place that carried me along to the next challenge. I created scripts—my personal set of heuristics—that became critically important once I set out on my own. Those scripts, my processes and guiding principles, have taken me far, and as I shared them with others, they took them far too.

The aha moment about the power of scripts—and this script specifically: "promises made, promises kept"—came in my first customer service posting at US Steel after completing the management-training courses. It proved to be the best place to start because customer service—serving the customer and meeting their needs—is the most essential process in any business.

Customer service can also be a company's canary in the coal mine. Customers don't typically call that department unless they are having a problem; somewhere, the company's promises haven't been kept. And that's why I've always kept my finger on the pulse of the business through the customer service department.

For example, when I was with St. Charles Kitchens, I learned customers were calling about their cabinets being damaged upon delivery. That was not technically my responsibility; we had a department to service such things. But as the company's vice president of sales and marketing, it was my responsibility, with a capital *R*, to make sure the promises we made to our customers were kept. Beautiful, functional cabinets delivered and installed without a ding or divot were what we promised, and apparently we were not living up to it.

So I made a surprise call at the warehouse one morning to ride along with delivery drivers to see what was really going on. I came dressed for the part in my ballooning jumpsuit, not my corporate suit, to make clear I meant business. I found out firsthand what was really happening and fixed it so that all products were delivered in top condition and the customer was happy.

"Promises made, promises kept" became an essential process for me, and I drilled that into everyone in my company. But I also had to create a process to define the scope of our promises.

That's where our company's mission and vision statements came in. Everyone needed to know what our promises were so there would be no doubt about whether they were living up to them. So through a process, we developed a mission and statements that defined our promises.

Our mission, vision, and promises defined our company's process. These ideals—our company's North Star—were so important that we printed little wallet-sized folding cards for every company employee to carry with them.

Just as in an orchestra, everyone in a company has their individual parts to play—their individual process. But the end result, as when the orchestra performs a symphony, is a harmonized company that works together for the benefit of all.

You, as the company founder, are the Bach, Beethoven, and Brahms writing the score for each instrument in the orchestra and leading the practice and final performance so that everything and everybody works together.

In working with young entrepreneurs—and I've worked with many—I have seen that they often don't grasp the importance of, or how to approach the process of, creating an enterprise. While they might be great at doing one thing or another (a superb solo violinist or a skilled conductor in an orchestra), they don't know how to write the score—that is the role of the entrepreneur.

So when I start working with a person who has an idea for a business, I pull them back to look at the bigger picture. Invariably, they have an idea of what they want to do, how they are going to do it, and what they will achieve, but they start with the *what* and *how*, not the ultimate question of *why*—why your idea is important, why it solves a real need in the market, why people will want to buy it and partner with you. Excuse me for using another metaphor, but they risk getting lost in the forest because they are looking only at the trees.

The first process for the entrepreneur is to define the mission of the company, the vision that inspires it and what it promises to the customers and its other stakeholders. Out of that comes the specific step-by-step approach to organizing any business, whether it be operations, marketing, sales, or finance.

Heavy responsibility rests on the entrepreneurs' shoulders, whether it's a one-person operation or many employees. The process starts with you: the chief architect of the company's mission, vision, and promise statements. Everything follows from that, and with it in place, all the other processes required of the company will fit into place.

The late Jack Welch, former CEO of General Electric who became a corporateneur when he established the Jack Welch Management Institute in 2009, describes the business founder's responsibility well: "Good business leaders create a vision, articulate the vision, passionately own the vision, and relentlessly drive it to completion."

Through Ken's effectual cognitive style, the mission and vision for his company evolved as new opportunities and challenges presented themselves. To manage those, he brought established processes with him that were proven throughout his corporate career.

Ken cut his teeth as a change agent in the companies he worked for. He knew how to transform a commoditized market by using different marketing processes, like he did for the DeSoto wallcovering business.

Setting out with a highly differentiated pullout kitchen faucet that was brand-new in the US market, he called on that experience to develop repeatable and proven processes to introduce new, innovative, and specialized plumbing products into a commoditized market that competed primarily on price. Price wouldn't be the differentiator for the pullout faucet; specialized value-driven features would.

He worked from what he knew—his ten-plus years in the kitchen industry—and set out to change a market that was filled with $50 plain-vanilla faucets. He had a product and process to introduce a more specialized, more luxury faucet to the market.

Ken's Key Takeaways

- Be aware of your thinking styles. Different strategies are needed for corporateneurs with a knowing versus a creative cognitive style. Entrepreneurship favors those with creating styles, while those who prefer the knowing style may be confounded by the many unknowns of starting a business. But the best approach is to use both knowing and creative cognitive styles.

- Beware of cognitive biases. Everyone is prone to them, so the corporateneur needs to seek out a network of advisors who can help avoid them.

- Take little steps to test your concept and create a repeatable business process for a sustainable business.

- Define your company's mission, vision, and promise from the customers' perspective and not your perspective.

Your Corporateneur Road Map

1. How do you like to think? Do you prefer working from the knowns to the unknowns?

2. Can you put together a range of things you know and create something new from them?

3. Is creative problem solving among your soft capital assets? If not, the corporateneur path may be uncomfortable for you.

4. Are you more risk averse or rewards driven? Are you more concerned with minimizing risk than gaining reward? If avoiding risk tips the scale, corporateneuring will be a challenge.

CHAPTER 3

Day One and Beyond

*"True voyagers are those who leave just to be leaving; hearts
light, like balloons. They never turn aside from their fatality
and without knowing why, they always say: 'Let's go!'"*

—CHARLES BAUDELAIRE

I t was February 1983 when Ken decided it was time to "fish or cut
bait" and set out on his own. He started Western States Manufacturing (WSM) as a distribution company headquartered in his
Irvine, California, home.

Only three months in, he got that fateful call from his son Lou
in Switzerland, which could have put the kibosh on the entire enterprise almost before it started. But failure was not an option, and
Ken boarded the plane to Switzerland with confidence that he could
convince the KWC board that they needed him, his expertise, and his
process to open up the potentially huge US market.

From the very beginning, Ken envisioned his company not as a solo enterprise but something the whole family had a stake in. Lou was officially the first full-time employee.

Lou's first WSM job assignment was to work a year in the KWC import/export department. It was effectively an apprenticeship to understand the business and facilitate a smooth partnership. With that secured, Lou returned to Southern California to help out on the operations and logistics side of WSM, which was growing fast.

"We started with our warehouse in a little aluminum shed in the City of Commerce, outside Los Angeles. For the first couple of years, I would pick up orders at our home office in the morning, drive up to Commerce to fulfill orders, and receive products," he relates. "That was the process for the first couple of years, and then we moved to a much bigger warehouse in Santa Ana, Orange County, where we needed a professional warehouse team, so I transitioned to sales."

Eventually, in 2012, Lou became the company CEO and carried over to the executive team after Fortune Brands bought the company in 2016. "I had the right last name and the depth of experience that gave me value to Fortune when they bought us," he shares.

Unlike Ken, who became an entrepreneur after a corporate career, Lou effectively followed a reverse career path, getting his start in an entrepreneurial enterprise and transitioning to a highly structured public-company environment. But Ken had prepared him well.

"A lot of companies in our industry are hardworking, entrepreneurial, family-owned businesses, but they miss a lot of the structure that Ken was able to bring to our company after his days in corporate America," Lou relates.

Firstborn Mark was the second son to join WSM. After college, he went to work for Marriott as a sales manager in their Palm Springs resort. "One weekend, Dad came to visit. After a round of golf, we got talking. My version is that Dad told me he *really* needed my help with the business. Dad tells a different story. He remembers that I said, 'I want to get on your train before it leaves the station. Please let me come to work for you now.' The reality is somewhere in the middle," he quips.

So in 1985, Mark joined the company. "I started during the day making local sales calls, then at night doing the accounting since I'd taken some accounting courses in college. It was a very grassroots organization, but as we grew, I got more involved with sales and marketing, eventually taking over national sales after we were able to hire a 'real' full-time accountant," he shares.

It wasn't long before the company outgrew its Western States Manufacturing name after one of its independent sales representatives said, "Enough of the acronym stew. Everybody knows Ken and the family. *Rohl* should be in our name." Ken listened and learned, and in 1993 the company became the Rohl Corporation.

As the company evolved, it added complementary products to round out its offerings to extend further in the kitchen and bathroom. It followed the same process proven with the pullout faucet: identifying specialty products from international suppliers that were unique to the US market. The objective was to become a one-stop shop for high-end, high-design decorative plumbing hardware.

"Our company was growing organically, adding staff and resources judiciously as the needs arose," Ken says. "By 1996 our sales exceeded $13 million, 90 percent of which was KWC kitchen-and-bath products. We had built an exclusive brand for our customers, our partner showrooms, interior designers, general contractors, and the media. We opened the doors across the country for authentically crafted, Euro-styled kitchen-and-bath products."

Speed Bump

On their sales, marketing, and distribution side, Rohl kept its promise to KWC, which was its cash cow. But over time, KWC wasn't living up to theirs.

"We started getting phone calls into the customer service department about leaking hoses," Ken relates. "At first, it was just a couple of calls, and even though they were out of our stated warranty period, we replaced them and thought little of it. Then the calls kept coming in about problems, not just with the hoses but the cartridges as well. That's when we knew we had a serious product-quality problem on our hands."

Immediately, fixing the literal leak was the top priority, with everyone across the company diverted to it. Besides the operations team, Lou, Mark, and third-son Greg (who was working full time at a publisher) were recruited to make plumbing house calls. In researching the issue, they found that the KWC hoses and cartridges designed for European water systems were failing because of the greater levels of chlorine in US water.

"We took it back to KWC, and after some tough negotiations, we got them to agree it was their responsibility to correct the problem," Ken says. "They agreed to supply not only replacement hoses and cartridges to us at no cost but also to subsidize the labor costs for replacements at $50 per appointment. But the biggest worry for us was keeping our integrity—our promise—to our customers."

Everyone in the family and the company rolled up their sleeves to correct the problems quickly and prove to their customers, beyond a doubt, that they were a company that could be counted on to do the right thing.

"These defective-product issues were a massive blow to a small organization and could have sunk us," Mark Rohl shares. "We had thousands of units in the marketplace with a significant percentage developing problems. But we had built a company that stood behind its promise. The fact that we were able to maintain good relationships with our customers and sustain our business was a testament to 'doing the right thing,' spelled out in our mission statement."

Pulling the Plug

With that hurdle behind it, the company grew nationally with Mark as national sales manager.

"I was spending a fair amount of time traveling from Southern California throughout the country, primarily in high-potential markets, following a guideline of my dad's to focus on where we were going to get the most bang for our buck," says Mark. "That was clearly New York City where the industry's largest distributor, Ferguson Enterprises, was king."

He made his first sales call on Ferguson in 1987, and it didn't go well. "I got beat up by those tough New Yorkers who said they wouldn't take on our product line unless we paid them, not the other way around."

Mark's more laid-back, California-surfer style didn't work well in uptight, hard-driving New York City. "When I got back to Orange County, I told Dad, 'If we want to open New York, we need an East Coast office.'"

Decision made, Mark traded his surfboard for NYC Yellow Cabs and moved to set up the office, hire locally embedded sales representatives, and build the East Coast business.

The company was growing from strength to strength. Then in November 1996, Ken got another alarming call from KWC. It was canceling its contract with Rohl when the January 1997 renewal date rolled around.

"So I immediately called Mark and a longtime friend who was an attorney in New Jersey and got on a plane to Newark, New Jersey," Ken recalls. "Between three o'clock on Friday to three o'clock Monday morning, we mapped out a lawsuit to protect our interests. We filed it with a judge in Newark, New Jersey, right before Thanksgiving."

It was an auspicious choice of judge and court. "Representing KWC was a German attorney working in New York City. For anyone who's dealt in the area, they know there is some rivalry between New Jersey and New York," Ken shares. "And their choice of a New York attorney, who speaks with a heavy German accent, coming into a New Jersey court with a Jewish judge worked in our favor. The CEO's deposition revealed how the company had pulled the same maneuver with other distribution partners in Italy and France, and now it was trying to do the same thing to us. The judge ruled for a stay and scheduled a jury trial for April 1997."

Ken decided not to waste time or money on a jury trial, and it was pretty clear the court would favor Rohl because the US has strong franchise laws that prevent offshore companies from taking business away from US partners. Seeing the writing on the wall, KWC settled for what Ken describes as a "favorable financial arrangement" out of court.

"As of February 1997, we shipped all the KWC inventory back. We lost $10 million in business in one stroke of the pen and were now a $2–$3 million company. We had to start all over again. That sadly meant we had to cut back our staff to a skeleton crew, and those who remained took salary cuts. But I wasn't going to allow the company to die," Ken declares, adding, "I remember feeling devastated seeing the empty parking lot afterward."

BACK TO SQUARE ONE

The company went back to its proven process of scouring the world for unique, differentiated, Euro-crafted kitchen-and-bath products to fill the pipeline for its growing network of dealers and customers.

"We always believed in selective distribution, protecting our partners' territory and not selling to every dealer on every corner," Mark says. "We had a track record of keeping our promises that built trust. We promised to make our dealers profitable with the best products and also the best service, then after the product is bought, the best service afterward."

The company didn't fall into the fatal trap of being just a product-driven company, which would have been easy to slip into because of its early reliance on the KWC pullout faucet. But Ken laid the groundwork to be a customer-driven company, and that required building a brand. He built his new team slowly and drilled them into his proven process and their shared mission and vision.

It also underwent another name change in 1998 from Rohl Corporation to Rohl LLC, now organized as a family partnership under Ken as chairman and his three sons—Lou (CEO), Mark (president, eastern division), and Greg (president, western division). Greg had left his publishing gig in 1993 and joined the company full time. Ken's stepdaughter Valinda had moved on.

Rohl LLC was well positioned for its next test: the 2008–9 Great Recession. "By 2006 we built the company up to $75 million, then like everybody else was experiencing, things started to turn in 2007," Ken reflects. "The bottom dropped out in 2010. We'd gone from $75 million before the recession to $40 million after."

That set up another round of building the business back up. But no radical moves were made because none was needed. The company had a proven plan, so it just kept working it.

By 2016, the company was back up to $75 million in revenues. And that was about the time that Fortune Brands came calling.

EXIT STRATEGY

At that time, Fortune Brands was in the process of building a global plumbing group with Moen as its flagship mass-market brand. It wanted to bolster its offerings in the higher-end luxury sector; Rohl and its roster of brands, now including Perrin & Rowe, of which Rohl owned 50 percent, would fill the bill.

In March 2016, talks began, and by August, Fortune announced the acquisition. "We understood our limits in growing market share through self-funded growth," Ken explains. "We saw unlimited potential with a market-leading company with its global footprint. Because of years of consistent performance, we were viewed as a valuable jewel to be added to Fortune's array of highly valued companies and brands."

The most important thing is you've got to stay relevant.

At least initially, Ken and family, along with the entire Rohl team, were retained. Mark and Greg eventually transitioned out of the company after several years, while Lou continued on until his retirement in 2021. Ken, however, knew he was going to be the first one let go and frankly was ready to move on because his side hustle with the University of California, Irvine, and nonprofit work was calling.

"As you move into these later years, the most important thing is you've got to stay relevant. I found that working with young people at

UCI; serving as chairman of the Irvine Barclay Theatre; and helping recruit local, state, and national political leadership let me stay involved and bring my business and operational skills to these causes."

 ## *Ken's Life Lesson Learned*

Teach What You Have to Learn

Throughout my life, I always kept a journal. It helped me see things in my life and my career from a different perspective, like the experience of looking down on the world from three thousand feet up in a hot-air balloon. Journaling lets me step out from the day-to-day fray, rise above it, and be in silence with my thoughts, like the quiet you experience floating in a balloon. It's how I tap my creative side.

You need that top-down perspective when building a company. You have to take a broader view, break the separate pieces apart, and put them back together in a new way to explain the information your people need to know and master to do their jobs.

Benjamin Franklin said, "Tell me and I forget, teach me and I may remember, involve me and I learn." The process of teaching what you have to learn is the ultimate way to be involved so you learn.

Training is essential for employees, but it does next to nothing to prepare them for their next job. That takes teaching. As Steve Jobs said, "Management is about persuading people to do things they do not want to do, while leadership is about inspiring people to do the things they never thought they could." Training is a manager's responsibility, and teaching is what a leader does. That's the prescription I follow.

Whenever I prepare to teach—whether employees, UCI students, the company founders I mentor, industry groups, or any other audience—I engage a different part of my brain than when I am going about my day-to-day business. It helps me see issues from a wider perspective and go deeper into the underlying whys and hows. I become a better leader by being a teacher. And just like other human capital, leadership grows with its use.

I teach through the age-old practice of storytelling, and I seal the stories in the students' memory—whether the matriculating kind or other—with simple catchphrases or scripts to live and do business by. That way, when next they are confronted with a problem or challenge, they have my guidance close at hand. It's how I teach people to move up the ladder or take the next step in their business.

After I joined the board of the Barclay Theater, having become involved through a personal passion for theater and the arts, I learned early on that they needed my teaching. When I came in, they were very close to bankruptcy, and the executive-management team trained in the nonprofit sector was not schooled in how to solve what were essentially business problems.

I spent a few weeks teaching them business processes, and through that, we developed a business plan to keep the lights on and the theater viable. While we were officially a nonprofit organization, to get out of our financial hole and keep operating, we had to take a profit-oriented approach. In other words, we had to make money.

As a community theater, partially taxpayer funded, the theater had a flat set ticket price for every show, no matter that the cost of one performance might be $25,000 or $50,000.

With about seven hundred seats available, we couldn't cover the cost for a $50,000 performance even if every seat in the house was filled. We would cover the high-cost shows with profit made by selling out lower-cost performances. The math assumed that some money-making shows would make up for the money-losing ones and it would all work out in the end. But it wasn't.

Fast-forward to today, and Barclay Theater prices every show differ based upon the individual cost for each show. That way, appropriate revenues are generated for every show. That is now our established pricing process, and at least until the pandemic shut the theater down, it was working. And now that things are getting back to normal, it is working again. It is a proven, repeatable process.

I've learned it doesn't take long to teach people 80 percent of what they need to know to be successful in business. To learn the other 20 percent is a lifelong process. But for most situations, that 80 percent is all that is needed.

Regina Clark is one of the many company founders who has benefited from Ken's mentoring. Regina runs a professional services business, A Clear Path, that helps people organize their homes and lives to maximize their productivity. Hers is an amazing success story—she was recently featured in *Inc.* magazine. She started her company in 2008 after her teaching job at UCLA was eliminated due to budget cuts.

Regina found herself at age fifty without a job but with a PhD. It was time to reinvent herself, and rather than continue along an academic path, she leaned into her personal passion: organizing chaos. She was great at helping people declutter and organize their spaces.

Doing her research, she connected with the National Association of Productivity and Organizing Professionals, and her passion became a business.

"People like me are needed in every phase of life, from womb to tomb, cradle to grave," she quips. "It could be families preparing for the birth of a new baby, or beleaguered parents trying to deal with their kid's mess. It could be professional women and their male counterparts who need help organizing their chaos, or seniors needing to downsize because they are moving into assisted living. We also do a lot of work in professional offices decluttering and setting up filing systems."

Organizing an Organization Business

Suffice to say, Regina knew how to organize for her clients, but she discovered she didn't know how to organize her business to maximize growth. Ken came alongside her in 2015 to help develop her business processes. "I had an 'OK' grasp on my numbers and enjoyed steady but unimpressive growth. If I hadn't met Ken, I'm sure I'd still be in business, but I probably wouldn't have the seven-figure business I have now, with fourteen employees and looking to hire another."

Working over the course of several years, they met quarterly. Every time they met, Ken wanted to see the numbers first. He read the tea leaves and taught her what she needed to learn. "His plan for me was to focus, to pick a track, narrow my vision about the services I want to offer, and then develop the marketing plan around my focus."

Regina had fallen into a trap that catches many new business owners: casting their net too wide and trying to be all things to all people.

Ken held her feet to the fire and demanded she focus, so she worked with a copywriter to create personas for her best referral partners and target customers. "Since then, every piece of marketing goes out to one of those four personas. Up until then, my marketing plan was to sit in a dark room with a handful of darts.

"The other thing he drilled into me was 'Always know your numbers,'" she continues. And the business process he taught her worked. "The proof is we stayed afloat during the pandemic and exceeded projections by 26 percent in 2021."

But most profoundly, what Ken imparted to Regina, besides his business process, was on the personal side. "Ken had the gift of making me feel visible," she says and admits she could be a tough student.

"I can be a bit of a 'smarty pants' with my head full of a thousand ideas. I'm not sure I would have known to ask anyone about how to do it better. But I'm so grateful to Ken that he taught me to be more focused and deliberate, to pick a track and stay on it," she says.

So now you've met Ken and learned about his background and experience becoming a corporateneur, moving from the corporate world to an entrepreneurial venture. You've got a sampling of the wisdom he has to share. It's time to get down to the nitty-gritty to explain the Rohl Model for the corporateneur and map your own path to success as a corporateneur.

 # Ken's Key Takeaways

- Teach what you need to learn. There is no better way to build expertise, authority, and understanding or to fill a skills/experience gap than to do the research, break down complex challenges into bite-size nuggets, and then put them back together, perhaps in different ways.

- Control the things you can control so you are always ready to confront the challenges you can't, like losing a major client or supplier or when the economy turns south. Never get too comfortable or confident because things can turn in an instant. And most importantly, don't get too dependent on only one supplier, client, or partner.

- There is almost never only one solution to a business problem, but there is one resource you can turn to for finding solutions: the numbers. Study them carefully and often, and don't browse the top or bottom line. Understand all the various factors (i.e., the key performance indicators, KPIs, that go into each line on the balance sheet; profit and loss statements; and sales reports).

 Your Corporateneur Road Map

1. Review your corporateneur résumé objectively from the point of view of a business owner looking to hire you to run their business. What skills are lacking? Where are you weak?

2. Take each area of weakness and prepare a lesson plan to teach yourself what you need to learn. Do the research, make notes, organize an outline, and get learning.

2

PART TWO

Getting Down to Business

CHAPTER 4

Path Forward

"Half the art of ballooning is to make your crashes so gentle that you can fool yourself into calling them landings."

—RICHARD BRANSON

We've all heard of the "Peter Principle," where one rises to the level of his or her incompetence. If you're a midcareer professional, you've undoubtedly seen plenty of Peter Principles at work. But as a corporateneur, you can't afford to become one. Whatever your respective incompetence is—and everyone's got some or many areas of incompetence—the corporateneur and the company he or she forms must overcome them.

We've shared the arc of Ken's career through the corporate world and into the entrepreneurial world—his corporateneur journey. We've given some highlights of his experience and learnings that have taken him from here to there. We've explained how you have to leverage your soft human capital to shore up your hard financial capital, often in short supply during the early days. We've looked at the factors that set the successful entrepreneur apart, most especially their unique cognitive processes.

With the sole purpose of this book being to help corporateneurs reach higher levels of success, we need to examine the root causes of why entrepreneurs fail. That will help recalibrate the balance toward new-venture success.

Numerous articles have been written over the years attempting to address this question, but most lack research rigor and validity. While statistics prove that a new business is far more likely to fail than succeed, very little research has been conducted about why the failure rate is so high and how to mitigate it.

Leo Tolstoy sums up the reason why such studies are rare in the opening line of his classic novel *Anna Karenina*: "Happy families are all alike; every unhappy family is unhappy in its own way." Successful companies, like happy families, are easy to study because they share similarities. But failed companies, like unhappy families, fail for a myriad of reasons. Because of that, it's extremely difficult to draw conclusions about them. However, entrepreneurship professors Dean Shepherd and Johan Wiklund took on the task.

BUSINESS FAILURE IS A PROCESS

In their study published in *Foundations and Trends in Entrepreneurship* titled "Successes and Failures at Research on Business Failure and Learning from It," the researchers point out the research shortfall is largely due to the lack of consistent and reliable data about business failures.

For one, there is no clear-cut definition of what constitutes new-business failure. Is it defined as business bankruptcy or simply failure to thrive? Business failure exists on a sliding scale that must be accounted for in research.

Besides the lack of a clear-cut definition, researchers also lack access to suitable data to conduct such research. Once a business closes, its data goes missing from databases. And to add to the confusion, entrepreneurs who fail do not make reliable research subjects. Their perspectives are anecdotal and subject to reporting biases. Nobody wants to talk about where their business went off the rails, and even if they do, they rarely have an objective perspective.

In their study, Shepherd and Wiklund set out with the goal of "producing prescriptive research that will help us educate entrepreneurs on ways to avoid business failure." Rather than seeing failure as a single event, they looked at failure as a process.

The researchers take an objective, thirty-thousand-foot perspective on the root causes of business failure. None is more important than another, but all contribute to the process of business collapse. Here are some of the root causes of business failure they identified.

Liability of Newness

The liability of newness often contributes to business failure. It applies a Darwinian survival-of-the-fittest spin to business failure, recognizing that new organizations face a number of internal and external factors that threaten their survival.

The internal factors include the need for everyone across the company to learn new tasks and design new systems and processes efficiently and cost-effectively. New businesses may run out of time before these numerous internal challenges are resolved.

The external factors are the barriers of entry any new business faces, including building brand recognition and market acceptance, countering competitor pressures, and regulatory and legal challenges.

Shepherd and Wiklund conclude, "The liability of newness relates to the *actions* and *learning* that the management team and employees must undergo to overcome the major challenges of adaptation to the internal and external environments of new organizations. Often, however, these liabilities of newness are so extensive that the new company fails despite attempts to adapt to the environment."

However, as much as newness can be a liability for a business, it also confers advantages, which the researchers call *the asset of newness*. These derive from a new business's ability to be more flexible and adaptable than established organizations, which may be unable to confront changes in the market that new businesses represent. "The strategic flexibility of young firms can represent an advantage," the authors conclude.

New ventures must leverage their strengths to overcome weaknesses. Ken would argue that includes building a business process that is flexible and adaptable. It also requires everyone in the company to have a clear understanding of its goals, objectives, and promises to the customer. That's the North Star that guides every business and its processes.

Ken also believes that the midcareer entrepreneur—a corporateneur—is better able to overcome the liability of newness because of their experience of once, or many times, being new in their corporate jobs and being successful, or not so successful, in adapting to an established business's structure and process. By learning on the job and on someone else's dime, the corporateneur figures out what works and what doesn't and can safeguard their own business ventures against the liability of newness and turn it into an asset.

Weakness of Human Capital

The corporateneur's human capital gained from their past experiences comes to the fore to navigate the liability of newness, Shepherd and Wiklund's research finds.

"Entrepreneurs with more experience will possess the knowledge to perform more effectively the roles and tasks necessary for success," they write. "In the entrepreneurial context, human capital refers to the knowledge and skills that assist in successfully engaging in new entries. It provides the entrepreneur with knowledge that assists them in identifying opportunities and knowledge of ways to more effectively and efficiently pursue new entry."

Having past experience in running a new business, whether as a serial entrepreneur or managing a business within a business—being an intrapreneur, as Ken did throughout his corporate career—provides significant advantages for the eventual success of a new independent venture.

Despite the many advantages human capital provides, it also can be a pitfall. For example, procrastination can be a leader's failing, as they are forced to make critical decisions with inadequate information. The researchers explain that procrastination is an avoidance/coping mechanism people use to relieve anxiety caused by thinking about and taking necessary steps forward when the path is unclear.

Sometimes it pays to wait, but more often than not, the business leader can't afford to and must be constantly poised for action to make uncomfortable and necessary decisions quickly. The midcareer entrepreneur's stakes are higher in their own venture than they ever were in their corporate careers, so greater decision-making anxiety is often the result. But by calling upon previous experience—their learned heuristic shortcuts—corporateneurs can avoid procrastination and make the hard decisions even without adequate information.

Persistence can be another stumbling block. The researchers point out that intrinsically motivated entrepreneurs, as opposed to those who are primarily extrinsically motivated, are more prone to persist in a course of action or business process that isn't producing the desired result.

Entrepreneurs with higher levels of extrinsic motivation take their cues and clues from the external environment. They are better able to read the signs about whether things in the business are working or not and more likely to make necessary changes than those intrinsically motivated where their work is its own reward. The intrinsically motivated leader can be prone to persist in an unproductive course and ignore the warning signs.

The intrinsically motivated leader can be prone to persist in an unproductive course and ignore the warning signs.

Reflecting upon Regina Clark's A Clear Path business, she was primarily intrinsically motivated to bring her organizational skills to help the disorganized. It wasn't until extrinsically motivated Ken came alongside her and helped her look objectively from the outside at her business that she discovered its true potential. Without his external perspective, she would have persisted operating her business at a lower level of success than she ultimately achieved with his help. He taught her to think extrinsically, to read the numbers and focus the business on a track that delivered better numbers.

When applied to a successful business, persistence is a virtue, but it can be a trap for leaders whose business is underperforming. So a leader's persistence must be tempered with flexibility to change course if the business is not working or not working as well as it should.

Failure to Learn

The entrepreneur must learn from both successes and mistakes, though Shepherd and Wiklund argue that mistakes are actually more powerful learning experiences.

"By seeking success and avoiding failure, errors are introduced that can not only inhibit the learning and interpretation processes but also make failure more likely or expensive than necessary," they write. "Failure is more important than success for learning. When failure occurs, the entrepreneur has an opportunity to learn from the experience."

Entrepreneurs can't indulge in avoidance behavior such as procrastination caused by undue anxiety. Nor can they persist on a course that is not delivering the results needed and desired. That's the definition of *insanity* often credited to Albert Einstein, that of "doing the same thing over and over again and expecting different results." Instead, you've got to learn from mistakes and take immediate corrective action.

Is it a failure to not make your numbers on the monthly, quarterly, or annual business plan? Not necessarily, though it might be a symptom that business changes are needed. Or it could be that the numbers in the plan are wrong and need to be adjusted.

Cognitive Bias of Overconfidence

"Entrepreneurs are overconfident," Shepherd and Wiklund write. They point to numerous research studies that conclude, "They consistently exhibit greater overconfidence than people in other professions."

One study found that 81 percent of some three thousand entrepreneurs studied rate the chance of their venture's success at over 70 percent, with one-third believing they have a 100 percent likelihood to succeed. Further, they are overconfident about the potential success of other businesses like theirs, with some 60 percent believing similar businesses would succeed, though the objective business-survival statistics argue otherwise.

"Overconfidence is a bias that, when exhibited by founding entrepreneurs, jeopardizes the life of their venture," they conclude. Overconfidence affects how they interpret information, allocate resources (putting too much toward one part of the process and depriving others), and overestimate the potential market reaction to their venture.

The authors call it the *hubris theory of entrepreneurship*, and the cure for that is to know yourself, play to your strengths, and compensate for your weaknesses.

 # Ken's Life Lesson Learned

The 80/20 Rule of Strengths and Weaknesses

The *Pareto principle*, also called the *80/20 rule* (80 percent of the effects come from 20 percent of the causes), was first identified by the Italian economist Vilfredo Pareto in 1896. It came from his discovery that 80 percent of the land in Italy was owned by 20 percent of the population. Intrigued, he conducted the same research in other countries only to discover the same 80/20 rule.

It was first applied to business by Joseph Juran. He stated, "You generally spend 80 percent of your time on 20 percent of the project." And since then, this idea of the "vital few" has been applied to guide innumerable business processes, like the adage that 80 percent of sales come from 20 percent of clients.

Throughout my career, I've found the 80/20 rule applies again and again. For example, I believe that a person can learn 80 percent of what they need to know to be successful in business in a short period of time. Learning the other 20 percent takes a lifetime.

However, the Pareto principle suggests that other 20 percent is the most vital for ultimate success. Yet no entrepreneur can wait a lifetime.

That's why Socrates's dictum "Know thyself" is so important for anyone starting a business. I like to think I know myself, having lived more years than many people have the privilege to. I also have made it a lifelong habit of keeping a personal journal that helps me work out problems and delve deeper into my thoughts.

PLAY TO YOUR STRENGTHS

Introspection is a critical quality for all entrepreneurs to develop. And even if they are blessed with plenty of it, it helps to quantify it by doing a detailed personal SWOT analysis: strengths, weaknesses, opportunities, threats.

Most of us have a good handle on our personal strengths and how they make opportunities for us, but we might be blind to our personal weaknesses and the threat they pose to making the most of our opportunities. In terms of the 80/20 rule, your personal weaknesses represent the "vital few" 20 percent that can be your business's undoing.

In building a business, you need to fill your personal-weakness void with people who have the skills and qualities that overcome your weaknesses. And you need to leverage your personal strengths in every way possible to overcome threats and maximize opportunities.

For me, one of my strengths is objectively seeing the big picture, looking outside in rather than inside out. Being a "forest" not a "trees" person, I was good at planting the forest but needed people around me who could tend, manage, and prune the trees. I was blessed to find task-oriented, detail-obsessive people to support me and the business. They became the 80 percent that kept the business running and serving the customers we depended upon.

That's how I was able to keep my focus on the outside, developing customer and partner relationships and identifying market opportunities by continually learning from those connections. And that was the reason I took to the road in the early days, and as the business grew, I tried to stay out on the road to make sure we were living up to our promises to our customers and partners.

DISRUPT YOURSELF

One of my strengths throughout my corporate career was challenging the status quo and fearlessly disrupting what needed to be disrupted. I took the same approach in examining the workings of my business. Any business is an interlocking system of interdependent parts and processes. A breakdown or weakness in one part of the system threatens the overall system, both upstream and downstream.

You don't want to disrupt a system that is working seamlessly—but almost none do over time. You've got to continually challenge and test the linkages in every process in the system. So I spent a lot of my time talking to customers and partners to measure the effectiveness of our systems and process. Everyone else in the company was also gathering insights from their outside connections. We knew that these sources could provide early warning signs of any potential breakdown or weakness in our business.

With a disrupt-yourself-before-you-are-disrupted perspective, we instituted a process for everyone in the company to perform a monthly SWOT analysis of their job and across their span of control. The management team and I did the big-picture SWOT analysis for the company, then folded in the SWOT analysis for each division in the company. This gave us a macro-micro understanding of where we were as a company and how we collectively and individually could do better in the future.

As always, I was keen on knowing our numbers. But just as when you go to the doctor's office and take your temperature and blood pressure, while those readings indicate potential problems, they don't diagnose the disease. Our routine SWOT analysis helped us diagnose what was driving the numbers up or down so we could quickly fix any weaknesses and overcome potential threats. And if the numbers were going up, we would double down on what was producing those positive results.

ALL HANDS ON DECK

We also built participatory management into our business system. I never thrived in a top-down management system and didn't expect anyone in my company to, either, so everyone had full responsibility and authority within their job function. And for everyone, serving our customers was always priority number one.

While I was the final arbiter, I needed and valued everyone's input. If we had a meeting and everyone at the table was in complete agreement and didn't have a different point of view, I would reflexively challenge them by asking something to the effect of "What are we doing here then, if we all agree? Why do we need you then?" I was never afraid of being challenged. On the contrary, I was more afraid of everyone just going along to get along.

Other people who were not as comfortable as I am with disrupting the status quo or challenging the boss needed some prodding. But it paid off in the end because no matter what you do and no matter how well you do it, there are always ways to do it better. It's that 80/20 rule again: 80 percent of the business is doing just fine, but that 20 percent, which inevitably isn't working as well as it should, could grow into the 80 percent that brings the business down over time.

It's my job and yours to see that doesn't happen, so build safeguards into your systems to not only know your numbers but understand why they are moving in one direction or another. Our disciplined use of the SWOT analysis combined with an 80/20 view kept us on course and will help keep you on yours.

One of Ken's early hires was Tom Duino, who augmented one of Ken's weaknesses. Tom joined the company in 1989 as a temp to do data entry as the company was computerizing its paper-based records system. "I had a general business administration degree from the University of California, but they hired me because I was adept at typing," Tom relates. "Then two weeks later, they brought me on full time. Ken saw something in me he valued, and I have been with the company ever since, now working with Rohl under Fortune Brands in quality control."

Tom filled a critical back-office function on which the success of the sales-oriented company depended. Ken says, "Tom contributed to the company's success in countless ways. He is one of the most diligent, dependable, hardworking, and detail-oriented people I have ever met."

As a generalist, not a specialist, Tom could be counted on to lend a hand wherever needed. "It was an all-hands-on-deck environment," Tom explains. "In a small company, you have to have people who will do what needs to be done, so maybe I was working the books for a couple of hours in the morning, then driving a forklift and checking in product for a couple of more in the afternoon, and taking out the trash at the end of the day. You just have to show up and do it."

Tom was most highly valued for his stick-to-itiveness. But he didn't just blindly follow procedures; he was always looking for ways to cut down on the 80 percent that yields little result and amplify the 20 percent that brings the rewards. "We didn't have a highly structured organization. Everyone knew their job, but they knew everyone else's, too, so we were always looking to find better ways of doing things and solutions that would simplify things and make them work better," he explains.

For example, Tom wasn't responsible for shipping out orders. That was handled by the warehouse managers who chose among various shipping services, like FedEx, UPS, or Consolidated Freightways, based on the immediate needs. But Tom saw the resulting bills and found the company was paying full list price on delivery. "When I found out we could get discounts of 60 to 70 percent by consolidating our shipments to one carrier, I had to say something. We were literally getting screwed every time we sent a shipment out," he says. By speaking up, Tom saved the company over a million dollars a year on outbound freight.

Every company needs a Tom who identifies opportunities beyond their direct span of control and puts the company's best interests first.

As Tom moved throughout the organization, he found his most valuable contribution played to his obsession for detail in keeping track of the company's price book. It was the company bible on which every transaction and all the salespeople and their customers depended. "Ken would joke that I was the 'chief impediment to sales.' The salespeople were always 'running and gunning,' but I was the one saying 'time out' because if we don't get the details right, we're going to stumble," he shares.

In reality, Tom was the company's chief facilitator of sales because without the price book being up-to-date and reflecting the current product selections and prices, the company's promises to customers couldn't be kept.

Reflecting on what made the company so successful for so many years, Tom says it was because everyone understood the company's goals, mission, and promises to each other and to business partners and customers. With those ideals constantly in mind, everything else was open for discussion.

"We would have 'doorway time' where anyone could stand in Ken's doorway, discuss an issue—so we were always thinking on our feet. That gave us the ability to make quick moves as circumstances dictated," Tom says. "Ken was the company hero, the master speaker and motivator. He has a 'silver tongue' and knows how to get the best out of people. He was always very engaged, but he didn't get down into the weeds. He trusted people to do the right thing.

"People in business talk about delegation, but Ken talked about responsibility, authority, and accountability. That's what he gave to all of us and that he trusted us with. And in turn, we completely trusted him," Tom shares.

 # *Ken's Life Lesson Learned*

Forget the Many; Be Important to a Few

In business today, a lot of new ventures put growth and scale before profits. The thinking goes that profits will naturally come as more and more customers are added to the list. Shockingly, in 2021 nearly 80 percent of companies filing for an IPO have yet to make a profit. And that high percentage of unprofitable IPOs has remained consistent over the last couple of years. Of course, some of those companies go on to succeed, but many others end up in the corporate trash heap.

I wasn't about to let that happen to my company. From day one, I positioned the company to be profitable. I chose a path of slower but consistent, sustainable growth with money always going to both the top and bottom line.

That goal drove all decision-making. I was fond of saying, "How do you eat an elephant? One bite at a time." And that's how we tackled entering what we saw as a multimillion-dollar market—by taking one small bite out of it at a time.

Throughout my corporate career, I found that the way to optimize my time and the company's revenue potential in a highly competitive market was to focus on major customers and consistently get hits with them rather than occasional home runs with a smaller player. Time spent cultivating relationships with high-performing/high-potential customers simply had a more measurable and impactful ROI.

So when starting my company, "high potential, high performing" became our mantra. Instead of spreading ourselves too thin, we started in our own backyard—California—and spread out organically by building a strong customer base there. We proved ourselves in that smaller market by testing and refining our processes so that we had a proven, repeatable business model. From that early success, we grew to other regions and eventually nationally.

Critical to our business model was to identify the most important potential customers in the chosen area and develop a program customized for their needs. We defined the best potential customers as those with the most influence in the market, who believed in us and would get behind us to help move us forward. We also were keen on finding customers who would benefit the most from us too.

Rather than being one of many plumbing products on big dealers' shelves, we aimed to be carried by dealers where we'd be one of a few, and out of those few, we were the best. This approach also gave us the ability to offer exclusive area dealerships, which was highly valued by the dealers we did business with. That way, we became important to a few, and those few were very important to us.

LESS IS MORE

Embedded in the Pareto principle is the concept that less—the vital few 20 percent—is really more. That idea was expanded upon by psychologist Barry Schwartz in his best-selling book *The Paradox of Choice*. The inspiration for that book came from a study done by professors Sheena Iyengar and Mark Lepper in their groundbreaking research "When Choice Is Demotivating," published in the *Journal of Personality and Social Psychology*.

It is widely known as the "jam study." The researchers presented consumers with an extensive selection of twenty-four varieties of jams and measured engagement (i.e., tasting) and subsequent purchase of the jars in a retail setting. The research followed with phase two where consumers were offered a limited selection of only six jars with the same measures taken.

The researchers found that in both the extensive-selection and limited-selection experiments, the level of consumer engagement was identical. Virtually the same number of people stopped and tasted the jams on offer.

But when it came to making a subsequent purchase, the results differed widely. About one-third of customers in the limited-selection group actually purchased a jar of jam. Only 3 percent of the extensive-selection group did the same. Paradoxically, ten times more jam was sold when customers were presented with fewer choices.

This has been my guiding principle in growing the business. Hire fewer people but make them people like Tom Duino, who can do more. Partner with fewer suppliers—where your business is more important to them, and likewise, they are more important to you. That is the basis of true business partnerships.

And when it comes to customers, focus on the few rather than the many. Our dealers were highly influential in their local markets. They valued our products and services and our partnership.

We were important to the vital few rather than spreading ourselves too thin by trying to be important to many. We may have grown slower than if we had gone another way, but we were always profitable, and that is what ultimately makes a sustainable business.

 # Ken's Key Takeaways

- Know yourself and your areas of weakness, and surround yourself with people who can make up for your shortcomings.

- Calibrate the business to maximize success and minimize mistakes. Learn from mistakes, and don't repeat them.

- New ventures can suffer from a liability of newness if they don't build adaptability and flexibility into the business's structure and processes.

- Corporateneurs must avoid procrastination when making decisions with incomplete information.

- Persistence can be a strength when the processes put in place produce desired results. Or it can be a weakness if the corporateneur doesn't read the signs that processes aren't working.

- Balance confidence with realism. Don't fall victim to the bias of overconfidence. Be confident but also realistic. Build feedback mechanisms like SWOT analysis and reading the numbers throughout the business, and objectively read the results.

- Make the 80/20 rule a guiding principle in your business. Focus your 80 percent on the 20 percent that produces results.

- To be a high-performing business, you must focus all efforts on the highest-potential prospects and opportunities in the market. Be important to a few, and forget the many, which will waste time and deplete resources.

 ## Your Corporateneur Road Map

1. Conduct a SWOT analysis for yourself and your business concept.

2. How prepared are you to overcome the liability of newness in your business? Is it new enough to make a real impression in the market? Be realistic. Too many new businesses simply tweak the status quo and don't disrupt it.

3. Are you more extrinsically or intrinsically motivated? Can you find the right balance to recognize when changes are needed in your business's process and systems?

4. Think about times in your career when you failed. What did you do wrong that caused the failures? How did you learn from them to come back and fight another day?

CHAPTER 5

Big Picture First

"When the air balloon was first discovered, someone flippantly asked Benjamin Franklin what was the use of it. He answered this question by asking another: 'What is the use of a new-born infant? It may become a man.'"

—CHARLES CALEB COLTON

A s founder and influencer-in-chief for the new enterprise, your span of influence includes those outside the organization— such as potential clients and customers, partners and suppliers, industry connections and influencers and the press and media who can influence them—and those inside the organization, in particular your employees. But *who* and *what* influences *you*?

For the *who*, Ken developed close personal relationships with business associates and colleagues, people he called "angels" who helped him along each step in his corporateneur journey. They were there to bounce ideas off of and to learn from. And now, he is giving back in kind through his mentoring and nonprofit work.

As for the *what*, you start with an idea for a product or service that you are convinced has more strengths than weaknesses and has enough of a difference to overcome threats and that will offer the greatest opportunity. You've done your homework, looked at the available market, identified competing products or services, and found white space where your venture can grow.

These early days are spent probing deep into your specific category, looking vertically up and down your defined market. But if you limit your view to only the vertical market, you may end up competing on the same plane as everybody else in the category. You run the risk of not being able to scale the category's barriers to entry. You'll be stuck only reimagining what already is, not imagining what can be.

In the early stage of business planning, you need to look wider across verticals to see what can be borrowed from strategies used by companies outside your category and applied to yours. This is where disruptive innovation comes from: a business model that turns the established one on its head.

BUSINESS MODEL INNOVATORS

Jeff Bezos at Amazon and Gary Friedman at RH are prime examples of entrepreneurs who imagined what can be, rather than reimaging what is within their vertical space.

Bezos started Amazon selling exactly the same thing as every other bookstore. He only changed the way to sell them: online. But from day one, he didn't limit his business model to selling books. That was the test of a much bigger concept: to become the "online everything" store.

People thought he was crazy in 1997 when Amazon went public. But his business model and guiding principles, from the start, carried the company through to what it has now become: the world's largest retailer. In following that path, Amazon also expanded into auxiliary services under different business models, including Amazon Web Services, Amazon Prime Entertainment, Amazon Advertising, and most recently, Amazon Logistics.

Bezos's founding principles for Amazon were the following:

1. Customer obsession rather than competitor focus

2. Passion for invention

3. Commitment to operational excellence

4. Long-term thinking

Gary Friedman took a near-bankrupt home furnishings retailer, called Restoration Hardware, and transformed it into RH, which he describes as an "ecosystem of products, places, services and spaces." He threw out the traditional business model for a furniture brand and home furnishings retailer and created something totally different and unique.

Ken was just such a change agent in the commoditized world of plumbing fixtures and supplies. His innovative Rohl Model elevated the kitchen faucet into a luxury appliance that set a new standard for the industry, which others followed.

THE BUSINESS MODEL DEFINES HOW THE COMPANY ROLLS

At its most elemental, a *business model* is defined as "a design for the successful operation of a business, identifying revenue sources, customer base, products, and details of financing." It is described in the business plan and includes the following:

- *Customer value proposition*, or what your business will do better for the customer than the competition.

- *Profit formula*, which defines how you create value in the business by providing value to the customer. It includes the cost structure and margin that will generate revenues and ultimately profit.

- *Key resources*, or the assets required to deliver value to the customer at a profit. It encompasses people, technology, products, facilities, channels, and brand.

- *Key processes*, which are the operational and managerial capabilities that enable the company to deliver value in a way that can be repeated and scaled. Manufacturing, budgeting, planning, sales and marketing, and customer service are among the key processes.

Writing in *Harvard Business Review*, Mark Johnson, cofounder of strategic consultancy Innosight and author of *Lead from the Future*, explained, "Every successful company, whether it knows it or not, owes its success to its business model."

> **"Every successful company, whether it knows it or not, owes its success to its business model."**

Challenging the assumption that a company's digital technology platform was the primary transformative value of their success (e.g., Amazon), he replied, "A digital platform, or a digital solution, may enable a new epoch of transformative growth, but when you get under a company's hood and look to see what's really driving it, the engine of transformation turns out to be its business model."

FINDING BUSINESS MODEL INNOVATION

Yet, unlike Bezos and Friedman, too few companies use the business model proactively to drive business transformation. Instead, business models are changed primarily as a reaction to external changes in the market, according to a study by Luis Martins, Violina Rindova, and Bruce Greenbaum at the McCombs School of Business, University of Texas. The researchers studied more than three thousand senior executives and found 52 percent reported that "exogenous shocks" drove business model adaptation.

"Business model innovation may not be the result of any grand master plan or a matter of superior foresight," the authors write, and offer a proactive approach to business model innovation by drawing upon cognitive psychology and schemas (i.e., mental shortcuts that enhance and simplify decision-making). They present a way to use "structured cognitive processes to innovate business models"—in other words, to take the lead, not to follow everybody else.

"Schemas can be changed, and entirely new schemas can be created through specific mental operations that enable individuals to reorganize their existing knowledge and cope with novelty," they continue. Business model innovation comes by leaders taking what they already know and reinterpreting it for their venture, as Bezos and Friedman did.

Business leaders can call upon innate cognitive processes to create business model innovation, specifically by using one of the following:

- *Analogical reasoning*, which relies on the identification of similarities (analogies in other business models) that can be profitably leveraged to broaden the understanding associated with the target concept (your business model).

- *Conceptual combination*, which represents a search for a difference between two concepts (different business models) that can be integrated into the target concept (your business model) to alter its attributes, thereby creating a new concept (an entirely new business model).

Using the analogical approach, entrepreneurs can find similarities between their challenge and other companies facing similar challenges, known as a *modifier concept*. By following the conceptual approach, entrepreneurs are able to identify differences and use those to develop their business model.

And both encourage leaders to look outside their existing industry framework to identify models to adapt and reconfigure for their businesses, just as Elon Musk and Howard Schultz did.

Tesla Used Apple as an Analogy

Elon Musk jettisoned the traditional automotive industry business model for Tesla Motors by using an analogical reasoning approach. He benchmarked against Apple Computers as a modifier concept. Apple, not General Motors and Ford, was the inspiration for the Tesla business model.

The initial challenge was to position Tesla's distinctive electric motor technology favorably against the automotive industry's dominant internal-combustion-powered technology.

He was inspired by Apple's emphasis on design and brought it to the Tesla car design. Musk called Tesla Model S "his Macintosh." He also followed its high-end pricing model—creating aspiration for the brand—by entering the market high and bringing prices down as volumes grew.

Musk copied Apple's method for introducing new models in well-choreographed, invitation-only "reveals" at company headquarters, rather than dropping new models at large auto shows. Like Apple's direct-to-consumer distribution strategy, he ditched industry-standard dealer franchises for company-owned stores in high-end malls and shopping centers.

Starbucks Used a Conceptual Approach

Starbucks started selling just roasted coffee beans in the Seattle Pike Place Market in 1971. It wasn't until the early '80s that it offered brewed espresso coffee alongside its beans and eventually expanded to six stores in the Seattle area. Then in 1987, Howard Schultz bought the coffee company after serving as its director of retail operations and marketing since 1982.

He immediately set out to transform the company from its traditional coffee-centric business. He defined the stores as coffee bars, applying a modifier concept of a traditional neighborhood bar to a coffee café. This meant a shift into the restaurant-service business from a more traditional retailer selling primarily packaged coffee beans.

During the company's early stage, Schultz used the analogical approach, borrowing the business model of the neighborhood bar. He substituted baristas for bartenders to mix customizable drinks, and the staff was trained to learn the names and preferences of their regular customers, rather than the more impersonal transactional approach in traditional retail.

A fateful trip to Italy clued him into the personal and social aspects of the coffee experience. "I couldn't believe that Starbucks was in the coffee business yet was overlooking so central an element of it," he said.

Then, Schultz transitioned to a conceptual approach to further refine the Starbucks business model. He identified the opportunity to elevate Starbucks cafés beyond a place to get your coffee fix—as a "third place" between home and office or, as he described, "an extension between people's lives, at a time when people have no place to go."

Schultz transferred the social aspects of stepping up to a bar for a drink into the entire space. He also adapted the idea of an office with tables to attract people to use the stores as their third place for work and expanded the product offerings to include coffee tools and accessories to take home, like a traditional retailer.

GREAT MINDS THINK ALIKE BUT COME TO DIFFERENT CONCLUSIONS

Using the analogical and conceptual cognitive approaches to creating innovative business models—as Bezos, Friedman, Musk, Schultz, and Ken did—is how each disrupted their industries. They took bits and pieces from other business models and put them together in new ways that allow for "more creativity in changing products or customer experiences and creating new market categories," the study authors write. And entrepreneurs have a distinct edge when it comes to developing new business models.

At its core, a business model is how a company unlocks value for the customer and the business through their product or service offering. One could argue that, in the early days, Bezos looked to Walmart as an analogy for the Amazon retail business, selling across a wide range of products at discount prices.

RH adopted a conceptual approach, as it reimagined a furniture store into an experiential gallery for home design and extended it into services, restaurants, interior design, hotels, spas, yachts, and residential real estate under its all-encompassing-ecosystem business model.

DEVELOPING THE ROHL BUSINESS MODEL

Like Schultz, Ken used a combination of analogical and conceptual approaches to develop the business model for his company. He looked to the luxury business model used by heritage brands such as Louis Vuitton, Chanel, and Hermès as a modifier concept and applied it to the mundane and commoditized business of plumbing.

He also drew inspiration from the kitchen appliance category, as he envisioned the individual components he was selling as a system, using and delivering water in the kitchen. The faucet-and-sink combination was conceived as the "water appliance" and further modified by borrowing from the smart-home concept to create the "water workstation."

In the commoditized plumbing market, Ken's concept was as revolutionary as Schultz's was in conceiving Starbucks as the "third place" between home and office.

Repositioning the faucet-and-sink combination as a system or workstation was backed up by research that found people interact with their kitchen sinks more than any other kitchen appliance.

By repositioning the faucet-sink combination as a system, Rohl was able to give its dealer network more ammunition to sell its higher-end offerings to their customers and clients. These customers were ready to invest significant amounts of money on high-end stoves and refrigerators, so it allowed dealers to encourage them to give more attention to what would be the most used kitchen appliance in the home.

And from Ken's accumulated corporate experience, he adopted the customer-first, always and forever, model of service.

 Ken's Life Lesson Learned ──

The Business Model's Three Legs: Product, Marketing, Financials

At the very outset, creating the business model for your new venture is the most critical decision you will make. But most design their business models as an inverted pyramid with the product or service carrying the most weight.

Virtually every entrepreneur starts out with a product or service idea that they believe fills an unmet need in the market or that they can do better than anybody else. Under that, they slip in marketing to enter the market and gain traction. And after that comes the reward—revenue-and-profit growth. But everything starts with the product or service.

While this may be the most prevalent way business models are crafted, I say they are wrong—dead wrong. It's out of balance. At its core, a business model is the method by which you are going to create value for your customers and ultimately extract value for yourself, your employees, and your partners.

The inverted-pyramid approach implies that the product or service is the most important aspect of the business model, but the product or service is only one part of the equation. Marketing is just as important as the product or service piece since that is how you reach your market and make sales. And making the sales supplies the needed financials.

Rather than building your business model as an inverted pyramid, it should be viewed as a three-legged stool. Value is delivered and realized from each leg of the stool. If it is out of balance, you know what happens: the stool falls over; it can't support the weight.

Product, marketing, and financials are the *what*, *how*, and *why* of your business because without attending to the financials by generating adequate profitability, the other two legs of the business collapse. Likewise, the marketing is essential because product alone will get you only so far.

The business model must give equal emphasis to all three: product, marketing, and financials. This, in essence, is the Rohl Model.

PRODUCT IS THE WHAT

Our business model was essentially borrowed from the luxury business model, except we were not vertically integrated and didn't manufacture the product ourselves. The products arrived at our warehouse ready to be sold.

It turned out to be a simpler and more cost-effective way to source products because we could identify unique, highly differentiated products from Europe that had no exposure in the US market. At the same time, we established exclusive distribution agreements with our partners, so we controlled that side of the business. And we were successful in bringing other product manufacturers on board because they appreciated our business model.

We relied on our business partners to be product design and manufacturing experts. We got involved in the manufacturing side only to make recommendations and suggestions for product features and enhancements. But we relied upon our partners to do the heavy lifting when it came to the manufacturing process.

This approach freed us up to devote all our energies to romancing the products and building benefit stories that we could take to the market in order to maximize profitability.

The luxury business model is the most value-intensive and value-producing one. Because of that, it generates the highest margins and profitability, and it was the right one for us to disrupt a traditionally commoditized market. And just like under the luxury business model, powerful, effective marketing was critical to our success.

MARKETING IS THE HOW

We may not have had our own factory, making products, but we operated a factory nonetheless: our "factory" manufactured sales.

Marketing unlocks the value in your business model. It's the engine that drives growth and profitability, and it is the process that encompasses every touchpoint with the customer.

As for all companies that sell through retail intermediaries, as we did, the customer profile is multilayered with distinct needs and perspectives. For us, it included dealers, showrooms, and retailers who stocked our products. It also included influencers, like interior designers and architects, who specified our products for their clients. Then, of course, we served the end user, including homeowners and commercial clients such as hotels. None was more important than another, so marketing had to be targeted on multiple fronts.

Because we sold through intermediaries, it was critically important that everyone throughout our distribution network—retail dealers and influencers—understood our product distinctives and the value of working with us. So we spent a lot of effort educating our partners throughout the network. By necessity, we became experts at storytelling, from the big picture down to the minutest details of how the products worked so well.

Importantly, marketing is not something that just sits in the marketing department. It's the responsibility of everyone throughout the company. I frequently told my team, "Nothing happens without the sale," and marketing is how the sale is made.

While we followed the luxury business model with its emphasis on marketing, we couldn't go all the way with its heavy investment in advertising. Too often, people mistake marketing for advertising and public relations. Advertising is a high-stakes gamble, and it takes a lot of money to get in the game, with no guarantee of success.

The problem with advertising is it just pushes your message out— and nobody likes to be pushed. We needed to pull customers in, so we adopted a different approach described by the familiar joke "How do you eat an elephant? One bite at a time."

We had a big addressable market—our elephant—and we needed to tackle it through small bite-size pieces with consistent messaging and an emphasis on the customers' needs and desires. That involved listening to our customers and potential customers so we were ready to share the right messages about how we could meet, and even exceed, their needs. That was our pull mechanism, and everyone in the company was part of the process.

I vividly remember meeting with a group of CEOs and former students who'd failed as entrepreneurs, organized by the University of California, Irvine, graduate school. The purpose was to learn how to better prepare its entrepreneurial-track students for success.

One young man got up and said, "My father sent me to UCI to get a great education. I got my MBA and came out with some great product ideas to set up my business. In three or four years, I'd given it everything I'd got, but it ultimately failed. In retrospect, one thing I didn't understand or have an appreciation for was marketing."

Many entrepreneurs launch their businesses, like this young man, as experts in the product or service they are selling. They take the inverted-pyramid approach to developing their business model.

But as he learned, product alone couldn't support the weight of his business. He needed an equally strong second leg of the three-legged-stool business model: marketing. And combined together, product and marketing would brace the third leg: the company financials.

FINANCIALS ARE THE WHY

We've talked about how making a lot of money is one of the worst reasons to start a business, but that in no way diminishes the importance of making a lot of money for your business. If your financial house isn't in order, then you won't be able to pursue the other reasons you started a business. Financials are the third leg of the stool of your business model.

Financials are the scorecard that tells how well or poorly the business is doing. Financials will alert you to problems in your business, but they can't diagnose them. Usually, the root causes relate to the other two legs in the business model—product or marketing or both.

The financials involve a lot of details, and many people can get lost in those trees. I preferred to stay above it and look down on the whole forest. The top-line revenues told me how well we were doing with marketing. The bottom line assured me that we were managing our business efficiently and generating profit. And our margins were the key performance indicator for that.

In the luxury business model that we copied, price and demand tend to rise and fall together, rather than have an inverse relationship as in traditional economics, where a price increase results in lower demand.

Under the luxury business model, higher prices signal higher value to the premium customer looking for the best. Higher prices stimulate greater demand among the customers who have the necessary means to afford luxury and value it.

However, we faced a roadblock in our business since the concept of a luxury faucet was so revolutionary. Some people got it right away,

120

but others just couldn't understand what the fuss was about, most especially the salespeople at our retailers' showrooms. Their bread-and-butter business was selling high-end kitchen appliances for which they got big commissions, not faucets or sinks that they viewed as simply add-on products.

As part of my traveling road show in the early days, I would meet with many showroom dealers who were more than willing to stock our product. But the salespeople responsible for moving them couldn't get excited. They were experts at selling $2,000 ovens, $5,000 ranges, and refrigerators. They didn't see the point of spending much time or effort talking about a $250 kitchen faucet, no matter how great it looked or how well it worked.

I would routinely take part in dealer training sessions to present our product range. I was joined in those sessions by other vendors, most especially luxury appliance dealers, who sucked all the oxygen out of the room. I listened and learned. I needed to "sex up" my presentation to make it memorable.

That was the genesis of the water appliance concept, borrowing from the appliance business model. Rather than just presenting individual components, I repackaged them as an interconnected system that managed water delivery and use in the kitchen. In marketing, it's called a *reframe*.

By seeing our products as a water appliance—including our premium faucet, sink, soap dispenser, cutting board, water purifier, and hot-water dispenser—the salespeople were looking at the potential of a $1,000+ sale, not just a $250 one. It raised our profile to the level of a Sub-Zero refrigerator or a JennAir six-burner gas stovetop.

The concept of a water appliance elevated our status, essential in the luxury space. We made the water appliance concept memorable because our research showed that people use their kitchen's water appliance more often than any other. And we codified it with a formula called the three *F*s: *f*oundation (the sink), *f*aucet (offering different styles), and additional *f*unctions (like filtered water and hot-water dispenser, disposal, soap dispensers, and others).

The good news for all was that our water appliance system offered even higher profit margins than is typical in the appliance business. And we helped them even more by giving them guidelines for how much they should advise their clients to spend on the water appliance. In a luxury home build or remodel, the typical appliance package ranges from $15,000 to $30,000 or even higher, and there's typically no price resistance there. We recommended the kitchen water appliance budget should be about 10 percent of the appliance package, so $1,500 to $3,000.

We overcame resistance to a luxury offering in a highly commoditized space by connecting the dots for the dealers and their salespeople. We helped our dealer and specifier customers communicate more effectively with their end-user clients, who ultimately appreciated the added value our superior offerings delivered to them.

STEPPING ONTO THE THREE-LEGGED STOOL

Everyone in the company is supported by the business model's three-legged stool. Likewise, everyone is part of the support system for the stool. A weakness in one leg threatens all. That's why it's important to have the right people overseeing the three critical functions—product, marketing, and financials—and good communications and support up and down each leg and across the legs.

We built a largely flat organizational structure, encouraging everyone to work across functionalities and within their specific span of control. I maintained an open door for everyone due to the great interdependence between each part of the business. I was always willing to listen and learn, and I modeled the behavior I expected from each team member.

As we got better at working together and our business processes proved effective, I devoted about 80 percent of my time outside the business, developing relationships with suppliers and dealers and talking with designers and specifiers about what their clients needed. My primary job was to keep the phones ringing because, without that, nothing else happens.

 # Ken's Key Takeaways

- The business model is your company's "secret sauce" through which you create value for your customers and profits for your company.

- The business model is the engine for disruptive innovation in any vertical category, and the best way to discover the greatest opportunity for disruption is to look across from your vertical category to others.

- Take a three-legged-stool approach to crafting your business model, placing equal weight on product, marketing, and financials. An innovative product alone will only take you so far.

 ## Your Corporateneur Road Map

1. What was the business model for the last company you worked for? What was good about it, and where were its flaws? If you

were going to build the company from the ground up, what would you do differently?

2. Which companies outside your vertical category do you admire? Study their business model. What's their business model? How did they innovate the category? What was their distinctive difference from the customer perspective?

3. What can you take from other successful businesses and their business models and apply to your category, your target market, and your business model?

CHAPTER 6

Make a Plan

"The jet stream is a very strong force and pushing a balloon into it is like pushing up against a brick wall, but once we got into it, we found that, remarkably, the balloon went whatever speed the wind went."

—RICHARD BRANSON

Ask anyone and they'll tell you the way to turn an idea in your head into a real business is to write a business plan. One widely cited study led by Andrew Burke found that new ventures with formal business plans experience a 33 percent uptick in growth, as measured in employment, not sales.

"Business plans help raise entrepreneurial capabilities and, thereby, enhance performance," the researchers state. But they conclude with this caveat: "By articulating goals and identifying strategies for exploiting entrepreneurial opportunities, written business plans appear to enhance entrepreneurial decision-making even in situations where *improvisation* [emphasis added] is important."

The problem with business plans is that they are out-of-date as soon as they are written. That's because of the *observer effect*. A business plan is written from the point of view of a market observer looking from the outside in. But once the business is launched, it becomes part of the industry system and will effect changes in the system.

Try as hard as you might, no one can anticipate how the market, competitors, or even the company's employees and internal processes will ultimately act and react after launch. A business plan can't control for the many changes the business must respond to down the line.

LEARN BY DOING THE PLAN

A study led by entrepreneurship professor Jan Brinckmann details two schools of thought on the value of business planning and business plans. The provocative title of his paper was "Should Entrepreneurs Plan or Storm the Castle?" where two approaches are explained: the planning school versus the learning school.

The planning school proposes "business planning is crucial for the survival and development of both new and established small firms" and argues that "a systematic, prediction-oriented and formal approach leads to superior venture performance."

The learning school, by contrast, challenges the predictive value of a business plan and suggests entrepreneurs should instead focus on "learning, strategic flexibility and controlling resources, especially when facing high degrees of uncertainty." To which must be added, every new venture faces high degrees of uncertainty.

While Brinckmann's meta-analysis of nearly fifty quantitative studies proves the value of the business plan and the business planning process, it also concludes that it must be combined with learning to adapt the plan to the arising contingencies.

Stressing the need for flexibility, continual learning, and adaptation, Brinckmann concludes:

> The output of the business planning (written plans) and the process of business planning (planning meetings, market and scenario analysis, use of computers, portfolio analysis) augment performance.

> Our findings reject the proposition that the value of business planning can be explained mainly by the formal-legitimating or signaling function of written documentation. It can be concluded that both the symbolic and the learning effects of business planning play a key role in augmenting small business performance.

This hearkens back to Ken's admonition to "Make a plan. Work the plan." Everything starts with a plan that describes the business, its goals, and the value it will bring to customers—benchmarks to be achieved and the processes it will follow.

But the plan must be worked to see if it is effective and then adapted

"Plans are nothing. Planning is everything."

as needed to improve it. As in a scientific experiment, the formal business plan is the control through which multiple business variables are measured.

Net net: the business plan is important, but even more important is the planning process that will prepare the business to make the most of the learning that will come from working the plan. Or, as Albert Einstein said, "Plans are nothing. Planning is everything."

ALWAYS PLANNING TO BE ON PLAN

Brinckmann cautions that entrepreneurs with more experience (i.e., the corporateneur) may be inclined to "storm the castle," relying upon their previous learning to see them through. They might favor a less formal, improvisational approach, rejecting the business plan "in the face of dynamic external conditions, formalized and predictive behavior might create internal rigidities."

Ken agrees the corporateneur brings more to that process than someone without in-depth industry knowledge and related career experience, but forgoing the formal business plan would be a mistake.

Ken views the business plan and the business planning process as an ongoing, repeatable process. It's a discipline that the corporateneur should borrow from their past corporate life—not a sign of rigidity but rather a facilitator for flexibility. By doing so, your business will be ready to adapt as conditions on the ground change, as they inevitably will.

Abraham Lincoln said, "Give me six hours to chop down a tree and I will spend the first four sharpening the axe." Business planning is how you sharpen your axe, so the first task for the corporateneur is to prepare a business plan and chop down that first tree. But to build a sustainable business, you'll need to chop down many. Planning must be a continually repeating process.

 Ken's Life Lesson Learned —————

Creating a Sustainable Business

Writing the business plan is the typical first step to turning a business dream into a reality. It's also typically a big undertaking, whether written for internal use or to get external funding. In essence, the business plan turns the business model from an idea into action.

Numerous business plan templates are available to help structure the document and make it a less grueling task. But those templates are generic and often miss some of the most important perspectives you'll need to nurture a sustainable business.

Our proven Rohl Model business plan includes ten essential sections:

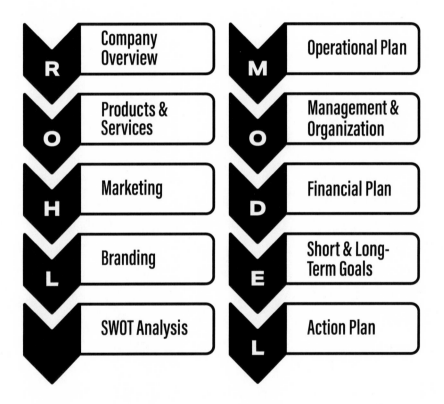

However, rather than being a once-and-done effort, the business plan must be a constantly evolving document subject to ongoing revisions and that is referenced often: more frequently in the early days and, at the very minimum, once a year once the business is established;

though given how quickly the market is changing, more often is always better.

For us, the business plan was constantly being updated. We established a process to do a SWOT analysis every month, and based on that, we would go back and revise the plan accordingly.

That's because the business plan is not just needed to launch a business; it is the guidebook to managing a sustainable business. The initial business plan is only the first step in a process that must extend over the life of the business.

Here are the guideposts I used to build an ongoing, sustainable business.

#1: IDENTIFY HIGH-POTENTIAL MARKETS WITH UNMET NEEDS

Your business's growth is limited not just by your internal resources and capabilities but by how great the market potential for your product or service is. That is the much sought-after white space you are looking to fill. New ventures can launch with one product or service, but that doesn't have the makings of a long-term sustainable business.

New business ideas need to be measured against whether they solve enough of a problem for enough people to reach critical mass. For example, some entrepreneurs start after confronting a personal frustration in the market, like Sara Blakely, who built Spanx into a $1.2 billion shapewear empire after cutting the feet out of a pair of control-top pantyhose to wear under slacks at a party. She created her business by recognizing many women were like her and needed a little bit of extra support. Her first pair of SPANX was an instant hit, but she didn't stop there and designed an entire wardrobe of comfortable shapewear undergarments.

Others bring special skills and talents to invent or refine new technology (e.g., Steve Jobs, Steve Wozniak, and Bill Gates in personal computers) or apply existing technology to solve new problems (e.g., Jeff Bezos and online shopping).

And other entrepreneurs take an existing commoditized product or service and add value to elevate it into another realm. Engineer James Dyson did it with his first invention—the bagless vacuum cleaner—which overcame deficiencies in traditional vacuum cleaner design. But he took his expertise from redesigning vacuum cleaners into a whole range of innovative household and commercial products around his core competency of moving and filtering air. His company remains private, but his net worth is estimated at well over $5 billion.

Basically, I followed the same model as James Dyson. Although I didn't invent a faucet that incorporated the spray function with the normal flow of water, I recognized its huge market potential in the US where nothing like it was available. I also saw a path to build a complementary product line around all the different ways water is used in the home.

Unfortunately, we learned a painful lesson not to become overreliant on our first product and original supplier, but we quickly recovered because our business plan included provisions for sustainable business expansion.

We created a product line that made a real difference in the lives of the customers we targeted—the discerning high-end homeowners, retailers, and commercial customers whose needs we were serving. We continuously searched the world for innovative, functionally superior, authentic, and appropriate water-management solutions that delivered more value to our customers. We went from the pullout spray faucet to farmhouse and fireclay sinks, total immersion showerheads, side-level kitchen faucets, Euro-styled bath products, culinary-styled sinks, and more.

As we grew in the luxury space, we widened our offerings to appeal to a more affordable lifestyle by downsizing the scale of our products and finding more competitive sources that could meet our expected level of quality and panache. These strategies worked together to increase our market penetration further.

A sustainable business is built on fulfilling unmet needs that other companies have overlooked or ignored. Your business must be expansive in vision, with a long runway, yet must be flexible and adapt to changes in the market, because as soon as your company enters the market, everything that you originally planned for prelaunch changes.

#2: FOCUS ON KEY PLAYERS IN THE HIGHEST-POTENTIAL MARKETS

Every sale is important, and considering every customer is key to business survival, but some customers and sales are more important than others. For a product business, having an internet presence is de rigueur today, but you still have to bring people to your site to make a sale.

Expanding to Amazon's third-party marketplace extends your reach, but it also is no guarantee you'll break through. Getting your products into local independent boutiques is good, but being carried by big national retailers is better. National retailers can order in quantity, provide maximum exposure, and be valuable partners to grow a sustainable business.

Likewise, with a service business, you can go small by serving smaller markets, but your greatest potential is found by thinking bigger and servicing major markets with bigger needs. I often advised start-ups to find the diamonds in their own backyard first. But once you do, then it is time to search in other backyards.

We started in our own backyard—California—where I personally knew the key dealers in the kitchen-and-bath industry. I didn't waste time trying to get placement in the maximum number of dealers. Instead, we targeted well-established retailers and specifiers who would get behind our products and be early adopters of our innovation.

One way we separated the wheat from the chaff in our dealer network was to require they purchase our display package. Most of our competitors offered a standard display package with a minimum order. That was the standard business model in our industry. But we wanted only dealers that would really commit to showcasing our line.

So we set an upfront price for our display and customized it to the specific products they wanted to feature. It was a revolutionary business model in the industry. That customization cost us more initially, but it gave us another competitive edge. Every dealer had their own exclusive range of products on display. And for each dealer, we'd offer a credit option so they'd recover the initial cost of the display by making sales.

It was a win-win proposition for all. We got dealers to invest and commit to us initially, and we invested in them by giving them a unique product display.

Through tenacity, persistence, and a relentless pursuit of leading influencers, we built our dealer base from zero to a select two hundred, giving us the exposure and support we needed to reach the most valuable plumbing contractors, remodelers, builders, kitchen and interior designers, and their clients.

Our mantra was "Be important to a few." We always made sure that those few were the ones with the largest potential in their geographical area and that we gave them the level of support and service worthy of their exclusive status. We followed that model as we expanded from

California, throughout the western states and then on to the New York metropolitan area. Eventually, we had exposure across the country.

The key to creating a sustainable business is to take it one step at a time. Don't diffuse your efforts in low-potential markets or with low-potential customers; instead, manage your time and resources carefully to maximize the return on your investment.

#3: RECRUIT ADVISORS WHO WILL CHALLENGE AND TEACH YOU

You may think you've got the greatest new idea since sliced bread. You've identified the highest-potential market and have found a path to reach it. With your confidence soaring, that's when you need to take a step back and reconsider.

As the saying goes, "Iron sharpens iron," and you need people around you who will challenge your assumptions, give different perspectives, and fill the gaps in your knowledge and understanding.

I've always surrounded myself with talent that goes beyond my wheelhouse. I've brought that talent in, both to work for me and to advise me through board and advisory board memberships and various informal relationships. They helped expand my understanding of finance, geopolitical matters, marketing, merchandising, business diversification, and information technology.

And it is critically important always to be open to criticism. At all costs, you must avoid confirmation bias. If everyone at the table agrees, somebody isn't necessary. The entrepreneur who isn't willing to hear that his or her business "baby" is ugly will not grow a sustainable business.

Ironically, I had to convey that tough "Your baby is ugly" message to a young lady in the beauty business. She had developed a new beauty product in her kitchen. It was so innovative that she got a patent for it.

But instead of taking one step at a time and growing the business organically, she invested immediately in a big office in an expensive downtown high-rise office building. She was trying to create an aura of success without having the success. And then, she planned to launch with a major national ad campaign. She had a business plan and grandiose sales projections that weren't well thought out or achievable.

She came to me for advice after the money she front-loaded into the appearance of success ran out. We went through her numbers. I showed her that too much money was tied up in making a first impression and nothing was left for marketing. Yes, first impressions are important, but she went way over the top.

There wasn't anything we could do about the initial overhead burden she put on the company. She'd created the shell of a company, but we needed to build the substance. We tore up the original business plan and created a new one. We focused on building her market locally in her own backyard and using that as the stepping stone to grow regionally and then nationally, so the business could go from strength to strength.

She didn't need and couldn't afford a national launch at the outset—or to try to make sales in Birmingham, Alabama, or Boise, Idaho, where the potential was low. She needed to focus first on high-potential markets close to home in the big West Coast markets that she knew and could reach easily.

#4: BUILD A BRAND, NOT JUST A BUSINESS

Building a business and building a brand are different. Being successful at building a business doesn't necessarily mean you've also built a brand. Becoming a brand is a more intensive process, but it gives lift and longevity to any business.

Herein lies the difference. A business is a thing—the organization that produces the products or offers the services. It belongs to the shareholders, the owners, employees, and partners that have skin in the game.

A brand is a concept. It is what the business stands for and the promises it makes and delivers to customers. Ultimately the brand is owned by the customers, and the business entity is effectively their trust holder.

Best-selling author and business-thought leader Seth Godin said, "A brand is the set of expectations, memories, stories and relationships that, taken together, account for a consumer's decision to choose one product or service over another."

For example, some companies own multiple brands, each with distinctly different promises to the customer, like Procter & Gamble. It is a business that manages over sixty brands in ten different consumer-product-goods categories, including laundry, home cleaning, and personal care.

Some companies are effectively brands. They may sell different products but all under the umbrella of a brand—like Apple, Amazon, Hallmark, Coca Cola, and Disney.

Our company was a mix of both. We sold other companies' branded products but under the master Rohl brand, which promised that every product we offered met our exacting authentic luxury standards.

Many national retailers operate this way. Consider Walmart, Target, Amazon, Macy's, Bloomingdale's, and Neiman Marcus. They all have established a master retail brand, and underneath their banners come the individual product brands carried.

Building a business requires an inward focus to get all the processes and people working together toward the business goal. Building a brand takes an outward focus to make sure the business is delivering on its promises and delivering on the customer's need.

Branding shouldn't be an afterthought and must be an integral part of business planning. But unlike business planning, where success can be measured quarter by quarter and year over year, building a brand may take years, yet it ultimately delivers extraordinary value to the company. Though there may be exceptions, *a sustainable business is built on creating a brand*.

And that inevitably elevates the role of sales and marketing in the business. Sales and marketing are two sides of the same coin; however, sales is transaction oriented and marketing has a long-term focus. Marketing is the process that sets the stage for sales so that a transaction takes place. Both are absolutely essential to building a sustainable business and brand.

> **A sustainable business is built on creating a brand.**

Throughout my career and advising other businesses, I've found that there is rarely enough integration between the sales and marketing function. Sales operates in their own world, and marketing in theirs.

In our company, we made sure sales and marketing worked in tandem, with sales having input on product development and marketing strategies and communications. Everybody talked the same language and communicated with one voice, which is essential to both the business and the brand. When sales and marketing work harmoniously together, nothing holds the business back.

Marketing and sales are mutually supporting functions in building a business and brands. Marketing is ultimately responsible for the story and creating the marketing support materials the salespeople need. The salespeople are constantly gathering needed input and customer feedback to bring back to the marketing department so they can refine the message.

Essentially the marketing department trains the salespeople, then the salespeople train the marketing folks. Sales and marketing create a virtuous circle for the business.

Unfortunately, too many businesses equate marketing with advertising, which like sales and marketing involves different processes. We never budgeted a lot on advertising, but we sure did lean into marketing. And we did that through the other three steps we followed for building a sustainable business:

- focusing on high-potential markets with customer needs just waiting to be met, which immediately brings awareness to your company and brand;

- aiming for key players in the highest-potential markets to make the biggest splash immediately and grow the business over the long haul; and

- getting valuable people to buy into our concept and provide needed expertise that fills the gaps.

So you've done your planning, got your business plan written, and are ready to put the *Open for Business* sign out. That's when reality sets in, and you'll discover how well or how poorly you planned.

Maybe the business plan needs only minor tweaks—or a complete overhaul, like Raghu Rai's health-tech venture.

READY, SET, RESET

Raghu was a freshman biomedical engineering student at University of California, Irvine, who was a team leader for a group of students that entered a business plan competition with the idea of developing an app to connect a patient's insulin pump with their iPhone. Having passed the first hurdle of the competition, the professor assigned Ken as their mentor and business coach to help them develop their formal business plan.

"The first time we met, I didn't have any idea what to expect. I never heard of Ken Rohl or his business and thought, What does a guy running a plumbing equipment company understand about what we were trying to do in healthcare?" Raghu says. "I learned pretty quickly that Ken had a wealth of knowledge about business, any kind of business. He taught us a systematic way to build and scale a business."

It was kismet from their first meeting. Raghu's team took second place in the competition, but in Ken's eyes, Raghu was the winner. "At the end of freshman year, Ken invited our team to his office for lunch and to meet with local community leaders and advisors. Sometime during that meeting, Ken gave me a wink, and I knew we were on the same page. I felt more than acceptance, but real chemistry based on shared values and understanding."

Fast-forward to graduation in 2005 when Ken offered Raghu a position at his company handling the hospitality side of the business. He also presented Raghu with a $5,000 check to continue to develop the healthcare mobile-app concept.

"Ken brought me into the company to get a real understanding of how the business world works," Raghu shares. "He also invested in the healthcare business. That first check was a huge amount of money to me at the time and gave me such a feeling of confidence in my potential because it came from someone I respected so much. People in business talk about 'angel investors,' but Ken was a true guardian angel to me, both personally and professionally."

In the early days, Raghu focused on developing partnerships with healthcare organizations, and Ken was actively involved in what was to become Jio Health. "Ken's cofounder DNA kicked in. He was always pretty hands-on, routinely meeting with healthcare leaders and hospital chief information officers. He really wanted to absorb as much as he could learn about the customers and the market. At the same time, he was always asking, 'Have you sold anything yet?'"

Raghu's answer was not enough. "Eventually, we recognized the opportunity in the US market was really challenging, and we didn't have the right product fit," he admits.

Revising and Expanding the Plan

Serendipitously Raghu had established connections in Vietnam for software development and visited there a number of times. Through that, he realized the opportunity for Jio Health was much greater in emerging markets, like Vietnam, where the healthcare information-and-technology infrastructure wasn't as well developed as in the US.

As Raghu and Ken researched further, they also saw the opportunity to expand their offering beyond healthcare tech into becoming a healthcare provider. It was a completely different business model but one that offered the maximum growth potential, and if it worked in Vietnam, it could work in other emerging Asian markets as well.

"We saw the opportunity to build the Kaiser Permanente for this emerging market and build it on an 'Amazon' technology chassis. We wanted to leverage the service excellence and high-velocity growth of a consumer technology company and apply it to a rigid and ossified industry like healthcare," he says. "And the best part is we didn't have any incumbents to compete with."

So they picked a new lane to sink or swim in and found they had a much easier time getting investor backing to keep them afloat in the meantime.

The next question was how to enter the market—either by partnering with existing healthcare providers, as they had tried to do in the US, or picking another route.

"We were trying to do something totally different that hadn't been done before. Based on our experience in the US market, we thought it might conflict with the interests of incumbents in the marketplace," he reflects. "So we decided it would be better to start our own licensed clinic and healthcare delivery system."

They searched and found an existing clinic with all the necessary regulatory licenses in Ho Chi Minh City. The only problem was that the clinic was "rundown and pretty bare-bones." They had the capital in place for the purchase of the clinic, but more capital would be needed to refurbish the clinic and bring it up to standards.

Jio Health got a round of $5 million in series A funding provided by a firm in Singapore to get to the next level. "It's never a linear journey going from step A to step B. There is so much that happens outside your direct control. You just have to be ready for it," he says.

Another Reset

What was outside their control was the COVID-19 pandemic, which halted the company's development.

"We had built a beautiful clinic and were growing our patient base. The next step for us was to build an online pharmacy business and expand clinical services, adding laboratory and diagnostics to complement our existing business. We were just about ready to close a round of series B funding when COVID hit and everything collapsed," Raghu explains.

Ken continued to have Raghu's back, providing hope when it was in short supply and giving real-world advice from when Rohl almost went under. "It was ironic that during the pandemic, we could have provided a lot of value in the healthcare market and for the consumer, but it turned out to be the toughest time for the business. Yet Ken kept us focused on making tough decisions in the face of so many unknowns. He stressed the need to be flexible and ready when the way forward eventually revealed itself. He kept saying, 'You can't get too comfortable.'"

Hitting Its Stride

Jio Health came through it, secured its series B funding, and exceeded its annual plan despite the pandemic.

"Ken helped us calibrate and sharpen our focus during the worst time. It's like Mike Tyson said, 'Everyone has a plan until they get punched in the mouth.' I feel like we took more than our fair share of punches since we launched in 2016. It takes tremendous energy to keep getting up after so many punches. But Ken gave much-needed perspective and had the forethought and patience to help guide us through this process," he concluded.

 # Ken's Key Takeaways ▬▬▬

- A business plan gives a 33 percent lift to a new venture's likelihood of success. Business plans are not a once-and-done affair for getting a new business launched. To build a sustainable business, business planning is an ongoing, repeatable business process.

- Once a new business enters the market, it changes in the market. That's why the original business plan becomes immediately obsolete. It must be continuously reviewed and revised as conditions on the ground change, as they inevitably will. The original business plan becomes the control against which progress is measured. Be ready to adapt the plan or throw it out entirely and start again if necessary.

- A continuously revised and updated SWOT analysis across all business functions is a powerful tool to bring innovation and change to the business. Make SWOTing an essential part of the business planning process.

- Make sure your business plan focuses on the highest-potential markets and that you influence the most important players in those markets.

- Recruit key advisors, both inside and outside the company (e.g., customers, suppliers, business partners), and listen to them.

- Building a business and building a brand are two different things. The corporateneur needs to do both.

 ## Your Corporateneur Road Map

1. Review the ten sections in the Rohl Model business plan outline, and draft your plan following each section. Prepare it in a format that feels comfortable for you, whether it's in thought balloons, a structured graphic diagram, or a written report. The ideas and concepts are more important than the format at this point.

2. Where is your business plan strong? Where is it weak? How can you teach yourself what you have to learn to fill in the gaps?

3. Some people are planners; others thrive by living spontane- ously. If planning isn't your thing, seek out people with the needed planning skills to help you.

4. What do you know about branding? Read some books, tap your network, and hire a branding expert to understand and internalize this critical process for your business.

CHAPTER 7

Managing Growth

"The man who goes up in a balloon does not feel as though he were ascending; he only sees the earth sinking deeper below him."

—ARTHUR SCHOPENHAUER

With the business model designed and business plan in hand, the desk work for launching a new venture is completed. Now it's time for doing, not just thinking, which means managing the business.

The late Harvard professor Peter Drucker, called "the father of modern management," invented the concept of *management by objectives* (MBO), which has been almost universally adopted in business circles.

Drucker defined MBO as a five-step, ongoing circular process:

1. Set organizational objectives.

2. Communicate organizational objectives to employee.

3. Monitor progress.

4. Evaluate performance.

5. Reward performance.

But he also said, "Management by objectives works, if you know the objectives. Ninety percent of the time, you don't."

As effective as Drucker is in teaching people the practice of management, the challenge is putting his theories into practice. But his definition of business management is hard to wrap your head around. In his book *The Practice of Management*, he defined management as "a multi-purpose organ that manages business and manages managers and manages workers and work."

Here's a more easily understood definition:

Business management is the coordination and administration of an organization. It is the art and science of managing resources of the business to reach its operational and financial objectives.

Libraries are full of books to help managers learn to manage more effectively. Some eleven thousand business-management books are published each year, and more than one million are in print. If you spend all your time reading about management, you'll never have time to do it.

MANAGING FOR GROWTH

The corporateneur's overriding business objective initially is to get the business off the ground and, after that, to manage growth to create a sustainable long-term business. Professor Karl Wennberg of the Stockholm School of Economics provided guidance in a paper titled "Managing High-Growth Firms." It is a comprehensive study of the last thirty years of academic research that identifies what managers of high-growth firms (HGFs) need to know. By definition, start-up businesses are HGFs because day one they start at zero sales or profits.

Even though the study of management and entrepreneurship is exploding, Wennberg writes, "There is a dearth of research addressing the unique challenges facing such firms. We still do not know much about management in HGFs." He offers research-validated findings to help managers of HGFs navigate the greater complexity they face due to rapid growth compared to managers of firms that are growing more slowly.

"The growth patterns of HGFs are highly erratic. Periods of rapid growth may be followed by stagnation or even decline," he explains. "This means the models of HGF management need to account for the often dynamic and rapidly changing organizational structure of HGFs. Major changes in systems, structures and capabilities are required to cope with the increased complexity that accompanies high growth."

Wennberg focuses on identifying the core competencies needed to manage the HGF and then delves into strategies to build those core competencies. It brings forward insights specific to both the science and art of managing a high-growth venture.

CORE COMPETENCIES CREATE COMPETITIVE EDGE

Calling core competencies an "imperative success factor in new firms," Wennberg defines them as "those resources and knowledge that are most vital to the production of goods and services in the firm, particularly those that are difficult to copy or imitate by competitors." They include leadership, organizational structure, skilled and motivated employees, and a growth-oriented organizational culture.

In other words, core competencies are based upon people and processes put into place to efficiently and effectively produce what the company sells. The good news is that the corporateneur with previous business-management experience and specific insider knowledge of the targeted market has an advantage.

Leadership Vision

The set of leadership capabilities of the CEO is the most essential core competence for an HGF. Leadership is the ability to influence, motivate, and enable others to contribute toward the firm's success. And it rises above management—controlling a group and processes to accomplish a goal—as key to an HGF's sustainable success.

Influence and inspiration, not power and control, distinguish leaders from managers. The HGF CEO must be both leader and manager, but being a leader comes first.

Influence and inspiration, not power and control, distinguish leaders from managers.

The talent of leadership, like musical or artistic talent, is largely innate, yet the research reveals that having a vision for the company and the ability to communicate it clearly and effectively across the organization is a defining characteristic of a CEO in HGFs as compared with non-HGFs.

The vision for the company must be crystal clear, as Warren Bennis, who founded the Leadership Institute at the University of Southern California, cautions: "The lack of a clear vision is a major reason for the declining effectiveness of a leader." And the clearer the vision, the easier it will be to communicate it to others.

Vision comes first, with the organization's management structure being designed to support that vision through the business's activities and processes. Regardless of the type of business, its management typically is divided into three areas:

- *Marketing and sales*, which include advertising, lead generation and conversion, product testing, and pricing. And because this function is constantly interacting with customers and the external environment, innovation through new-product concepts and market research typically operates here. "An important activity in driving innovation in new firms constitutes a systemic process through which such firms acquire knowledge of the market," Wennberg reports. "Understanding what customers want and how a firm can deliver products or services to them is critical for HGFs to establish a sales-revenue base."

- *Operations*, which includes production, customer service, purchasing, and—depending upon the industry—manufacturing, inventory management, and quality control. Operations assure that the company mission, vision, and promises can be delivered to the customer.

- *Administration* is the back-office operations that support the other organizational functions—marketing and sales and operations. This includes finance and accounting, human resources, payroll, and collections.

Wennberg stresses the need for "functionally balanced" management teams across these responsibilities. *Balance* is a key word here. The corporateneur must maintain the right balance within the company, where each team is often competing for attention and resources.

Ken was obsessive about his vision for the company and measured every decision by that yardstick, as longtime employee Tom Duino observes. "We didn't nickel-and-dime little decisions when we could make big decisions that would help the customers make more dollars.

"I don't remember hearing the word *budget*, as in 'We have to stay within this budget,' related to some needed expenditure to deliver what we promised the customer. Ken took care of the big picture, and he let us go at it. Ken had a commonsense perspective on doing the right thing and making good decisions for the sake of the customer," he continues.

Nothing can substitute for vision. As Jack Welch said, "Good business leaders create a vision, articulate a vision, passionately own the vision, and relentlessly drive it to completion."

To which entrepreneur Tony Hsieh, who founded Zappos, added, "Chase the vision, not the money. The money will end up following you."

Industry and Business Experience

The research found little benefit accrued to the HGF from founders who have previous experience starting new business ventures. In other words, serial entrepreneurs have no significant advantage.

However, prior management experience and experience in the respective industry entered provide measurable benefits that yield a greater likelihood of success (i.e., the corporateneur). The HFG founder's human capital "provides managers with the skills and know-how necessary to overcome problems in the context of that industry," Wennberg writes.

That lends the corporateneur significant advantages entering either an industry or a segment of the industry where their previous corporate experience was. They not only have insider knowledge and understanding but also greater reach into the industry to gather and activate resources that will lead to future success.

"Managers of HGFs more often have longer industry experience in the same sector and larger leadership teams than their non-HGF counterparts," Wennberg states. The leadership teams may be both internal managers within the formal business structure or informal networks of contacts and advisors from outside the company.

Ken relied heavily on his extensive network within the plumbing industry to know who the movers and shakers were and exert influence with them. His network grew through leadership in the industry's trade association and always being present at trade shows.

"I've always been a big believer in industry associations and trade shows as a quick way to gather industry insights and build relationships with customers and potential business partners," Ken says.

Innovation Edge

By definition, HGFs generate high growth through innovation. But being innovative is not just measured in the number of patents held or spending on R&D. The research suggests that "there might be more intricate relationships between innovativeness and growth."

For example, Wennberg found that R&D activities focused on developing new products and processes were positively associated with growth. But product innovation *alone* didn't necessarily translate into high growth; however, the active and innovative use of marketing to launch the new product did.

Ken would second the importance of marketing since a company will get nowhere introducing new products without effective marketing behind it that generates demand. Innovative products need innovative marketing approaches to yield high growth.

Wennberg suggests that HGFs need to lean into innovative business strategies, target profitable niche segments, and focus on customers to develop unique products and services, rather than formal R&D. That is just what Ken did at his company.

And Wennberg concludes, "It is not necessarily the most technologically innovative firms that become HGFs but rather firms that are able to create close contacts with customers." That was always Ken's North Star.

Profitability Challenges

Not surprisingly, the research finds profitability is a key challenge for high-growth firms. Citing conflicting studies, Wennberg poses a fundamental question: "Is profitability needed to engage in high growth or may high growth lead to long-term profitability?"

And there is no definitive answer yet from the research; however, having enough money to grow is always a challenge for companies starting out. As a result, the HGF needs a firm handle on how they are going to manage not just sales coming in but profits retained.

Neither high growth in sales nor number of employees relates to firm profitability, one study referenced by Wennberg found. And in another: very rapid growth can lead to financial distress and eventual failure unless the firm is properly managed.

The odds are against HGFs that don't keep their financial systems in order, which means attending to both the top and bottom line. "Only one in seven firms achieves sustained growth while remaining profitable," he shares.

Building the Management Structure for the HGF

A business's organizational structure is how business activities and the people who accomplish them are organized and ordered to achieve the goals of the company. The organizational structure defines each unit making up the company, each employee's role, and how information flows within the business.

There are numerous business structure models—hierarchical, functional, horizontal (or flatarchy), divisional, matrix, team based, and network—each having their pros and cons. But they are divided into two groups: centralized or decentralized models.

A centralized organization model places management authority, decision-making, and strategic planning under a single manager or leadership team with information flowing from the top down.

Decentralized structures, on the other hand, distribute decision-making across multiple units or teams within the organization. Units are empowered to make their own decisions without getting approval from above; however, even decentralized structures have some hierarchy built into the system. And within decentralized structures, there tends to be a more even flow of information up and down and across organizational units.

Unfortunately, Wennberg finds there is no one-type-fits-all solution for management structures for an HGF. Referencing tension in the current research, he writes that some studies argue that "HGFs need to establish formal managerial structures to manage their growth, while other studies highlight 'the capacity to adapt' as being more important. No conclusive evidence can be drawn about the relative merits of these two general claims."

The research suggests there needs to be a mix of more-formal and informal structures for the HGF. For example, more-formalized structures are recommended in human resource management (HRM) and cost-control systems.

Regarding the human resource function, a more-formal structure better facilitates recruitment and hiring from outside the organization quickly. This is the typical requirement for HGFs because high-revenue growth usually requires growing staff quickly.

HGFs also benefit from more-formal accounting systems. Wennberg warns that sales revenue can get tied up in accounts receivable. With effective accounting-management systems in place, those receivables can be rapidly transformed into cash. Otherwise, financial distress can result. "HGFs need to build formal management control structures as well as reporting and billing systems to 'manage growth,'" he advises.

No matter the organizational structure, it must be able to cope with the increased complexity of forecasting and predicting changes that affect high-growth firms. HGFs need to focus on "capacity building" to adapt to rapidly changing conditions on the ground with their attendant greater complexities.

Capacity building includes not just hiring in or contracting out functions but also developing skills and capabilities from within the existing workforce. A more-formalized human resource department can help develop such training and personnel development systems.

To reduce the negative effects of complexity facing the HGF, diffusing decision-making throughout the organization helps keep any one group from being overwhelmed. It also helps to bring together different people from a variety of functional perspectives and capabilities to build a deeper understanding of operational problems and how to resolve them.

Ken would call that teamwork.

Ken's Life Lesson Learned —

Push Authority and Responsibility Down

Throughout my career, I worked under many different managers with different management styles. I observed what worked and what didn't, but no matter the weaknesses of the managers above me, I never let their failures become my own. And in starting my company, I didn't want to repeat the management mistakes I experienced that could have set me or my company off its game.

The business-management structure—the org chart—is like the frame of a house. As the company founder, you're the architect responsible for designing the different operational units of the business and how they work together.

Like a building's frame, the organizational structure provides structural integrity so that the business can withstand the stresses and strains that will come. It defines workflow, as a building plan supports traffic flow so that one room's function flows seamlessly into another.

After the business model and business plan, defining the management structure for your company is the next most critical factor for creating a sustainable business. Your firm's ultimate success or failure will be realized through the organization that you build.

But as important as the management structure is to support the business, it can also be limiting. Like in a house, the building frame keeps the outside out and the inside in. And once walls, doors, and windows that define rooms are in place, they stay in place and can't be easily moved around. Likewise, in a company, the management structure may

159

incline people to stay in their lane and not look across their lane to ways they might contribute to the whole.

I believe the business structure must be freeing, rather than limiting. It must support and enable everyone to do their best work and achieve their personal goals while also fulfilling the business's goals.

Rigidly hierarchical business structures are the limiting kind. They separate authority from responsibility. In a hierarchy, the boss is the authority who assigns jobs, gives orders, enforces rules, and makes the decisions. He or she also measures the performance of those under them with the responsibility to perform the specified tasks.

Some people thrive in a hierarchically structured environment. Task-oriented individuals who need to be told what to do and how to do it feel comfortable there. Command-and-control types, like my first boss at US Steel, are another.

But I wasn't fitted for that kind of environment. I didn't like working under such command-and-control constraints, nor did I like working with those who flourished under them. I determined to structure my company differently.

Unlike my first US Steel boss who admonished me to either "sink or swim," it was my responsibility as a leader and manager to make sure everyone on my team learned how to swim first. So I looked to hire people with potential and who would thrive in a company where they were going to have both authority and responsibility to achieve their individual and the company's goals.

Rather than the hierarchical top-down approach, I wanted people who could reach their maximum potential through autonomy, giving each individual freedom to make decisions and fulfill their objectives.

I guided rather than dictated. I gave everyone room to do their own thing in their own way as long as they were meeting the responsibilities they had to everyone else in the company, our business partners, and our customers. I gave them room to try new things and take on new responsibilities—I encouraged it—all the while, holding everyone to their promises. People said I had very high standards, and I did, and I wanted people working with me who had the personal drive to meet those high standards.

I never wanted to force people to do something; I wanted them to want to do it and do it better than before, better than anyone else and better than they thought they could do. The measure of my success was seeing people rise to the occasion and reach and exceed their potential.

And critical to their individual success, their coworkers' success, and the company's success was that everyone understood our mission, our values, and our promises. That was the ideal we all were striving for.

Ken's Key Takeaways

- The business model is your company's "secret sauce" through which you create value for your customers and profits for your company.

- The business model is the engine for disruptive innovation in any vertical category, and the best way to discover the greatest opportunity for disruption is to look across from your vertical category to others.

- Take a three-legged-stool approach to crafting your business model, placing equal weight on product, marketing, and financials. An innovative product alone will only take you so far.

Your Corporateneur Road Map

1. What was the business model for the last company you worked for? What was good about it, and where were its flaws? If you were going to build the company from the ground up, what would you do differently?

2. Which companies outside your vertical category do you admire? Study their business model. How did they innovate the category? What was their distinctive difference from the customer's perspective?

3. What can you take from other successful businesses and their business models and apply it to your category, your target market, and your business model?

CHAPTER 8

Mentor Leadership

*"The balloon seems to stand still in the air, while
the earth flies past underneath."*

—ALBERTO SANTOS-DUMONT

C orporations are beset by a new problem, though some would argue it's an old problem that is just getting the attention it deserves: quiet quitting. *Quiet quitting* is defined as "employees doing only the minimum requirements to keep their job and putting in no extra time, effort, or energy than is absolutely necessary."

Gallup conducted a study about the quiet quitting phenomenon and concluded that at least half of the US workforce are quiet quitters, if not more. It measured the percentage of employees who were engaged, 32 percent, as compared with those actively disengaged (i.e., quiet quitters), 18 percent, and found the gap between those engaged versus disengaged reached its highest level in 2022 over the past decade.

Quiet quitting is particularly prevalent among younger employees below age thirty-five, with the number of engaged employees dropping 6 percentage points from 2019 to 2022, and the same number of those actively disengaged rising by the same number of points.

Gallup's diagnosis: "Quiet quitting is a symptom of poor management. The overall decline [in engaged employees] related to the clarity of expectations, opportunities to learn and grow, feeling cared about, and a connection to the organization's mission and purpose—signaling a growing disconnect between employees and their employers."

Gallup may be misstating management for leadership. Organizations have plenty of managers running around doing what managers do: managing workflows and processes. What they lack is leadership: influencing people so that business objectives are willingly and enthusiastically achieved. Another way to put it is that leadership is an art and management is a science.

"Leadership is about making others better as a result of your presence and making sure that impact lasts in your absence," said Sheryl Sandberg when she was Facebook COO.

That is mentor leadership, building a more robust and more capable workforce by helping each individual achieve their maximum potential within the organization.

Management by Mentorship

Ken's success in the science of management is measured on the company's balance sheet. His success in the art of leadership is gauged by the relationships he built both inside and outside the company. For those working with him, he came alongside each of them, imparted wisdom and his experience, then let each take it from there and see how far each could go. He taught them how to swim in the Rohl pool.

The measure of Ken's mentor leadership is best explained by those who worked with him over the years, like Al Rykus in sales, Paul Satkin in accounting, and Skip Johnson in marketing. Each grew personally and professionally under Ken's mentorship.

Mentoring Sales

Al was one of Ken's first outside hires after family members. He joined the company's sales team and stayed with the company for the next ten years, until parting with Ken's blessings to launch his own venture.

Al was pivotal to the sales function during the early high-growth period when the innovative KWC pullout faucet was being introduced, working first in California, then on to Florida as the company's footprint spread. Despite his abilities and success at the company, Al had to be let go after KWC pulled the plug and the company was forced to pull back and start over.

> The only way to succeed in sales is to establish a personal relationship with the customer and get them personally invested in the product.

But Al bears no hard feelings. Quite the opposite: his time with Ken prepared him to start his own business, acting as a consultant and an independent sales representative for brands in the plumbing-and-hardware industry.

"Ken was more than a boss; he was a trainer, a mentor, and gave me the feeling of being part of the family," he shares. "He gave me confidence that I could easily do what I did with Rohl for other brands."

Al came to Rohl experienced in sales but had to learn the ins and outs of the plumbing industry and its dealers. Yet sales is sales, regardless of what is being sold. "The only way to succeed in sales is to establish a personal relationship with the customer and get them personally invested in the product," he says.

After Ken's road warrior days testing and fine-tuning the company's sales strategy, he gave Al and other members of the sales team their mission, objectives, and a road map for success. With everyone understanding the big picture, each individual had the opportunity to fine-tune how they accomplished it.

"Each of us had the right of first refusal. We'd meet weekly to go over the past week's sales, discuss any issues that cropped up, and plan the week ahead. If anyone wanted to try something new or do it differently, he let us go with it after we explained our reasoning," Al recalls. "And if it didn't work, he gave us another opportunity to get it right. We all learned through that process."

Ken's style wasn't to give orders or present ultimatums. He had a clear idea of the best path for the sales staff to follow, and if they got off course, he'd lead them back to it.

"Ken made it so inviting to go along with his ideas," Al continues. "He'd lay it out and follow it up by telling us the reasons why we are doing it this way and not that way. He'd always bring in examples and stories about what he'd learned from his experience over the years.

"It was a pretty simple formula, really. He wasn't judgmental; he taught, encouraged, and brought out the best in each of us," he continues.

That approach inspired innovation and allowed each individual to meet and even exceed their potential. Al tells of implementing a local radio show for its dealers. The objective was to help local dealers reach out into the community to connect with people thinking about remodeling their homes. As host, Al invited people involved in remodeling projects to discuss their experiences and how they navigated the many decisions along the way.

"It was a podcast before anyone had ever heard of a podcast. It helped our dealers, and it helped us by helping them. It put us way ahead of our competition," he shares.

Al produced the radio show for a year, then as cable television started to take hold, the idea evolved to move to television with the same interview formula and share the broadcast with cable stations nationwide.

"It seemed like a great opportunity. Ken planted the seed, and I began to fill in the steps to get there," he continues. "But I quickly discovered television was way outside my wheelhouse. Radio was one-dimensional, but television is three-dimensional. I had bitten off more than I could chew."

So with stress mounting, he approached Ken. "I can still see him sitting at his desk, leaning back, and just listening. Then he said, 'It's okay to move on and not do this. You've already been a success and become more important to your dealer base than any of the competition. You don't need to go to this next level.' He gave me permission to accept defeat and move on. He did it in a reassuring, positive way."

In bringing new people on, Ken looked for tenacity, people who'd take the bull by the horns and wrestle it down. If they got into trouble, he was always there as a sounding board, and he never forgot to reward individual and team accomplishments.

"Ken wouldn't tell you what to do. He would guide you and give you opportunities to see how you could succeed. If you came back and asked for help, he was always there," Al says. "But if you got into trouble and didn't ask for help, he wasn't pleased. He knew how to position people so that he could get the best from them and they could make the most for themselves."

Mentoring Finance

On the operations side, Paul Satkin joined Rohl in 2000 to take over the accounting function from Tom Duino, whose span of control was stretched thin. Paul came with credentials in accounting, having worked in that function for both large corporations and small companies. He also had experience with an accounting and manufacturing resource planning (MRP) software consulting firm and helped manage its clients' conversion to the new system.

Paul was the right person at the right time because Rohl was in the process of upgrading its accounting-and-operations computer system. After meeting Ken and being duly impressed, he was still hesitant to join a small entrepreneurial firm, figuring the opportunities would be better with a bigger firm.

"I'd seen the good, bad, and ugly with small businesses. I worked for a good one for five years, but after we reached a certain level, it went into maintenance mode, sales growth flattened, and I got bored. I didn't want the same thing to happen again, and fortunately, it didn't," Paul shares, and he retired only after Rohl was acquired by Fortune Brands.

Ken knew Paul had just what the company needed and pursued him intently. "Ken was everything you'd want in a CEO. He had vision. He knew where he wanted to go, and I knew I could help him. More importantly, I wanted to help him. I really wanted to work with him," he recalls.

Ken's hiring approach was to first find the best people with the right personal qualities and work ethic. Their résumé experience came second. Who they were, rather than what they did before, was of primary importance because with the right stuff, Ken could mold them to do the job.

"Because of his corporate background, he established a good structure for the company, having meetings when we needed to work through issues. But he gave people autonomy to do their jobs," Paul says. "He was always ready to listen to new ideas—he relished them—and he was always there if you needed some advice or direction."

Paul put Ken to the test after only about one month on the job. At the time, he wasn't reporting directly to Ken but to Tom, who still had oversight of the accounting function.

As he started handling the accounting details and workflows, he identified redundancies and inefficiencies across the other company departments. He saw a way to make things run more smoothly and drafted up a new organization chart and took it to Ken. Being a change agent himself, Ken appreciated it in others. He rewarded Paul's initiative and saw the benefits of making changes.

Paul recalls that as keen as Ken was on the company's financials, he wasn't a trained finance guy. "Ken had great business instincts and understood finance fundamentals, but he didn't get down into the nitty-gritty of accounting. For Ken, it was always about maintaining profit margins and collecting the money we were owed so we'd have cash flow and could pay our bills. I saw him make deals on just a handshake with international suppliers who knew Ken's word was his promise."

"Promises made, promises kept" applied to both Rohl's customers and suppliers. And after learning from the experience of having a big corporation like KWC pull the rug out from under him, Ken chose to develop close working relationships with smaller, often family-run suppliers in Europe. It led to long-term, mutually beneficial relationships based on trust.

And Ken even stepped in to acquire half of one of its major suppliers, Perrin & Rowe, when that company got into trouble. It turned out that when Fortune Brands came calling, its part ownership of Perrin & Rowe made Rohl an even more attractive acquisition target.

While reflecting on what he learned working with Ken, Paul says he gained a new understanding of the importance of customer service and building a brand, which is interesting since Paul's job didn't involve much face time with customers, sales, or marketing. "We would literally do anything for a customer. If a customer was upset or dissatisfied, we'd do what it took to remedy the situation at whatever the cost. That was what the Rohl brand was built on: relationships. People buy from people they like, and that saved us during the bad times," Paul says. "We didn't just talk the talk of customer satisfaction; we walked it day in and day out."

Mentoring Marketing

"Managing for growth was always top of mind for Ken, and as a result, it was top of mind for everyone else in the company," shares vice president of marketing Skip Johnson, who worked with Ken for some fifteen years. "He was always asking, 'What's our next step for growth? What are the unmet needs for our customers and the market? How can we meet those unmet needs?'"

Ken's business model aimed for growth, and he structured the different working parts of the business to achieve it. "It was always about teamwork—everyone up, down, and across the organization was primed to contribute to his growth goal," Skip explains.

The organizational structure was designed for everyone to look not just within the scope of their job description and responsibilities within their department. They needed to (1) understand how their department and their job fit into the bigger corporate picture and (2) take responsibility horizontally across departments and functions and vertically up and down the corporate hierarchy.

That's why before he talked about marketing, sales, and branding, Skip spoke first of his responsibility to help manage the company supply chain and strengthen the customer service department, build industry alliances, and develop programs to generate consistent revenue growth.

His marketing job extended way beyond the traditional four *P*s of marketing—product, price, promotion, and placement—to every engagement with the customer and potential customer.

"Managing every customer touchpoint fell under my marketing responsibility, throughout their prepurchase experience, purchase experience, and postpurchase experience," he says.

It's not that he didn't have marketing's four *P*s firmly in mind, but he never let it restrict him. "Ken always said, 'Make marketing simple, not complicated,' so we worked with the four *P*s model to manage our activities," Skip reflects. He goes on to explain in the following sections.

Product: Be Uniquely Differentiated and Best in Class

"We offered nearly fifty different product collections, reflecting traditional, transitional, and modern faucet fixtures and accessories for upper-tiered customers' homes, including kitchen, prep bar, bath, spa, and laundry. Every collection was handpicked to be both uniquely positioned and best in class," Skip says.

The point of difference was that the company's products were mostly from small, independent European firms unknown in the US market. Their products offered uniquely different styles and features that made them stand out here. And they were all expertly crafted with old-world traditions. These points of difference provided the company with engaging stories to wrap presentations around, elevating Rohl offerings above commodity products that were afterthoughts, not top of mind.

"Everyone in the company fully understood each product's unique selling point, and we would focus on that. Our products really resonated with showroom consultants, designers, and consumers alike because they were so clearly different. Authenticity, innovation, and value were our products' touchpoints."

Price: Be Profitable for All Partners and Rewarding for Customers

Price, first and foremost, impacts profitability, so in communications with showroom dealers and product suppliers, the company always made that a unique selling point for dealers to carry the company's products and for suppliers to partner with Rohl. With the promise that everybody would make more money and profit working with Rohl and backing up that promise with proof, the decision to partner with Rohl became a simple one.

"We were always uniquely positioned to offer a profitable combination of benefits for all of our partners," he says. "Ken would always say, 'Make it valuable and profitable for everyone,' so we priced products right to reinforce that mission."

Price also played to the psychology of the more discerning, high-potential customers Rohl targeted. Consumers' perception of higher product quality was embedded in the products' higher price. The entire luxury industry hangs on that hook: higher quality + better materials + superb design + craftsmanship = higher price. And it becomes essential to propel demand when a product's quality is hard to measure, like for faucets that the typical customer doesn't understand.

Rohl's higher price tag assured all partners would make a profit and counterintuitively drove higher demand for its products with its precisely targeted, high-end customer base.

Promotion: Share Information

"We did all the usual things for promotion, like running ads in *Architectural Digest*, digital marketing, social media, website optimization, and public relations. But the most impactful was to spend time training our showroom dealers and providing an abundance of promotional materials to support sales," Skip says.

While every company sales rep made training a part of regular showroom visits, the company established a special program for its highest-performing and most committed dealers. Every month, a group of about a dozen of these dealers were invited to California headquarters to tour the facilities, meet the Rohl family and staff, and get in-depth training on the product line.

This program made each of the participating partners feel special and provided a chance for the company to gain valuable feedback on how well they were doing and where they might improve. This allowed for immediate correction, if needed, and increased dealers' commitment to the company and its products.

Place: Right Place, Right Time

"Of all the other four *P*s, *place* is my favorite and the most critical," Skip shares. "When it comes to marketing, it's all about putting the right product at the right price in the right place at the right time.

"You've got to be constantly reviewing your current channel strategy, product movement, and supply chain to see if it's working for you. If not, you've got to take action immediately," he continues.

The company followed a carefully measured step-by-step plan to grow its network of dealers, starting first in its own California backyard and growing from strength to strength as its network expanded regionally, to ultimately covering the entire country.

MANAGING ALL CUSTOMER TOUCHPOINTS TO INSPIRE SUCCESS

As Skip explains, his marketing responsibilities touched every aspect of the company's operation and each touchpoint with partners and customers. With this broad cross-functional perspective, Skip and the Rohl marketing team developed what was called the "Rohl Wheel of Fortune," which defined every customer touchpoint with the company.

Divided into three quadrants, it took what most companies define as the linear customer journey—prepurchase experience, purchase experience, and postpurchase experience—and turned it into a virtuous circle. Each step in the customer journey should circle back so the customer takes another turn at the purchase wheel.

Within the three quadrants, it defines twenty-three specific touchpoints in the customer's purchase experience. The company established processes to measure success and performance at each step on the wheel.

This overcame what is a challenge for many marketing departments that have difficulty measuring the return on investment for their budgetary expenditures. By measuring success at each step on the wheel, Skip's marketing department could show in dollars and cents its contribution to each company operation.

Based upon the "Rohl Wheel of Fortune" and its ability to measure marketing's overall contribution across the entire company, weaknesses could be identified in specific departments and corrective action taken. But more importantly, the company could identify and double down on its strengths.

"Ken always said, 'Focus on what we do best.' He knew, from his corporate experience, it is often hard to measure marketing expenditures and whether you are investing it right. But he also knew marketing was essential to everything we did and the path to continued growth."

Ken's Life Lesson Learned ———

Everyone Counts

"Everybody counts or nobody counts" is the motto Michael Connelly's fictional detective Harry Bosch lives by. Long before Connelly introduced his Bosch character in his best-selling book *The Black Echo*, I adopted a similar motto for my company: "Everybody matters or the business won't matter." In our case, our everybody included the end-user customers, our retail and manufacturing-supplier business partners, and our company employees.

That's why the concept of participatory management is so big to me. There are all kinds of definitions and interpretations of participatory management. For me, it is pretty simple. It comes down to teamwork and speaking in one voice. And my job was to inspire everyone to do that.

BUILDING THE TEAM

Like in baseball, everyone in the company has an assigned position to play, but they must also be ready to pitch in if a play goes sideways. And as in baseball, individual performance statistics are important, but nothing is more important than the team's score on the scoreboard. Everyone needs to work together to put the most points up there.

In bringing new people onto our team, they were slotted into a particular job function. That was determined by our company's need and the candidate's work and educational experience. But I was always looking for people with extra personal dimensions and inner drive that went beyond their résumés. Sometimes people would come in with excellent qualifications for one position yet be better suited to another job. They could have been routed into one career track for a variety of reasons besides their natural interests and capabilities.

With new employees, it's essential to take their measure by assigning them challenging tasks and putting them on cross-functional teams to see what they can contribute in other areas. I often discovered that people would excel in areas of the business I couldn't predict otherwise. And giving people a chance to expand both vertically and horizontally can keep the business-killing silo effect from occurring.

As a company leader, it's critical to have the best people on your team and make sure that each one is also the best at performing their job. "A chain is only as strong as its weakest link" is a cliché, but it applies to business. Make sure all the links in your business chain are strong, and be sure to test their limits.

Cross-functional experience helps everyone understand the company's mission. They gain insight into the inner workings of the company, its processes and procedures, and how each team member contributes directly to the mission. That's why the "Rohl Wheel of Fortune" was so important; it gave everyone a visual so they understood how they and their job function fit into the bigger picture.

I was devoted to making sure that all our people grew in a holistic way. We weren't going to throw someone under the bus because they made an error.

LEARN FROM MISTAKES

They say you learn more from failure than success, and that is true. But I also found people are so quick to put failures behind them; they don't take time to process the valuable lessons failures can teach them. They also say, "Fail fast. Fail often." But by emphasizing speed, you can get shortchanged in the learning process.

When new strategies, processes, and procedures are put into place, it's important to conduct a thorough analysis of improvements gained and weaknesses or failures exposed. It's not enough to realize the changes didn't work as planned, then move on or, worse, play the blame game.

When a shortcoming or failure is detected in a plan, you've got to go beyond the superficial reasons, dig into the root causes, and take the learnings from it. Cross-functional teams, including staff members who weren't necessarily involved in the decision-making process, can be especially helpful in looking at the overall project and assessing what went wrong. An in-depth failure analysis will teach what everyone in the company needs to learn from the failures.

Not only were we constantly looking for ways to let our people do their best work and make the greatest contribution to the company. We were also constantly looking at ways for the whole company to do better and make an even greater contribution to our customers, dealer showrooms, and business partners.

ALL VOICES HEARD

No matter what we were working on—and we were always working on improving our processes and performance—I would bring teams together in the decision-making process. I wasn't looking for everybody to nod in agreement so they could get out of the meeting and back to their desks.

I demanded real participation in the decision-making process. I wanted to hear, and even encouraged, dissenting voices. Everybody in the company had their own personal experiences in their work and from the customers and partners they interacted with. Their perspective was critical to making not just the right decision but the best decision for us all. I needed everyone's point of view, arguments for and against, and an open discussion about alternative solutions before making the final decision.

The more challenges that arose in such team meetings, the better the ultimate results of our decisions would be. You've got to push everyone to reach excellence and can't ever be satisfied with just being good enough. To achieve excellence, everyone must be involved, everyone must be heard, and everyone must contribute.

MISSION UNDERSTOOD

To make participatory management work, the company leader must be open to not just hearing but really listening to what members of their staff say. And every member of the staff has to be playing for the team and fully understand the rules of the game. Like Peter Drucker said, too many people in the business don't understand its overall mission and objectives.

I wasn't about to let that happen in my company. That was the sole purpose of the "promises made, promises kept" note card every staff member was given during their onboarding process and encouraged to refer to on a regular basis. It clearly defined our company's mission, vision, and promises.

Because of it, everyone in the company spoke in one voice to our customers, dealer partners, and product suppliers and understood what was expected from them. We made it as simple and straightforward as possible, so nobody had an excuse for not living up to it.

TO OUR SUPPLIERS & CUSTOMERS

We pledge courteous, efficient and ethical behavior and practices, respect for your interests, and an open door. We pledge to build and uphold the trust and goodwill that is the foundations of successful business relationships.

Authentic Luxury for Kitchen and Bath

www.rohlhome.com

OUTSIDE

WELCOME TO ROHL

ROHL markets high-end kitchen and bath products that define authentic luxury. Through exclusive relationships with the best designers and craftsmen in Western Europe, North America and New Zealand, we offer product lines that span the market.

MISSION

To be the supplier of choice for new and classically differentiated faucet and fixture products that deliver outstanding quality and overall value to our customers.

VISION

To be the most recognized brand in the luxury category for faucets and fixtures. Achieve this vision through selective distribution, consistent trade and consumer communications, innovative products, a passionate commitment to customer service and consistent attention to meeting unmet needs of the marketplace.

INSIDE

Looking across corporate America, I see company executives giving lip service to it but don't necessarily see it practiced well. As business leaders, we must practice what we preach.

Yet in your corporateneurial venture, participatory management—having everyone in the company truly invested in the enterprise's success and understanding how its success is achieved—is nonnegotiable.

Ken's Key Takeaways

- Managing a high-growth entrepreneurial business requires a mix of both science and art. A high-growth business presents many challenges and demands and different types of competencies than managing in a more established, slower-growth company.

- In a new venture, having a vision for the company is the first priority, and as the business begins to grow, every person brought on board must understand and share that vision.

- Business leaders who bring insider industry and market knowledge to their venture have a greater likelihood of success. They have connections that may prove valuable down the road and can identify white space where they can flourish.

- Profitability is a major challenge for high-growth businesses. Be sure to have your financial house in order.

- Based upon the current research, there is no best way to structure the management of a high-growth firm. Regardless, no matter what structure is put into place, be sure that all the connecting parts of the business understand where they fit into the company's overall vision and mission.

- The business structure must free each individual to do their best work and make their personal greatest contribution.

- A participatory management structure can take a company from good to great if it allows each member of the team to give their best.

- The success of marketing impacts every aspect of business operations. Make sure marketing is given tools and resources to maximize its potential.

Your Corporateneur Road Map

1. Looking back, which manager stands out as exceptional? What qualities did he or she exhibit that inspired you? Likewise, do any managers come to mind who failed you? What can you learn from their failures that you don't want to repeat?

2. How do you like to work as a member of a team? How did you lead from behind as a team member?

3. When hiring, do you focus primarily on educational and past-experience qualifications? How can you develop skills at taking a full candidate's measure, including their personal qualities and personal drive?

CHAPTER 9

Marketing and Sales Intersect

"When one steals a flying balloon and animates it to fly over Paris, one should, ideally, have some idea how said balloon normally works."

—CASSANDRA CLARE

Managing a business's various organizational functions is important. Managing them so that they work effectively together, even more so. But the marketing-and-sales function stands above the rest as most critical to building a sustainable business.

That's because, as Peter Drucker explains, "The purpose of business is to create and keep a customer." Marketing sets the stage that creates the customer so that sales can close the deal. They are two sides of the same coin.

One can't exist without the other, so these two functions need to be structured together, not separately. In fact, Drucker argues that marketing subsumes sales, and if applied effectively, marketing makes sales almost redundant.

"Marketing is not a function; it is the whole business seen from the customer's point of view," he said. Ken wouldn't go quite so far but believes Drucker is absolutely on point with the need for business to be structured from the customer's point of view. "Customers first, customers always" was a credo Ken lived by.

PHILIP KOTLER ON MARKETING

While Peter Drucker is called the "father of modern management," Philip Kotler is the "father of modern marketing." When recruited by the Kellogg School of Management at Northwestern University in 1962, he was offered a job teaching either economics, in which he holds a PhD, or marketing. He chose marketing because it was the discipline that needed him more.

> "I realized that economics was pretty well settled in its structure. Big new ideas were not likely to happen and revolutionize the discipline. Marketing, on the other hand, was underdeveloped. It was full of description and prescription but not very analytical and scientific. Marketing was the right subject for me because it needed new frameworks, new tools, new methodologies, a new purpose."

And that's what he has given to the discipline of marketing over the last sixty years. He's published over 150 articles and 90 books, including the most widely used textbook in marketing, *Marketing Management*, originally published in 1967 and now in its fifteenth edition.

Through that textbook, he introduced generations of marketing students to the four *P*s marketing mix: product, price, place, and promotion. Since then he's considered other models, like the four

Cs—customer value, change, convenience, communication—but he asserts the four *P*s still hold up in this digital age.

"The four *P*s seems to cover anything," he said in a recent interview. "For example, the internet. Are you going to blog, do a podcast, a webinar? All of those are promotional channels. The *P* of promotion handles both messaging and media."

The beauty of the four *P*s model for marketing is its simplicity. "It's easier to remind companies [of the four *P*s] when they are looking at a marketing or brand plan. What's the product? What's the place it is going to be available, and what's the promotion we're going to use?

"It works. I have no interest in protecting it. If something better comes along, I'm very happy to use it. But [the four *P*s model] is actually quite good and something we can still rely on in this day and age," he asserted.

Beyond the Four Ps

Yet as Kotler's prolific writing and speaking suggests, the scope of marketing goes far beyond the four *P*s. In a speech at the 2008 London Business Forum, he provided an expansive definition of the marketing function that encompasses every department and function of the organization:

> Your job is to create, communicate, and deliver value to a target market at a profit.

Everything—all processes and all people—must be focused on creating value for the customer, communicating it at every customer touchpoint, delivering it with promises made and kept, targeting the customers who most value the values promised, and delivering it to make a profit for the company so that the business is sustained and continues to grow.

In other words, marketing is the engine that drives the business train.

The marketing function is to create the "value package" that is uniquely differentiated for the target customer. Differentiation from the competition that offers similar values to the same customers is a marketer's superpower.

"Marketing managers are so important because they manage intangible assets. They manage your brands, your customer relationships, your networks, your market position, your market information," Kotler said.

Visible Difference

For example, Trader Joe's is a brand that maximizes differentiation by putting Kotler's principles of creating, communicating, and delivering value to a high-potential target market into practice. It starts with the Hawaiian shirts employees wear.

"We wear Hawaiian shirts because we're traders on the culinary seas, searching the world over for cool items to bring home to our customers. And when we return home, we think grocery shopping should be fun, not another chore," its website states.

Customers shop there to discover interesting, differentiated products, not commoditized grocery items found elsewhere. Its products are presented in limited quantities and called out with colorful, handwritten signs telling their stories with a humorous flair.

Trader Joe's products aren't necessarily cheap, but they deliver significant value, unlike Whole Foods, where every product carries a premium upcharge by being in its stores. Done right, differentiation doesn't just set a company and a brand apart. It leaves the competition in the dust.

"You've got to decide your segments, your targets, and positioning before you get to the four *P*s," Kotler asserted. "Our aim is to know enough about potential customers to develop the right offer expressed in the right message to reach a prospect at the right time and place."

Marketing Evolves

"The future of your company is going to be a function of how good a marketing organization you have. Marketing is not just a strategy. It's actually driving the business," Kotler asserted in an extensive presentation titled "Marketing Strategy 2021," where he delivered any number of actionable takeaways for the audience.

Based upon his expansive vision of marketing's role in the company, Kotler maintains that sales, which has been around since the beginning of time, was the first iteration of marketing (i.e., Marketing 1.0). "Marketing was really sales and it was the study of advertising and the sales force."

By the mid-twentieth century, marketing progressed to the 2.0 stage defined by the four *P*s. "It was still at a mass-marketing stage where everyone could buy your product," Kotler explained.

Then it evolved into Marketing 3.0, becoming more sophisticated with segmentation, targeting, and positioning. It also grew more focused on the human element to emphasize how a company's products and services improve people's quality of life.

"Brand inspires everything you do. It's emotional, and there's a new direction. We want mindshare and heart share," he explained.

Looking to marketing in the twenty-first century, Kolter proposes businesses must adopt a "holistic marketing concept" that recognizes the expanding breadth and interdependencies of the marketing function across all aspects of the business.

Holistic marketing includes

- *internal marketing*, where everyone in the organization, including senior management, embraces marketing principles;

- *integrated marketing*, which ensures that multiple ways of creating, communicating, and delivering value are used and combined in the best way;

- *relationship marketing*, through which deep, multifaceted relationships are fostered with customers, channels, and other business partners; and

- *performance marketing*, which measures returns to the business from marketing activities and programs and that addresses broader legal, ethical, social, and environmental impacts of the business.

Holistic marketing extends far beyond the four *P*s. "More than just making a sale, today's marketers must engage customers and build deep customer relationships that make their brands a meaningful part of consumers' conversations and lives," he wrote.

Kotler said, "Authentic marketing is not the art of selling what you make but knowing what to make. It is the art of identifying and understanding customer needs and creating solutions that deliver satisfaction to the customers, profits to the producers, and benefits for the stakeholders."

Authentic marketing is not the art of selling what you make but knowing what to make.

Those are the underlying principles on which Ken founded and ran his company. Marketing and sales weren't just processes carried out by individual departments. Marketing and sales, in big ways and small, were the responsibility of everyone in the company.

 *Ken's Life Lesson Learned*

A Systems Approach to Marketing

Philip Kotler had a powerful influence on me throughout my career. Seeing the evolution of his thinking on marketing over the years—he is a few years older than I am—proves that "You *can* teach an old dog new tricks."

Back in the early '60s, when I was at US Steel, we didn't have a marketing department as such. We had advertising and product management, and I worked in sales for a time there. As I moved on in my career, Kotler's work began to influence the business world, and my subsequent jobs expanded to include both marketing and sales. I always viewed marketing and sales as part and parcel of my responsibility, so that's how I structured Rohl.

For me, as for Kotler, marketing and sales cannot be separated. Kotler once said, "The sales department isn't the whole company, but the whole company better be the sales department." Based on the full breadth of his work, it's likely he'd revise that to say, "The whole company better be the marketing department." I certainly would.

Marketing has evolved from being a profession, a discipline, and a department to driving the whole business.

MARKETING AS A SYSTEM, NOT JUST A BUSINESS PROCESS

Marketing isn't a thing; it is *the thing* that runs the business. I think of it as system. A marketing department carries out the marketing-and-sales processes (i.e., it does them), but the business must operate from a marketing systems approach with an overarching objective of creating, communicating, and delivering value to a target market at a profit.

In Kotler's words, "Every company ought to be run by marketing, not necessarily a marketing person, but Marketing." In other words, like the air in a hot-air balloon, marketing provides the lift that gets the business off the ground and keeps it in the air.

In my experience, marketing is often perceived as subservient or secondary to sales. Sales gets the attention and rewards, and marketing is looked upon as that group of people squirreled away in the marketing department working behind the scenes. They often operate independently, often fighting for resources and support.

When I started my company, the marketing-and-sales functions were closely aligned and codependent. While they operated as separate departments and the sales department had a larger staff than marketing, a marketing systems approach ran the show, and it was implemented across all departments.

The "Rohl Wheel of Fortune" gave everyone throughout the company visibility into our marketing systems approach. It showed how each individual and their departments were essential to the smooth operation and success of the whole.

Critical to our marketing system was the routine SWOT analysis performed by each department, and it helped strengthen every department's service performance to our current and future customers. Every individual and each department needed to understand their strengths, where they and our company were weak and vulnerable, what opportunities they had to overcome weaknesses, and how our strengths could prevail against threats as the market and we changed.

Then the executive leadership team and I analyzed the results together and conducted scenario planning to understand where we stood now and how we could move forward over the next three to five years.

As the CEO, you need foresight to see what is coming straight at you but also peripheral vision to see what may hit your business from the side. Our process of SWOT analysis gave both.

BE DIFFERENT

We shared our marketing systems approach throughout the company—across those in the warehouse, administration, finance, and customer service—with a formula so all would be familiar with marketing concepts and terminology:

$$D + C + P^s = \text{Success}$$

The D stands for "differentiation." We wanted every customer experience with our company, whether in the products offered or the way we answered the telephone, to be different and better than what customers expect and get anywhere else.

Many companies get stumped by the concept of differentiation, but I don't think it should be so hard. Just study what everybody else is doing, and do it differently. Trader Joe's does it by everyone wearing Hawaiian shirts. It's such a simple difference but one that perfectly tells the brand-differentiation story of Trader Joe's.

And that points to the C value in the formula: "consistency." You've got to understand the points of differentiation in your company—your products and services and your brand—and communicate them consistently.

To do that, we developed our "promises made, promises kept" note card that every employee carried. It made our differences crystal clear and provided a consistent language to communicate our differences.

The next value in the formula—P^s—has a multiplier effect. The P represents "problems" and the superscript ^{s} (its exponential factor) are "solutions to problems," and together they equal "problems solved."

Every customer problem solved exponentially multiplied our success, at the employee, brand, and company level. And those problems may be small, like how a call is answered, or big, as in the company's policies and processes. Put simply, the more problems you can solve for your customers and business partners, the greater difference you make in their lives and their businesses.

This simple formula—$D + C + P^s$ = Success—was originally developed specifically for our marketing-and-sales department. Marketing was charged with (1) anticipating the problems our partners faced in their business and the problems our customers faced in their homes and (2) identifying the unmet needs we could satisfy.

Sales took the ball forward to communicate our differences consistently and demonstrate to our direct customers—plumbing supply dealers, contractors, specifiers, and interior designers—how we were better at satisfying their customers' unmet needs. We also understood our partners needed to generate more profits through better margins, which we gave them.

As we discovered the power of the formula, we spread it further throughout the organization because everyone in the company had opportunities to solve customers' and partners' problems, giving that exponential multiplier effect to the business.

Every interaction with the customer was an opportunity to uncover potential problems that we could, should, and must solve to build a sustainable business that was consistently different from every other company.

MARKETING WITHOUT SALES AND SALES WITHOUT MARKETING ARE DOOMED

Addressing the causes and cures for potential conflicts between marketing and sales, Professor Kotler, along with coauthors Neil Rackham and Suj Krishnaswamy, published a seminal article in the *Harvard Business Review* titled "Ending the War between Sales and Marketing."

They wrote, "Senior managers often describe the working relationship between sales and marketing as unsatisfactory. The two functions, they say, undercommunicate, underperform and over complain."

They observed that this resulted from organizations splitting the two functions so that there is a "handoff" between where marketing's responsibilities end and sales's begin. So, for example, marketing's responsibilities are generating customer and brand awareness, leading to brand consideration and preference. Then sales takes the handoff to be responsible for purchase intention, purchase, customer loyalty, and ultimately customer advocacy.

"This division of labor keeps marketing focused on strategic activities and prevents the group from intruding in individual sales opportunities," they wrote. But when things go sideways, "The blame game begins. Sales can say that the [marketing] plan was weak, and marketing can say that the salespeople didn't work hard enough or smart enough."

Kotler and his coauthors described different types of relationships between marketing and sales that organizations put into place, but the optimum relationship they found was an "integrated" model of marketing and sales. It was the model that Ken followed for Rohl.

Specifically, an integrated marketing-and-sales approach means the two functions work hand in glove by

- *involving* marketing and sales in product planning and setting sales targets;

- *working* together to develop value propositions for different market segments;

- *assessing* customer needs together;

- *signing off* on advertising and sales materials jointly; and

- *analyzing* key opportunities by market segment.

The *HBR* paper goes into detail to help businesses determine their level of marketing-and-sales integration and provides steps to transition from one to another. While the authors note that not all organizations need to move to a fully integrated marketing-and-sales model, greater rather than lesser integration is best.

Kotler and his coauthors concluded:

Every company can and should improve the relationship between sales and marketing. Carefully planned enhancements will bring salespeople's intimate knowledge of your customers into the company's core. These improvements will help you serve customers better now and will help you build better products for the future. They will help your company marry softer, relationship-building skills with harder, analytic skills. Best of all, these improvements will boost both your top-line and bottom-line growth.

Ken's Life Lesson Learned ——

To Influence: Where Marketing, Sales, and Management Intersect

Say "influence" in the context of marketing, and people assume you're talking about "influencer marketing." Today, brands spend upwards of $4 billion annually to hire social media mavens to post glowing reviews and endorsements across their Facebook, Instagram, and other social media accounts. Despite claims that influencer marketing helps brands drive more engagement and better-qualified customers, I'm suspicious.

Influencer marketing is just another form of paid advertising, and consumers are becoming smart enough to realize there is little difference between an influencer or company-sponsored post.

Influencer marketing has an authenticity gap because consumers understand paid influencers are mere shills for the company, not necessarily authentic endorsers.

AUTHENTIC INFLUENCE

The influence I'm talking about is authentic, not just paid advertising in another form. It is "the power or capacity of causing an effect in indirect or intangible ways: *sway*," as defined by *Merriam-Webster*. That, in a nutshell, is what marketing and sales must do together. Its purpose is to persuade consumers that your company is the best and that they want to do business with your company.

The marketer takes a macroapproach to make specific target-market segments aware of your company and influence them positively toward your company. The salesperson focuses on persuading individual prospects to take the next step and become customers. And both are responsible for carrying the relationship forward to repeat business and hopefully onward to customer loyalty, the holy grail of marketing and sales.

And just like marketing and sales are in the business of influencing customers, the role of the business manager is to persuade company employees to carry out their assigned tasks so that the company meets customers' needs.

Another definition of *influence* applies to them: "the act or power of producing an effect without apparent exertion of force or direct exercise of command." Command-and-control management may be comfortable for some managers, but it rarely is comfortable for those who fall under their control.

The manager's influence is directed inside the company, whereas the marketer's and salesperson's are directed outside. But all need to be master influencers, skilled in persuasion, with the corporateneur being both CEO and Chief Influence Officer. And like any skill, how to influence people can be learned.

INFLUENCER-IN-CHIEF

Professor of marketing and psychology at Arizona State University Robert Cialdini, PhD, has written a best-selling book on the subject, *Influence: The Psychology of Persuasion*, which I highly recommend.

But I prefer to go back to 1936 and the first and most influential book on influence of all time, that of Dale Carnegie, *How to Win Friends and Influence People*. Some might say his stories are hokey—he grew up dirt poor on a farm in Missouri. But they get his points across.

Carnegie taught a commonsense way to win friends and influence people; much of business is just plain old common sense too. He was a master marketer and understood branding long before it became a "thing."

He was born Dale *Carnagey*, but intuitively understanding the power of positioning, he changed the spelling to *Carnegie* to capitalize on the image of success evoked by the Gilded Age steel tycoon Andrew Carnegie.

I first picked up Carnegie's book while living in St. Louis and working for US Steel. The local chamber of commerce asked me to compete in a debating contest. At the time, I had no experience in debates or even giving speeches, so I thought I'd better read Carnegie's book before taking the stage.

It was a simple enough read but powerful in its message. Each of its thirty chapters presents one simple and succinct principle to apply to all relationships, be they personal or professional.

The one that stuck most with me was his admonition to be a good listener. If you are wrapped up in yourself and what you want to say, you can't win a debate, let alone influence people to buy your product or service.

In business, you accomplish far more by listening rather than talking. That gives the other person a chance to tell you what they want and need. From there, it is easy to unfold a solution for them.

I didn't win the debate that evening, but I got second prize, which I considered a success given my lack of debating experience. I never had to debate again, but I carried forward the principles I learned from Carnegie to business success over the years.

MANAGEMENT BY INFLUENCE

To be a successful employee, a successful manager, or a successful CEO, you have to be an expert at influencing people. Carnegie wrote,

"There is only one way to get anybody to do anything. That is by making the other person *want* to do it."

In business, we talk a lot about consumer needs, but their wants (i.e., desires) are ultimately more important. Business success comes from more than satisfying customers' specific needs in the moment; it comes from gratifying their emotional needs as well.

Let's face it. Everyone needs water faucets in their homes. But some want the best faucets money can buy. These select few, not the many, were the potential customers we needed to influence and persuade to buy our products. So we targeted advertising in publications they were likely to read, like *Architectural Digest* and *Departures*, but more importantly, we aimed to influence the plumbing dealers that catered to our exclusive target market to carry our line. It was very simply an influence-the-influencers strategy.

Regarding management, my philosophy was always to get employees to want to do what we needed them to do. Carnegie devotes a whole section of his book to that, under the title "Be a Leader."

One of my favorite principles in that section is to ask questions instead of giving direct orders. That was something I did repeatedly, both individually and in groups. No matter if things went right or wrong, I always posed questions, like "What can we do better?" or "What have we learned?" We formally instituted this perpetual questioning process through our monthly departmental and corporate SWOT analyses.

I've learned that mistakes can and will occur whenever fallible human beings are involved. Putting systems, processes, and procedures in place, as well as anticipating where breakdowns can happen, are ways to avoid mistakes, but no system is foolproof.

When inevitable breakdowns occur, managers should begin with honest appreciation for trying, then lead into questions to let the individual discover and own their mistakes. I never penalized anyone for trying and failing. But I couldn't abide employees not trying at all.

INFLUENCE NEEDS TRUST

Trust is the essential element that underlies influence. Stephen Covey of *The 7 Habits of Highly Effective People* fame said, "Trust is the highest form of human motivation. It brings out the very best in people." You want to use influence to motivate specific behaviors, which requires trust on both sides.

In marketing and branding circles, we hear the repeated call for *authenticity*. Somehow the meaning of that term has morphed from the simple idea of "promises made, promises kept" into a whole host of environmental, social, and governance issues (ESG) that companies hope will result in consumers trusting the company or the brand. But instituting all the popular ESG policies in the world is no substitute for the kind of trust I'm talking about, which is "My word is my bond."

Getting people to trust you—really trust you—maximizes your influence, and it starts with trusting yourself. As a corporateneur, you have many responsibilities to your customers, business partners, and employees. You've got to balance competing priorities and make hard decisions, aiming to find the best solution for all, but sometimes what's best for one may not be the best for someone else.

It's at those decision crossroads when you need to gather as much data as you can and input from those concerned. Then trust yourself to make the right decision.

Ken started his company as a sales and marketing company. He sold out of the trunk of his car and called on the most influential dealers serving high-end customers in the booming California housing market.

In those early days, he discovered a repeatable process to generate sales by telling stories about his products' old-world origins, craftsmanship, and quality. These stories clearly differentiated the products in his "trunk" from all others. Philip Kotler calls them PODs—points of differentiation—and they are important not just in marketing and selling a product. They are critical to building a brand.

As the Rohl company grew and more differentiated product brands were added, the balance in the business shifted from "sales first, then marketing" to "marketing and sales." The company was becoming the Procter & Gamble of high-end home water-management products under the umbrella of a master Rohl brand with a family of individually crafted product brands underneath.

As the company grew and product lines expanded, Ken recognized the company needed help to build the master Rohl brand. Enter Sherry Qualls and the White-Good MARCOM agency specializing in luxury home furnishings and building products branding and marketing.

Building a Brand

"It was kismet when Ken and I met," Sherry relates. "We were seated together at a kitchen-and-bath industry meeting. After some small talk, he asked me about what I did, and I proceeded to tell him how we helped a family making kitchen-and-bath cabinets out of their basement grow into a major player in the luxury cabinetry market. And he said to me, 'I'd like to have someone tell our story like that.' Obviously, he was impressed."

Shortly after that fateful meeting, a business partnership was formed. Ken explained his company had mastered marketing and sales, but now it needed to build a brand:

We've done an amazing job of becoming a trade brand and building strong relationships within the distribution channel, but now we need to build a brand, one that consumers and especially design professionals understand and recognize as a leader in the luxury space.

He was looking for an expanded influence-the-influencers strategy to go beyond dealers to reach kitchen-and-bath design professionals as key influencers for the purchase decisions made by and for clients. While reaching the end-user consumer was a goal, they also recognized that the Rohl brand would never be able to reach the level of awareness of a mass-market brand like Moen or Kohler.

"Rohl was a discovery brand positioned for a certain type of customer that would appreciate authentic luxury. That became our differentiating strategy: to define authentic luxury for the kitchen and bath. And we saw design professionals as best to carry that message forward to the end consumer," Sherry says.

"Ken stayed focused on that mission. He is one of those people who trusts their instincts and surrounds himself with people he can trust to move the company forward," she continues. "And his instincts are backed up by great insider information from within and outside the industry. He gets that by turning conversations with everyone he meets into one about them, not him. The information he gathers allows him to make the right decisions quickly."

Sherry worked with Rohl for fifteen years until the Fortune Brand acquisition. Over that time, her relationship with Ken and the company was transformational for her agency and her personally.

"Ken brought out the best in me and gave all of us at the agency a chance to find the best in ourselves," Sherry related. "He was never didactic. He'd throw an idea out there, like the authentic luxury concept, and he'd expect you to grab it, take it, and make the most of it. His message was 'You're someone I trust to figure out how to make it happen. You'll figure it out.'"

Ken's management style is a living example of Dale Carnegie's assertion that the only way to get a person to do anything is to use your influence so they *want* to do it.

"Everyone who worked with Ken wanted to do the absolute best for him," she shares. "He was a mentor to all. Ken's got some kind of magic or chemistry that brings the right people into his orbit so that great things happen. Everyone is better for knowing him."

Sherry tells how Ken encouraged her to take charge in digital marketing when her agency faced the collapse of its print advertising business, the bread-and-butter for most MARCOM agencies at the time.

"Ken is hardly a techie guy, but he recognized that digital marketing was the way of the future. He said to me, 'Don't be afraid of it. With a little bit of work, you can figure it out. I believe you can figure it out.' And that encouragement is what I needed to start the agency all over on a digital platform," she says.

> **How can you grow a company if you don't have faith in other people and they don't have faith in you?**

People have a lot of different names for the qualities that Ken reflects, be it positive thinking or the law of attraction. Sherry describes him as a "When one door closes, another opens" individual.

Ken credits it to trusting in himself and others. "I'm surrounded by nothing but positive karma. I create an aura of who I am and what I am all about, and that builds trust. How can you grow a company if you don't have faith in other people and they don't have faith in you?"

Ken's Life Lesson Learned —

Business Is Always Personal

We tend to think of business as business, separate and distinct from the personal, as Michael Corleone said in the *Godfather* movie: "It's not personal, Sonny. It's strictly business."

Then later—only in the book, not the movie—Michael reveals the truth. "Tom, don't let anybody kid you. It's all personal, every bit of business. Every piece of shit every man has to eat every day of his life is personal. They call it business. OK. But it's personal as hell."

Managers want to build a wall between business and the personal. They hide behind the wall to justify that which may appear harsh, unprincipled, exploitative, even unscrupulous. But inevitably, what goes around comes around.

Business is always personal because any business is created for people, made by people, and run by people and ultimately answers to people.

Business coach Brad Sugars said, "Business is all about relationships. How well you build them determines how well you build your business." I couldn't agree more. And all relationships are based on trust—whether with customers, clients, partners, or employees—in business or in your personal life.

DIVIDE AND CONQUER

I've done a lot of thinking about trust of late through the course of a mentoring relationship with a young man—I'll call him Bob—who's grown a nice-sized service business in his local market with an elite list of clients, both consumers and commercial customers.

Bob now wants to scale the business and extend into other markets. He's developed a repeatable business process in one market with a proven service offering that appeals to both consumers and commercial clients. Now he believes it's time to take it further.

His first step was to engage the services of a professional business coach, who after a series of meetings, delivered him a three-page to-do list. Bob was confounded by the length of the list and frustrated that the coach didn't give him more direction other than to check off the next box on the list. Instinctively, he didn't trust the business coach he paid a pretty penny for, so he sought my help.

I took a cursory glance at the list and found it wasn't worth the price of the paper it was printed on. A to-do list is not a business plan. Granted, maybe the items on the list were things Bob should do, but a critical element was missing: prioritization. He needed to know what things to do first, second, third, and so on, plus contingencies for every follow-up step along the way.

I introduced him to the Eisenhower grid and how we adapted it for our business. The grid was conceived initially as a time-management tool in a four-part matrix defining tasks as important/unimportant and urgent/not urgent. It was named after Dwight D. Eisenhower, who said, "I have two kinds of problems, the urgent and the important. The urgent are not important, and the important are never urgent."

At Rohl, we adapted the grid to manage personnel, products, markets, and customers according to their performance (x-axis for high-performing and low-performing) and potential (y-axis for high-potential and low-potential). Bob and I studied the business coach's original three-page to-do list and narrowed them down to the essential five or six that would be high-performing and high-potential.

USING THE EISENHOWER GRID

- We can control two things—time and resources.
- Originally created to prioritize time, Rohl used the EG to manage personnel, products, markets, and customers.

	URGENT	**NOT URGENT**
IMPORTANT	**DO** *These are the things you need to manage right now.*	**PLAN** *Take your time in here. These tasks will be the ones you want to pay special attention.*
NOT IMPORTANT	**DELEGATE** *These things take your time without contributing. Delegate and free up space for more important tasks.*	**ELIMINATE** *These are pure distractions. It's super important to identify these and eliminate them completely.*

ORIGINAL MODEL

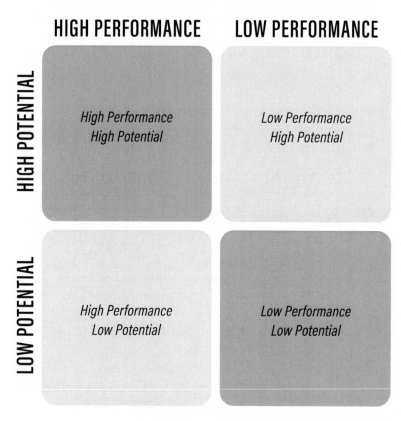

HIGH PERFORMANCE   **LOW PERFORMANCE**

High Performance
High Potential

Low Performance
High Potential

High Performance
Low Potential

Low Performance
Low Potential

ROHL MODEL

In reviewing where Bob was and where he wanted to go, we found he had developed and refined a specialized service and proven there was a demand for it. He'd recruited a team of workers who could follow his plans. His marketing-and-sales efforts needed refinement with more precise targeting, but we could get there with some work.

However, when I assessed Bob's own performance and potential, it was clear he needed to change his perspective from one of being an expert in the service he provided to acting the role of a business manager.

KNOW YOURSELF, TRUST YOURSELF

He had yet to give up hands-on control of every project and every sales engagement and delegate specific tasks to someone else to carry them out. He was micromanaging the business and not allowing others to rise to their potential.

To scale his business, Bob needed to stop being the best player on the ball field and become the best coach. He lacked trust that others could do as well or even better than he could. Instead of coaching, he was trying to play every position on the team, and it was holding him and his company back.

Bob was afraid of looking at his own weaknesses and failings, but without that intense self-examination, he'd always be trapped by those weaknesses and never rise above them.

In growing my company, I was always keenly aware of what I do best and where I needed support. While I had every confidence I could manage any specific task I set my mind to, spending time and effort to fill my personal weak spots didn't fit the high-performing/high-potential box on my personal Eisenhower grid. My time was better spent finding the right people who could deliver high performance to the high-potential tasks we needed.

Some of those high-performance/high-potential people I found outside the company, like Sherry, but I considered it even more desirable to grow them from the inside. So I worked to move people into different functions and throw them tasks that challenged them to see if they could swim instead of sink. Those "swimmers" I moved ahead, but I didn't punish those who failed. Rather, I discovered through trial and error what they were and were not capable of and managed to that.

Bob needed to bolster the skill sets in his fledgling company, either by developing the raw talent within or going outside to recruit the needed skills. Unfortunately, he had never worked in a structured organization—he wasn't a corporateneur—and didn't have experience to learn how delegating responsibilities worked. That is what he needed to learn. He needed to develop trust in order to delegate responsibilities to others.

My hope is that in trusting me, he could begin to trust himself and extend that trust to people in his company so they all could perform the high-potential tasks necessary to take the business to the next level. Otherwise, he will stay where he is, with a good business but not a great one able to scale.

Ken's Key Takeaways

- Marketing is the most critical function of the business. It impacts every aspect of the company. The job of marketing is to "create, communicate, and deliver value to a target market at a profit," which also describes the purpose of the company.

- Corporateneurs need to take a holistic or marketing systems approach in structuring their businesses.

- Differentiating the business and brands, communicating that difference consistently, and solving customers' problems will yield business success. And solving problems has a multiplier effect: the more problems solved, the more loyalty customers will give.

- The sales and marketing functions need to be fully integrated. Their job is to influence customers and potential customers to the business. In turn, the corporateneur must be influencer-in-chief, influencing everyone within the company to solve customers' problems, big and small, and to communicate the company's difference in big ways and small consistently.

- Being able to influence people is a skill every corporateneur needs to master. Like any skill, it can be learned.

- Trust is the foundation on which influence builds. Trust yourself first so that people will trust you, and with two-way trust established, you can trust others.

 ## Your Corporateneur Road Map

1. How well do you understand marketing? Get a copy of Kotler's *Marketing Management*, and invest the time to read and make notes on these eight hundred-plus pages.

2. How influential are you? Get a copy of Dale Carnegie's *How to Win Friends and Influence People.* It's a quick read but well worth it, then digest Robert Cialdini's *Influence: The Psychology of Persuasion*.

3. Create an Eisenhower grid for your business where it is today. What are the high-performing and high-potential tasks you need to do? What are the low-performing/low-potential things you are trapped by? Get rid of them, and focus 100 percent of your attention on those high-performing/high-potential tasks that will get you where you need to go.

4. Are you ready to coach a team rather than just be the best all-round player on the team?

5. Do you talk more than you listen? Develop the habit of listening more than you talk. Being skilled at asking questions is one way to develop the listening habit. Develop a list of standard

questions you can ask anybody that will start a conversation and get them talking.

6. How comfortable are you at delegation? Think about times when a manager trusted you and delegated responsibility to you and how you grew through that process.

3

PART THREE
The Art and Science of the Corporateneur

CHAPTER 10

Mapping Corporateneur Success

*"We should all have personal hot-air balloons and
drift serenely through the clouds."*

—RHYS BOWEN

We've said it before and will say it again: the odds are stacked against long-term entrepreneurial success. The midcareer corporateneur has a distinct advantage, nonetheless. "Entrepreneurship is an irrational pursuit," as *Entrepreneur* magazine columnist Jennifer Wang wrote. "Founding a company entails insane amounts of risk, ridiculously low chances of success and zero work-life balance." And that is magnified for those who dream of rich rewards in scaling a business to make it attractive as an acquisition target or to go public.

Maybe your ambitions in starting a company don't fly that high, but nobody sets out to be a failure, even if the goal is to operate a comfortable solo venture. You want to stack the deck for success, whether big or small.

On these pages, we've shared Ken Rohl's entrepreneurial journey, how he leveraged his corporate experience into a successful company that caught the eye of a *Fortune* 500 company and how he followed that up by mentoring aspiring entrepreneurs to launch their own ventures.

Ken brought a unique skill set and personal qualities to his business, setting the course for his company's ultimate success. Throughout this book, he's taught what corporateneurs must learn. Yet he's also been learning alongside you, as he distilled the many disparate elements that led to his and his company's success.

"It comes down to interweaving the science of business and the art of innovation and emotional intelligence when dealing with people," he shares. "It requires developing two cognitive styles: the analytical knowing style (i.e., the science) and the intuitive creative style (or art). Not only must each cognitive style be well developed, but both styles must work well together, continuously complementing and reinforcing each other. The entrepreneur needs both the science and art of business. It's not either/or but both, and both can be learned."

NATURE OR NURTURE?

Neurobiologist Dr. Roger Sperry won a Nobel Peace Prize in Medicine in 1981 for his work on the split-brain theory. He identified the left side of the brain as responsible for speech, writing, and the main language center and calculation, while the right side controlled spatial construction, simple language comprehension, and nonverbal ideation.

Sperry further found that both sides of the brain perceive, learn, and remember separately; each has different skills and functions; and both sides are simultaneously conscious and processing. Both sides are necessary to perform the full functions of the brain, yet we are unaware of how their complementary functions operate.

However, as Sperry's split-brain theory spread through the popular culture, it got misinterpreted. Stereotypically, we think of the entrepreneur as a creative, right-brain-dominant person, driven by their creativity to build new businesses, invent new products, and find innovative solutions to existing problems. They are thought to flourish in unstructured environments and wither in structured ones.

Analytical left-brain-dominant people are believed to be the exact opposite. Logical and linear in thinking, they use those qualities to solve problems and are not necessarily given to creative endeavors or innovation. They are said to thrive when things are defined, structured, and orderly.

It turns out, however, that this concept of dominance by one side of the brain or the other is a myth with no proven validity. Humans, by nature, are both creative and logical and require different skills, talents, perceptions, and consciousness to perform to the max. However, many individuals have a tendency (or, more correctly, a habit) that favors one or the other side.

And that's where the problems arise, suggests neuroscientist Paul King who's headed up data science for Quora, Uber, and Apple.

"Children have a more active imagination than adults, and young adults are less constrained by their own prior patterns of thought," he explained. "As people become 'good at life,' they develop habits of thought that serve them well. These habits are thought styles that 'work' (get results, impress people, carry us through difficult situations)."

Societal norms and business tend to favor more logical ways of things—adulting—so childlike imaginative approaches are left behind.

Once those rational cognitive or thought styles take hold, adults get stuck using what worked in the past, which can ultimately inhibit creatively discovering new solutions and unexpected outcomes, the very thing that corporateneurs must do.

King says people can develop personal systems, or what Ken calls "repeatable processes," to nurture their creativity. "This is a lifestyle choice to stay in the uncomfortable territory of the unknown," King writes. That includes pursuing hobbies and divergent interests, getting to know people outside your business and profession, spending time in nature, and giving yourself the freedom to smell the roses.

"This systemization of creativity doesn't have the bizarre arc of childhood imagination but does combine life experience with creativity in a way that can be more impactful (and higher paying) in modern society," King concludes.

FINDING YOUR PATH

If, as King suggests, younger people tend toward greater creativity, then it's easy to see why we think entrepreneuring is a young person's game. The media has provided proof of concept by mythologizing young entrepreneurs, like Mark Zuckerberg, Steve Jobs, Jeff Bezos, Elon Musk, and Bill Gates. They started companies in their twenties or, like Bezos, at age thirty.

And venture capital firms tend to favor investing in ventures launched by young people. "People under 35 are the people who make change happen," said venture capitalist Vinod Khosla in the *Washington Post*. "People over 45 basically die in terms of new ideas."

He was expressing what is known as *Planck's principle*, which holds that younger people are less bound by existing paradigms of thought and so are more capable of transformative ideas.

But nothing could be further from the truth. The average age of a company founder is forty-two years old, according to research led by Pierre Azoulay for the National Bureau of Economic Research (NBER). That study focused on firms with employees, thus eliminating noise from sole proprietorships. Further, the most successful company founders in the lot (i.e., those leading one of the top one thousand largest companies) started their businesses at age forty-five.

Dispelling the notion that entrepreneurial success favors the young, Azoulay and his coauthors concluded, "Younger founders appear strongly disadvantaged in their tendency to produce the highest-growth companies."

The research showed that someone who starts a company at fifty years old has nearly twice the likelihood of becoming a high-performing, fast-growth company than a company starter at thirty years old, and the possibilities decline further for those in their twenties.

The research also found that entrepreneurs with previous experience in their particular industry had a leg up to achieving success. "Prior employment in the specific [industry] sector predicts a vastly higher probability of an upper-tail growth outcome or success exit, with success rates rising up to 125 percent. Moreover, the closer the industry match, the greater the success rate," the researchers write.

This conclusion only makes sense. An industry insider understands the conventional wisdom that predominates in their industry and is best able to see its flaws. That's where transformative business ideas are born.

And finally, the researchers tested the idea that youth confers advantages from greater energy, deductive abilities, originality, and creativity—a bias expressed by Mark Zuckerberg, who remarked, "Young people are just smarter." They looked at young entrepreneurs, such as Musk, Jobs, Bezos, Gates, and Larry Page and Sergey Brin of

Google fame, and found, far from peaking in their youth, they only got better with age, like fine wine.

"There is no fundamental tension between the existence of great young entrepreneurs and a general tendency for founders to reach their peak entrepreneurial potential with middle age," they write.

> That's the definition of a corporateneur: "a midcareer professional with a transformative business idea and a compelling need to start a company to address it."

To put it simply, extremely talented young people get even more talented as they accumulate more work and life experience.

And for the rest of us, it pays to get a good ten to twenty years of increasingly responsible work experience before setting out on your own and then targeting an industry that you know well. And if you've got your eyes on another industry, invest some time learning the ropes by working inside it.

That's the definition of a *corporateneur*: "a midcareer professional with a transformative business idea and a compelling need to start a company to address it." It takes both a great idea and fire in the belly to turn that idea into reality.

THE ART AND SCIENCE OF THE CORPORATENEUR

It is blithely said that there is an art and science to business, and when starting a new business, people assume more creativity—art—is required. If that were the case, neuroscience suggests the youthful would have an advantage, but that is clearly not the case, as Azouley's NBER study found. Both the art and science of business take time for people to develop and master.

The art is the soft skills needed to imagine creative solutions to problems. But emotional intelligence is also required to develop meaningful personal relationships. Young people may be more creative by nature, but emotional maturity arrives later in life than a person's cognitive abilities, and some people never get there.

As for creative business ideas, Jeff Bezos said, "Ideas are cheap. Execution is everything." That is where the hard skills of business—the science—come in, and just like the art of business, they can take years to master.

Ken believes the best way to master the hard business skills is by gaining experience working for someone else before starting out on your own. College courses and book learning provide a useful foundation, but nothing replaces the sweat equity from working in one or many businesses. That's why many MBA programs require professional, full-time work experience. To fully benefit from the academic learning the MBA program provides, students need real work experience.

While every entrepreneur must understand the many business-specific functions required to operate a business—such as finance and accounting, marketing and sales, product management and development, customer service, and more—Ken sees that the value of corporate experience extends beyond just gaining the skills needed to perform specific business functions. It can yield a broader perspective for how to think about and approach business.

It's a *work style*—"the way a person thinks, structures, organizes, and completes their 'work'"—and in the case of a corporateneur, their work is founding and running their own business.

The hard skills needed to launch and succeed in the business include the ability to organize and develop processes and strategies with fierce discipline to execute the business idea. The soft skills required include an innovative approach and an imaginative mind that sees things not as they are but as they should be. The corporateneur must also be flexible as their dreams become a reality, since things rarely go exactly according to plan, and trust in their intuition, that gut feeling that guides decision-making.

And most of all, the corporateneur must work for the good of all the people the business touches. No matter the product, service, or industry, a business is simply an organized group of people doing, making, or selling something that makes a difference to other people both inside and outside the company.

"Of the people, by the people, for the people," as Abraham Lincoln said in the Gettysburg Address, applies not just to government but to businesses too. And it's on the human, people-to-people level that the corporateneur's soft, creative, and emotional skills and their hard, logical, and analytic skills intersect.

Just like the human brain needs both the left side and right side working in concert to function fully, the corporateneur needs to be master of the art and science of business.

CORPORATENEUR CIRCLE OF SUCCESS

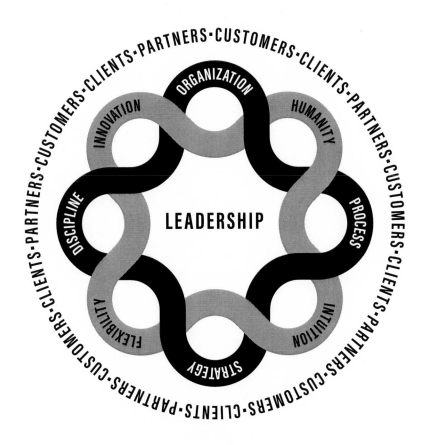

The art and science of business becomes a virtuous circle of qualities and attributes that intertwine and loop back and across each other. These eight qualities must be directed separately and in combination, to work for the good of those both inside the company and outside of it, as well as to customers, clients, partners, and ultimately for the good of society.

In the chapters that follow, we will examine each of the attributes in the corporateneur's *circle of success*, including the hard skills (black ribbon) and the soft skills (gray ribbon).

You have to use all the tools in your toolbox to build your business and achieve greater business success faster and with less blood, sweat, and tears.

 # *Ken's Key Takeaways*

- The human brain has a left-brain (rational, analytic side) and a right-brain (creative, imaginative side). Every person has and uses both sides of the brain regularly, consistently, and unconsciously, making the idea that some are right-brain or left-brain dominant a myth.

- The split-brain theory has also led to the assumption that entrepreneurial success favors the young. Research proves otherwise. The most successful entrepreneurs start their businesses after age forty and after being employed through their twenties and thirties. That is the definition of the *corporateneur*: "a midcareer professional with a transformative business idea and a compelling need to turn that idea into a business."

- A successful corporateneur is skilled at both the art and science of business, and both are skills that can be learned.

- Eight key attributes make up the circle for corporateneurial success. The science includes organization, process, strategy, and discipline. The art includes intuition, flexibility, innovation, and humanity.

CHAPTER 11

The Organized Corporateneur

"You will rise by lifting others."

—ROBERT INGERSOLL

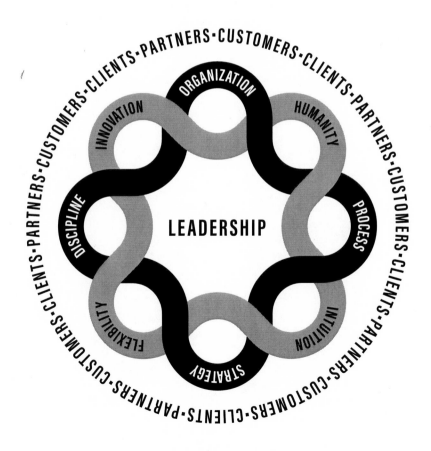

Building a business means building an organization, usually starting small with the intention of growing larger. That takes *organization*, meaning "the ability to arrange things in a systemic order according to a plan."

Marie Kondo is organizing's reigning queen, only in her case, it applies to organizing things in your home. Through her trademarked KonMari method, she provides a simple principle to systematically order all the stuff surrounding you: "Ask yourself if it sparks joy." If so, keep it. If not, toss it.

After following her method, people typically end up with far less stuff than they started with. While her method was developed for household organization, her principles can be applied more broadly to all organizing challenges, even business ones.

Granted, *joy* isn't a word commonly associated with business, but when it comes to customer service, it certainly is. A step above customer satisfaction is customer happiness, delight, and joy. And when it comes to employees, joy results from feeling rewarded and supported by someone having your back.

It's fair to say that joyful employees create joyful companies that bring joy to customers.

ORGANIZING FOR JOY

As corporateneur and company founder, organizing starts with you. At the outset, you are the most important resource in your venture, so your time and energy, both physical and mental, must be carefully organized and managed. Time spent worrying about things you can't control is time wasted. Better that time be applied to things you can control, manage, and organize.

Kondo provides useful guidance. She said to sort things into one of three piles and use the joy principle to decide whether to keep, donate, or trash a particular item.

In business, a traditional Eisenhower grid can use the same joy principle, but instead of three piles, organize tasks into four:

THE EISENHOWER DECISION MATRIX

- Do. Urgent things so important you need to do them yourself.

- Delegate. Less important but still urgent things to assign to another.

- Decide. Nonurgent but important matters that need to be scheduled for further attention.

- Delete. Nonurgent and unimportant things to be eliminated entirely.

Managing your time and resources wisely is always urgent and important. Following that, Kondo's joy principle can help you decide whether to do or delegate: Does it bring you joy? If the answer is no, then delegate it to someone else whose joy it is.

For example, at the start, it's urgent and important to prepare your business plan. Maybe writing it doesn't bring you joy, but conceptualizing your business certainly does. So draft the plan any way that brings you joy, using key words and phrases or thought balloons and pictures, then delegate the writing part to someone who gets joy from writing.

Use the same principle to bring new people on and to organize your business as it grows. As important as it is to find people with expertise and previous work experience in the roles needed to be filled, it is also important to find people who will take joy in that work.

So instead of hiring the person with the most impressive résumé but who takes little joy in their career path, it is better to give an opportunity to someone with less experience, even no experience, but who wants to experience the joy of trying. And those people will feel doubly rewarded by being given the opportunity to grow and learn. And they will reward the trust you place in them with trust in you.

Another way to bring joy to the people you hire is to give them both the responsibility and authority to do the jobs entrusted to them. Trust is a two-way street: trust given is trust returned. Giving responsibility and authority to those who work for you takes a load off your back and gives you time and freedom to do the things that bring you the most joy in running your company. And ultimately, the person doing the work will be more joyful for being given the responsibility and authority to get the job done.

Marie Kondo's organizing method helps people discover they can find more joy by having fewer things. The same concept applies in business with the idea of doing more with less. Businesses with rapidly growing revenues also tend to add manpower rapidly.

But Ken advises not to get caught up in the excitement by bringing in new people too fast. There are a lot of hidden costs in hiring and training new people, and it takes time to get them to perform up to speed. Better to think first about how the existing organization and resources can be leveraged to handle more throughput.

As in all human systems, there are often redundancies and inefficiencies built in. These need to be addressed and resolved before adding more staff, which can lead to the point of diminishing returns.

JOY FOR CUSTOMERS AND PARTNERS

The organization must serve the needs of customers, and that's where Kondo's joy principle shines. Every customer interaction should bring them more than just satisfaction—but joy.

Customer satisfaction results from giving the customer what he or she wants, when it's wanted, how it's wanted, and at a price they want to pay. That's the basics, but customer joy or delight elevates customer satisfaction to the next level. Customer satisfaction is not only giving people what is expected but giving them an unexpected "something more" that results in customer joy.

Joy is contagious. For example, if the person answering a customer's phone call sounds like they are delighted to take the call and resolve any issues, the joy is felt by the customer and is returned.

Unfortunately, our reliance on the internet and digital communications has effectively eliminated much of the person-to-person interaction that leads to emotional connection, so other ways must be found to deliver delight. Researching how your company's direct competitors serve customers or studying other companies known for excellent customer service will give ideas about how to elevate your company's customer-joy level.

The same joy principle must be applied to organizing the business for the joy and delight of your company's business partners. Ken did more than just offering dealers exclusive high-quality products and access to the highest-quality product suppliers. He also gave each partner, whether dealer or supplier, extraordinary personal attention to their special needs.

And to the ultimate joy of all partners, he provided each a way to make more money and profit by working with his company.

STAYING ORGANIZED

As corporateneur and company founder, it feels like the full weight of your company rests on your shoulders. That can be a heavy load to bear, and one way to lighten the load is by being organized personally. Another is to bring along coworkers to help carry some of the load.

Corporateneurs can be challenged managing and organizing their workday because of the added responsibilities. Pulled in many different directions, the corporateneur may find the time-management habits that worked well in their previous corporate jobs don't work so well managing their own venture.

Here are some practical ideas to get and keep organized.

Themed Days

Theming—the practice of formally scheduling a workday or major portion of one and devoting it to one specific task—is how Elon Musk manages $2 billion companies (Tesla and SpaceX and, with the acquisition of Twitter, another). It was also the way Jack Dorsey ran Twitter and Square back in the day.

For example, Elon dedicates two days a week to Tesla and two days to SpaceX. Dorsey themed his workdays around activities: so Monday was meeting day; Tuesday for products and design; Wednesday for marketing, growth, and communications; Thursday for partnerships; and Friday for company culture. Saturday was his day off, and on Sunday, he prepared for the coming week by reflecting and planning strategy.

Theming is a personal productivity enhancer that overcomes the inefficiencies inherent in multitasking and context switching. By grouping similar tasks into concentrated blocks of time, you stay focused. And this also provides structure for those working with you. They learn not to interrupt you with extraneous matters not related to that allotted theme.

Gatekeeping

Countless distractions can be the biggest time waster for the company CEO and make them less efficient in their jobs. A dedicated executive assistant can be invaluable in managing your calendar, handling distracting staff interruptions, filtering emails, and dodging bullets that can draw your attention from more important matters. Having a gatekeeper to handle the little stuff frees you for the big stuff.

Ken had an open-door policy in the office, but those who worked with him understood when it was appropriate to walk through that door. At the same time, he delegated responsibility and authority to the managers under him, so they effectively acted as Ken's gatekeepers within their domain.

Delegation

Ken has always been a big believer in delegating responsibility and authority. It was good for him but even better for those he delegated to because it gave them a chance to see what they were capable of, and most of the time, they rose to the challenge.

The corporateneur can too easily fall into the trap of holding on to too many tasks. You'll build a strong company and a more capable and dedicated workforce by delegating responsibility and authority. And you'll be relieved of extra burdens by giving them some of the load to carry for you.

Meetings

Research found that the typical knowledge worker attends some sixty meetings per month, adding up to four days of working time on average. And more than one-third of those meetings are rated as having "no value to the organization."

Establishing an "essential meetings only" culture at your company can be a huge time saver and productivity enhancer. And when a meeting is deemed essential, a clearly defined agenda should only be shared with those people who are essential to attend.

The typical knowledge worker attends some sixty meetings per month, adding up to four days of working time on average.

Another useful trick is to schedule meetings at an off time, like ten or fifteen minutes after the hour or fifteen or twenty minutes before, instead of on the hour or half hour. That can have the added benefit of reducing the scheduled time from the typical thirty-minute or hour-long meeting to twenty or forty-five minutes. If everything can't be covered in the shorter time allotted, use the "parking lot" method to park issues not covered to a later time.

Journaling

The bullet journal, known as BuJo, has replaced the old to-do list as the business executive's productivity-enhancing tool. A bullet journal typically includes a monthly overview of upcoming events and tasks to complete over the course of the month, followed by daily logs to track daily to-dos along with thoughts, ideas, and random notes to retain.

By design, it should be in old-fashioned pen-and-paper format, forcing you to slow down and contemplate as you record it. And it supports doodling, mind maps, and any other format that taps your brain's logical and intuitive side.

Designer Ryder Carroll literally wrote the book on the bullet journal method. He describes it as the productivity app for the digital age but in analog style.

"Inevitably, we find ourselves tackling too many things at the same time, spreading our focus so thin that nothing gets the attention it deserves. This is commonly referred to as 'being busy,'" he writes. "Being busy, however, is not the same thing as 'being productive.'"

He adds, "For most of us, being busy is code for being functionally overwhelmed," that feeling that every corporateneur can fall victim to easily. Using a bullet journal can help alleviate stress, worries, and to-dos till tomorrow when they can't be done today.

Self-Care

Taking care of yourself—your mental, emotional, and physical well-being—is the corporateneur's first priority. But with so many demands on their time and energy, the corporateneur can too easily let their own well-being slip by, prioritizing the well-being of the company ahead of their own. That is a misplaced priority; you come first.

Unplugging from the business is critical. Even five minutes of free time between scheduled activities can be a refresher to prepare for the next scheduled task, rather than using it to answer a couple of emails or make a quick call. Distractions such as these make it harder to attend to what's important now.

It's also vital to disconnect for longer periods during the workday, like taking a walk, working out at the gym, eating in peace, or even catching a twenty-minute power nap when your energy fades. And, of course, vacations should be used for vacating the business and not taking it along as your vacation travel buddy.

Taking care of your mental and physical health will ultimately benefit your company and make you a more valuable and effective leader.

Ken's Key Takeaways

- As company founder, the corporateneur is the business's most valuable resource. Managing your time and energy is critical to the success of your venture.

- Marie Kondo's organization method based on the joy principle can help the corporateneur manage their own time, decide when to delegate tasks, and guide them in bringing on new people as the business grows.

- The same joy principle can be applied to strengthen relationships with customers and business partners.

- To stay organized, the corporateneur should use some effective, proven time-management tools—such as themed workdays, having a gatekeeper, delegating tasks, establishing an "essential meeting only" culture, using a bullet journal, and practicing self-care.

Your Corporateneur Road Map

1. How inherently organized are you in your daily life? If it's a weakness, seek help in time management.

2. How can you bring more joy to your customers, business partners, and employees?

3. What's your business's key differentiating factor? What's its Purple Cow?

CHAPTER 12

The Intuitive Corporateneur

"One can never consent to creep when one feels the impulse to soar."

—HELEN KELLER

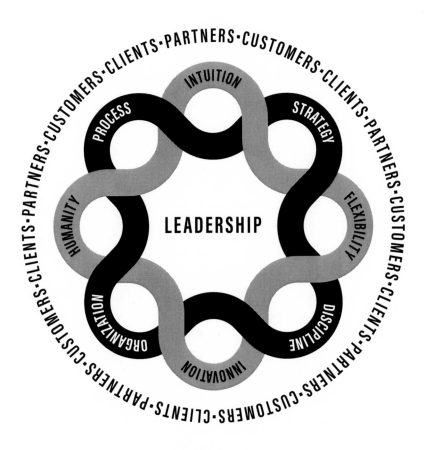

S ince mechanical engineer Frederick Winslow Taylor applied scientific measurement to work in his 1911 book *The Principles of Scientific Management*, business management and decision-making have been overtaken by Taylor's analytical, logical approach.

Taylor's work profoundly influenced Alfred Sloan, who applied scientific principles to the management of General Motors from the 1920s through the 1950s. In the annals of business management, Alfred Sloan might best be remembered for implementing GM's decentralized organizational structure, said to be the most ground-breaking and studied organization chart in business history.

Peter Drucker, who followed Taylor as the most prominent business-management thinker in the twentieth century, was well versed in Taylor's scientific method. "Frederick W. Taylor was the first man in recorded history who deemed work deserving of systematic observation and study," he said. But ultimately Drucker found the scientific method too rigid and went on to envision business management as a "liberal art." He drew inspiration for his thinking from history, sociology, psychology, and philosophy.

Drucker challenged the scientific approach Sloan instituted at GM after he was invited into the company to study it in 1942. The resulting report, published in book form as *Concept of the Corporation* in 1946, was more than rejected by GM management. It was scorned.

"GM's managers were so greatly offended by it that it became 'unmentionable' in GM for many years," Drucker wrote in a foreword to the 1990 edition of Sloan's autobiography, *My Years with General Motors*, originally published in 1964.

As much as Sloan and Drucker bumped heads professionally, they maintained a harmonious personal relationship until Sloan's passing in 1966. Drucker recollects, "When his associates attacked me in a meeting called to discuss the book, Sloan immediately rose to my defense. 'I fully agree with you,' he said to his colleagues. 'Mr. Drucker is dead wrong. But he did precisely what he told us he would do when we asked him in. And he is entitled to his opinions, wrong though they are.'"

About Sloan, Drucker added, "He asked for my opinions and carefully listened—and he never once took my advice."

Ironically, Sloan's book, which was written ostensibly to refute Drucker's, didn't do the job well. The cold and impersonal face of the professional manager that Sloan portrayed in the book "is really not Alfred P. Sloan as he was," Drucker observed.

Citing one of Sloan's core management principles, "Real leaders are swayed by facts, not personalities," Drucker found the book most powerful in Sloan's largely unconscious revelations about the man behind his stoic professional manager's mask. "To be sure, Sloan was not 'touchy-feely.' But he was 'people-focused' to the point of being quixotic."

While Sloan was obsessed with the discipline of scientific management, he was also highly intuitive when it came to managing people, picking the right person for the right job, and adjusting for their strengths and weaknesses in order to get the best results from them. His profound intuition is evident, too, in GM's organizational structure, which is designed to get the most out of each corporate operating division, its executive leadership, managers, and employees.

For the corporateneur, as valuable as following standard business practice to establish your business, your intuition is equally, if not more, important when confronting new situations and challenges, like building a new company.

POWERED BY INTUITION

Since the publication of Sloan's book, which downplayed the power of intuition in business, its superpower for leaders has been explored more deeply in academia, as well as in the popular press, such as journalist Malcolm Gladwell's *Blink: The Power of Thinking Without Thinking*.

Intuition is partly that God-given, gut instinct every human is blessed with. But it also is acquired through a subconscious cognitive process psychologists call "pattern matching." When exposed to a new situation, our minds unconsciously process stored memories to find similarities or patterns from past experiences to respond accordingly.

Nobel Prize winner Dr. Herbert Simon explained it this way:

> Experts often arrive at problem diagnoses and solutions rapidly and intuitively without being able to report how they attained the result. This ability is best explained by postulating a recognition and retrieval process that employs a large number—generally tens of thousands or even hundreds of thousands—of chunks or patterns stored in long-term memory.

These are intuitive mental shortcuts known as heuristics, used to make decisions quickly and efficiently, which was explored in chapter 3. Pattern matching makes the process possible.

Theoretically, the corporateneur with past work experience comes to their new venture with a well-stocked memory database ready for their subconscious to tap. Unfortunately, many midcareer professionals—having graduated from business schools or worked in organizations filled with analytically minded, data-driven managers—may have been taught to distrust their intuition.

Business schools and corporate environments have long favored the rational cognitive style. Stephen Robbins in his textbook *Organizational Behavior* wrote, "The optimizing decision maker is rational."

However, Roy Rowan, author of *The Intuitive Manager*, warns, "Business schools, of course, still put heavy emphasis on developing left-brain talents. The lesson of all this for business leaders is, don't let the left, monitoring side of your brain overanalyze problems or talk you out of moving intuitively into an exciting new venture."

Tapping one's intuitive power starts with knowing yourself, what you're really good at, and where you are weak. While you play to your strengths, you must decide if making up for your weaknesses is worth the time and effort or if somebody else can fill the gap.

Being a careful manager of his time and energy, Ken overcame his weaknesses by recruiting others to join the company and fill the gap. But when he determined that a personal weakness needed filling, he chose the "Teach what you have to learn" path. He figured if he didn't know something and needed to, then others alongside him probably needed to know it too. So he studied and mastered it by becoming the teacher.

Self-confidence in the face of what might seem overwhelming odds is also required. Ken was born with it, but for the rest of us, he advises that we "fake it before we make it." It's a variation on the "dress for success" model popularized by Thomas Molloy in his 1975 book of the same title, where he counseled people to dress up for the job they wanted, not the job they had.

People are drawn to self-confident people. They trust them and want to get to know them, so you need to put your self-confidence "suit" on every day in business. Save your doubts for private time, and always show your positive, self-confident side, and after a while, you will begin to feel it and be it.

INTUITIVE LEADERSHIP STYLE

By every objective and analytical measure, Ken had great success as a corporateneur, but he did it primarily by excelling as an intuitive leader and business manager. A characteristic of an intuitive leader is keeping their inner vision for the business always in focus. That vision becomes the yardstick to make decisions, big and small, short-term and long-term. A vision can never become an external reality without a clearly defined vision.

Equally important is to share that vision far and wide throughout the organization and with business partners. It becomes the "promises made, promises kept" reality for the venture.

As an intuitive leader, Ken set trends in the industry and refused to follow the industry's conventional wisdom. Every industry has got its own inbred conventional wisdom. It helps maintain the status quo and is a barrier to entry, keeping potential disrupters out.

Early on, he was met by people telling him nobody needed a "luxury" kitchen faucet, and what's more, nobody would pay the price for it when perfectly good faucets are available for half or even a quarter of the price. He didn't let the naysayers hold him back, rather he followed his intuition. He believed the world was ready for a luxury faucet and there were plenty of people who'd pay for the privilege. He was proved right.

Along the way, Ken also made more friends than enemies in the industry that he effectively disrupted. Part of his vision was to help the whole industry grow, not just take market share from other players. In doing so, he became more than only the leader of the Rohl company, but also a leader in the kitchen-and-bath industry.

And by being an intuitive leader, Ken knew how to get the best out of all the people who worked with him, including employees, dealers, and product suppliers. To accomplish his goals, he needed to help all the people working for and with him accomplish their goals too. As much as he needed to understand each individual's strengths and weaknesses in their specific roles, he also needed to intuit their personal goals.

For business partners, that was easy—help them make more sales and profits and treat them as equal partners. For employees, it was about helping them grow personally and professionally, allowing them to contribute and get the credit when it was due. Praise is a far greater motivator than punishment, so Ken gave everyone he worked with ample opportunity to garner praise through performance.

One of the superpowers of intuitive leaders is they know they don't have all the answers. So they are not afraid to ask questions to learn. Asking the right questions to get the best information and insight is an art, not a science, but Ken applied some science to help, such as SWOT analysis and the modified Eisenhower grid the company used. While he always wanted to

The intuitive leader needs to be able to think and manage the business across multiple dimensions, having a three-dimensional rather than a two-dimensional approach.

know how to grow the business, make more sales, and find new dealers and partners to build a more robust organization, he also mastered asking short, thought-provoking questions that could lead to bigger answers. He'd ask, "What are we doing now that doesn't need to be done or that we can do better?" or "What can we do today to make our customers happier and to serve them better?" Such open-ended, stimulating, and challenging questions empowered innovative thinking across the organization.

The business goal is to see revenues and profits grow linearly in two dimensions, rising steadily month after month, quarter by quarter. But the intuitive leader needs to be able to think and manage the business across multiple dimensions, having a three-dimensional rather than a two-dimensional approach.

Ken made a habit of always imagining "What if ..." scenarios when making decisions. Through the intuitive scenario-analysis process, he could envision multiple plans and directions to move the business linearly forward by taking a lateral, multidirectional approach.

INTUITIVE POWER NEEDED

Many respected experts—such as Nobel Prize–winning psychologist Daniel Kahneman and author of the popular *Thinking, Fast and Slow*—warn against making snap decisions or what Kahneman calls "fast-think" decisions.

Kahneman believes intuition is a poor guide to handling risk and it makes people more prone to cognitive biases. Further, that overoptimism—a quality necessary for the corporateneur—can be the intuitive decision maker's downfall. He concludes, "People are consistently bad at dealing with uncertainty. Surely there must be a better way than using intuition."

Yet uncertainty is the steady state confronting every business founder, and that is where Dr. Weston Agor's research comes in. He has conducted extensive studies of intuitive leadership and developed a survey tool to measure it, called Agor's Intuitive Management survey.

Agor says intuition in business decision-making is most necessary and powerful when applied under the following circumstances, which define the corporateneur's world:

- where there is a high level of uncertainty;

- where there is little previous precedent;

- where reliable facts are limited or totally unavailable;

- where time is limited and there is pressure to be right;

- where there are several plausible options to choose from, all of which can be supported by factual arguments.

Interestingly, Agor also found that as managers move up the ladder and gain more work experience, their tendency to rely on intuitive management increases. Research psychologist Gary Klein, author of *Sources of Power*, concurs. "Intuition grows out of experience," he wrote. And despite Kahneman's doubts about intuition in management decision-making, he concedes that prior experience can overcome some of its inherent weaknesses.

Or as Bill Gates puts it, "Often, you have to rely on intuition."

 # *Ken's Key Takeaways*

- Business schools and management-training programs downplay the role of intuition in decision-making, favoring a more analytical, logical approach. But intuition can be a business leader's superpower.

- Intuition derives from an unconscious mental process called "pattern matching," where past experiences influence responses to current situations.

- Tapping one's intuitive power requires self-knowledge and self-confidence, both qualities that can be learned.

- Applying intuition in business decisions requires a multidimensional approach that measures future actions against the overall vision for the company. Scenario analysis is an aid in this process.

- Intuitive power grows through experience, giving corporateneurs an advantage.

- Intuition is most important for business leaders facing uncertain business conditions with little previous precedent and the lack of reliable facts. It also comes into play when time is limited and where different options are available that cannot be supported by available data. That describes the world the corporateneur confronts every day.

Your Corporateneur Road Map

1. Think back on decisions you've made where your analytical "head" conflicted with your gut instinct. What did you decide, and what was the outcome?

2. If intuition failed you or if you often default to rational decision-making, read some of the resources listed in this chapter.

CHAPTER 13

The Process-Driven Corporateneur

*"Flying solo, you have a fair workload. I'm not only flying
the balloon but doing the navigation, communications,
repairing the burners, taking care of the equipment."*

—STEVE FOSSETT

J ulia Child was a paradigm-shifting change agent who shaped modern American food culture from her Cambridge, Massachusetts, kitchen, now installed in the Smithsonian's National Museum of American History.

While she wasn't the first television chef, she perfected the "recipe" since the 1963 premiere of *The French Chef* on WGBH, Boston's public television station. She went on to star in three hundred shows from 1963 through 1973, then kept reinventing herself through a series of sequels. She continues to inspire celebrity chefs and home cooks in PBS's *Dishing with Julia Child* and the Food Network's *Julia Child Challenge*.

Julia got her television start by appearing on a WGBH book review show to discuss her recently published *Mastering the Art of French Cooking*, which became a best-selling classic.

During the show, she demonstrated how to cook an omelet, which has little to do with the recipe and everything to do with the cooking technique—the process. After meeting Julia virtually on the screen, viewers were hungry for more, and her first series was born.

What set Julia's classic book and television presentations apart was her focus on teaching the cooking process, not just sharing recipes. She showed people how to take both familiar and sometimes unfamiliar ingredients and turn them into exceptional dishes to serve family and guests.

Her original thirty-minute series was recorded live in her kitchen, just Julia and a camera crew, unlike today where assistants operate behind the scenes to ensure everything goes according to plan. That made for dramatic and realistic television because inevitably something went wrong and Julia expertly showed the process to recover.

Dan Aykroyd's iconic *Saturday Night Live* sketch where he donned a wig, frilly blouse, and apron to parody Julia deboning a chicken was inspired by such an incident. He'd seen Julia and Jacques Pépin on Tom Snyder's late-night *The Tomorrow Show*.

Just minutes before their on-air segment, she had an accident while prepping ingredients and suffered a serious cut. Insisting that the show must go on, she explained to the audience her bandaged finger was caused by a mishap chopping shallots and let Jacques do the cooking while she provided commentary from the side. After the show, she headed to the hospital where five stiches were required.

Aykroyd said the sketch "was a tribute," coming from deep respect for Julia Child. "I was a huge fan of hers, of course," he said. And Julia and her husband got that when they watched the segment live. Chef Sara Moulton, who started her television career working with Julia, said that the couple retained a video copy of the skit, and Julia would play it for laughs at dinner parties.

As much as Julia taught viewers the cooking process, she also taught professional chefs the process for producing a television cooking show. Her influence is everywhere, from cooking shows on PBS, the Food Network, and the Cooking Channel to food segments on talk shows.

And while there is clearly an art to fine cooking, as the title of her first book implies, Julia really taught the cooking process. However, she probably wouldn't have sold over 1.5 million copies of her cookbook if it had been titled *Mastering the* Process *of French Cooking*.

FOLLOW THE PROCESS

Every human activity involves some kind of process, whether cooking dinner, producing a television cooking show, or starting and running a business. Mastering the process first requires envisioning what you are trying to achieve—the big picture—regardless of whether it's a pot of beef bourguignon or a thriving, sustainable business.

For each endeavor, there are micro- and macroprocesses. For example, a microprocess in business makes for efficient workflows for repeated tasks, like the procedures for handling a purchase order or hiring a new employee. In cooking, it's the printed recipe, including the ingredients needed and step-by-step instructions to put them together.

Ken was always keen on establishing workflow processes throughout his business, but his primary concern was the macroprocesses of establishing and running the business. That involved business strategy, business planning, managing staff and resources, distribution, partner relations, marketing, and financial results. And he approached each of them as an ongoing repeatable process, not a once-and-done task. He believed these processes must be continually revisited to learn from the past, to inform future decisions and processes.

Ken was the ultimate "business process engineer," concerned with engineering processes to improve productivity, efficiency, and operating costs across the current activities and operations of the business. But they aren't much use until the business is operating. For that, the corporateneur needs to develop macroprocesses for business development to turn an idea into a real business.

Ken's repeatable business-development approach is what he shared with University of California, Irvine, students and mentees, like Daman Starring.

Daman met Ken while playing basketball for UCI. "The university likes to introduce players to people who support the school and its athletic program, so that's how I originally met Ken. I knew immediately that he's a special man, so I wanted to stay connected with him and build a relationship over the years."

Daman's basketball career took him overseas to play professionally for several seasons, then he returned home to help his mother with a family-owned vending company, which was eventually sold, leaving Daman to search for new opportunities.

He hit upon the e-commerce space, and since he was also engaged to be married, he and his future wife decided to launch an online party-planning business targeting engaged couples.

Many successful corporateneur business opportunities grow like this, from people's personal needs. That perspective provides a unique position to identify the white space in an existing market.

With an idea in mind, Daman met Ken, and the first thing he asked was to see the business plan. Daman had a few ideas jotted down, but the plan was mostly in his head.

"Ken basically yelled at me like I was one of his kids, which I appreciated because it showed me how much he cared and was willing to invest in me throughout the process," Daman shares. "What he taught me was anytime you set out to do something—in business, on the basketball court, or anything else—you have to have a goal and a plan to guide you throughout the journey. Otherwise, you're going to lose your way."

Ken held his feet to the fire, and the next time they met, Daman had a full-blown business plan in hand. "My college degree was in psychology, so I didn't have any background in writing a business plan like you'd get in an MBA program. But Ken gave me an outline, I did the research, and then I wrote the business plan. I worked hard so that it would be good enough for Ken."

Afterward, Ken took him through each phase in the plan, sharing the good, bad, and ugly, identifying what needed changing and the parts of the plan to double down on to carry the business forward.

"Ken just knows, after more than fifty years in business. He's figured out a process that works across the board, whether the business is in clothing, food, party planning, or insurance," Daman says. "He knows exactly what needs to be done in certain situations because he's been there and done that."

Daman's engagement-and-wedding-planning business, called Starr Celebrations, got off the ground officially in April 2020. It has been so successful that he is planning on repeating the business process he learned from Ken to extend into other celebratory events, such as birthdays, anniversaries, and graduations.

REPEATABLE PROCESS FOR BUSINESS DEVELOPMENT

Ken has developed a step-by-step process for business development. It's a macro "big-picture" process to create a business. It starts with the business plan. Then once the business is up and running, other processes to execute the business plan and modify it as necessary carry the business forward.

It's a master recipe for midcareer professionals who've toiled away in one or many different corporate departments to get a CEO's overall perspective—a thirty-thousand-foot view from above—on how to build a sustainable business. We've talked about each of these processes before, but it's worth reviewing.

Identify Your High-Potential Market

Ken always took a long-term vision in business, aiming high to get the widest picture of opportunities for his company. He employed the modified Eisenhower grid to identify high-performing/high-potential opportunities and lean into those.

Aiming high for the highest-performing and highest-potential market can be daunting for the corporateneur starting out with limited resources. That's where the eating-an-elephant trick of taking one bite at a time comes into play. You can't do it all, but you need a big vision of where you want to go and to figure a path to get there one step at a time.

For Daman's Starr Enterprises, his vision is to be the online version of Party City, the $2 billion company with over eight hundred retail stores. But he started with the highest-performing/highest-potential party opportunity that he personally knew the most about: engagement and wedding parties. Using that as a foothold and a test for his business process, his company can strategically expand into other party and celebration opportunities.

Develop Differentiated Products/ Services to Fit the Market

Too many new businesses fail because they don't push hard enough to develop a truly unique, differentiated product or service offering.

In traditional marketing and sales, it's called the *unique selling proposition* (USP) or *unique value proposition* (UVP). Business coach Tony Robbins calls it the "X factor," and marketing guru Seth Godin says it's a "Purple Cow":

> Cows, after you've seen one, or two, or ten, are boring. A Purple Cow, though ... now that would be something. *Purple Cow* describes something phenomenal, something counterintuitive and exciting and flat-out unbelievable. Every day, consumers come face to face with a lot of boring

stuff—a lot of brown cows—but you can bet they won't forget a Purple Cow. And it's not a marketing function that you can slap on to your product or service. Purple Cow is inherent. It's built right in, or it's not there. Period.

Too many businesses create just-good-enough offerings or become so enamored with their idea that they don't see its failings and weaknesses. In other words, they fall in love with their idea when they need to fall in love with the customer instead.

Godin stresses that your Purple Cow products and services must offer remarkable value to the customers, and by that, he doesn't mean cheap or me-too but something of real meaningful, measurable value. That makes consumer research an essential part of the differentiating process.

Daman's Starr Enterprises differentiated by offering a party-in-a-box solution so that customers get the decorations and doodads needed to start their party just minutes after opening the box. It sure beats going into a Party City and trying to select from its overwhelming array of products to create a themed party.

For Rohl, Ken differentiated by moving upmarket and turning commoditized plumbing offerings into essentials for the luxury homeowner.

Channel Strategy That Focuses on Key Players in the Highest-Potential Market

Use the same high-performing/high-potential principles to design your venture's distribution strategy. Don't waste time and effort playing in the margins, but look for the highest-value partners. Ken developed a process to identify the right fit for his dealers. He needed only dealers that would devote ample selling space and commit staff resources to learn about and promote the Rohl product line. That meant he sometimes said no rather than yes when approached. He was focused on reaching only the highest-performing/highest-potential dealers in their markets.

Ken relied upon forming partnerships with key players consistently throughout his career. A relentless networker, he used his wide-ranging connections inside and outside the home-and-plumbing industry to identify and cultivate relationships with the players that mattered most, and he tested his assumptions about the market and his business potential through them.

He also understood that success in networking means not just taking but giving back, which he always did generously, following the principle of making the overall market "pie" larger, not slicing it into smaller and smaller pieces.

Seek Advisors and Use Them

Unless you move from the highest levels of corporate management into an entrepreneurial venture, you've probably not had much experience in corporate board meetings. Virtually any corporation of any size has a board of directors, not just to meet legal obligations but because of the immeasurable value they bring.

Company founders tend to be headstrong individuals with a keen sense of what they want to do. But by going solo, they can get so caught up in the business that they ignore signals in the market that will impact critical decisions. A formal *board of directors* (BOD) or a less formal advisory board can guard against that.

At the outset, a formal BOD is probably not required for a corporateneurial venture, but an advisory board is essential. Typically members are recruited among people that have a genuine interest in the success of the fledgling venture. This will include key business partners, like product suppliers, key distributors, retailers, and influencers.

These outsiders bring specialized skills and expertise to shore up the corporateneur and his or her team. They can also provide access to their networks and contacts, which can greatly expand the new venture's reach.

The advisory board becomes a sounding board for strategies, both big and small, and can often identify weaknesses and issues the founder is blind to. "The purpose of an advisory group is to integrate different points of view from people with different vantage points on the business and create a unified whole and do it in a constructive way."

The business will be stronger and work better when different perspectives influence the ultimate decision maker: you.

Be Confident

"Any plan or process depends upon the firm belief by the one who initiates it that the company has the capability to execute it successfully," Ken advises, and that takes having confidence in one's own capabilities and also requires that the leader nurture confidence in employees and business partners.

Confidence grows from experience, and it grows as new challenges are confronted and overcome. Building self-confidence is a process all its own.

Once, during an advisory meeting, Daman asked Ken anecdotally about the biggest mistake he made along the way. Daman recalls, "He said, 'I haven't made any mistakes,' and he said it not in an arrogant way, just as a matter of fact."

Ken didn't recall mistakes, not because they didn't happen but because of how he processed them into his memory. He followed the process described by Rabbi Harold Kushner. "You cannot control what happens to you in life, but you can always control what you will feel and do about what happens to you."

Or more simply, when life threw Ken a lemon, he figured out how to turn it into lemonade.

BEST PROCESSOR WINS

The cooking show format originated by Julia Child has continued to evolve with cooking competitions, now a fan favorite. The cooking competition format started with *Iron Chef*, which debuted on the Food Network in 1999, and its success spawned many others, including *Chopped, Cutthroat Kitchen, Guy's Grocery Games*, and the popular British import the *Great British Baking Show*.

The chef who's mastered the best process inevitably wins these cooking competitions. Perhaps that is most evidenced in the *Beat Bobby Flay* show. The concept is simple: two master chefs compete against each other, with the winner moving on to battle it out against Bobby with the dish of their choosing.

The show is made even more dramatic because everyone—the celebrity guest hosts, the competing chefs, and even the audience—are out to see Bobby beat. Yet nine out of ten times, if not more often, Bobby shuts down his chef challenger and beats him or her at their own signature dish.

That's because Flay has perfected the best cooking processes—in a career that started at age seventeen after he quit high school to work in various restaurants, until a New York Theater District restauranteur recognized his talent and paid his tuition to study at the French Culinary Institute.

After graduating from culinary school in 1984, Flay took a number of increasingly responsible restaurant jobs, eventually getting promoted to executive chef. In short order, he found himself underwater, not yet ready to manage the responsibilities of running a restaurant kitchen.

While he had perfected his cooking skills, he recognized he was missing organizational and management skills. So he went back to apprentice under the guidance of more-experienced executive chefs. He hit his stride in 1991 when he became executive chef at the Mesa Grill and became a part owner in 1993. The rest is history.

By definition, the fifty-eight-year-old Bobby Flay is a corporateneur. He was blessed with native talent and shored it up with formal chef training followed by years of hands-on experience in professional kitchens. But that wasn't enough to run a restaurant successfully. He continued to work as an employee to gain

Take the best you've learned through your professional career, leave the worst behind, and have the insight to recognize which is which.

experience and an understanding of all restaurant processes before setting out on his own. Through the process, he added business skills to his cooking skills.

That's the process that you are on. Take the best you've learned through your professional career, leave the worst behind, and have the insight to recognize which is which.

Ken's Key Takeaways

- Every human activity involves a process, whether it's cooking dinner, producing a television cooking show, or starting and running a business.

- The corporateneur must be a "business process engineer" at the micro level to operate the business efficiently and effectively and at the macro level to get the business off the ground, through the concept and planning stages to implementation.

- Ken's repeatable process for business development includes
  - identifying your high-potential market,
  - developing differentiated products and services to fit the market,
  - focusing on key players in the highest-potential market, and
  - seeking advisors.

- The successful corporateneur must approach all aspects of developing and operating his or her business with a high level of self-confidence. Building that self-confidence is a process all its own.

Your Corporateneur Road Map

1. Are you more comfortable following processes and procedures or creating them?

2. What processes do you have in place to make yourself more productive?

3. Who do you turn to for help and guidance when your processes fail?

CHAPTER 14

The Flexible Corporateneur

"You don't need a weatherman to know which way the wind blows."

—BOB DYLAN, "SUBTERRANEAN HOMESICK BLUES"

Flexibility in business is critical to creating and maintaining a sustainable business over the long haul. Or as Bill Gates said, "Success today requires the agility and drive to constantly rethink, reinvigorate, react, and reinvent."

Business flexibility is the ability of a company to adapt to changing circumstances in order to remain profitable. It requires the capacity to anticipate market changes and adjust effectively to meet those shifts. Flexibility is one of the *key performance indicators* (KPIs) for a strong business that can endure.

However, it is in short supply, as suggested by the history of the *Fortune* 500, the definitive ranking of the country's biggest public and private corporations. In 1955, when the first list was published, it was headlined by General Motors, Exxon Mobil, US Steel, General Electric, and Esmark. At the time, no one knew how long these companies would hold their position, but it seemed certain they would withstand the test of time.

But most didn't. Out of that select group of five hundred, only about fifty companies—10 percent—have maintained their top five hundred rank. All others have gone bankrupt, merged, been acquired, or simply fallen off the list. For example, US Steel's last year on the list was 1982, and Esmark fell off after 1984. Further, over 50 percent of companies on the list in 2000 are now extinct.

The Standard & Poor's 500 index, which ranks only public companies, shows a similar pattern. In 1958, McKinsey found the lifespan of an S&P 500 company averaged sixty-one years. By 1965, it had fallen by about half to thirty-two years; in 2016, it was down to under twenty years. By 2027, McKinsey predicts 75 percent of the companies on the S&P 500 list will have disappeared through a buyout, merger, or bankruptcy.

There are any number of reasons why market leaders fail, such as those formerly on the *Fortune* and S&P 500 lists, but many failures can be traced to their inability or unwillingness to adapt to changing market conditions. They lacked not just foresight but flexibility to adapt.

SPECTACULAR FAILS DUE TO INFLEXIBILITY

Over the course of the *Fortune* 500's history, about 1,800 companies have earned a place on the list. There have been some spectacular successes—like Walmart, which made its first appearance in 1995 and has held the number one slot over the last ten years, or Amazon, which entered the list in 2002 at number 492 and by 2020 worked its way to number two.

Then there are spectacular fails, like Blockbuster, which entered the list in 2006 only to drop off in 2010.

Blockbuster Goes from Boom to Bust

Blockbuster was the category killer in the movie rental business, founded in 1985 with one video rental store. By 2004, it had reached some nine thousand stores. Today it's back to square one—literally, with only one Bend, Oregon, store.

Blockbuster successfully managed the transition from video cassette format to DVD, but then crashed and burned when it failed to respond to disruptive competitors, such as Netflix and Redbox, which offered easier access to movie rentals without hefty late fees.

That was the original pain point that Reed Hastings addressed with the launch of Netflix in 1997. At that time, Netflix was an e-commerce company where customers ordered DVDs online that were delivered and returned through the mail. Blockbuster didn't see the potential of Netflix's e-commerce model, figuring brick-and-mortar stores were essential to the movie rental business, and turned down the opportunity to buy Netflix in 2000.

Netflix went on to pioneer in-home streaming services, which put the final nail in Blockbuster's coffin.

Kodak Had It, Then Lost It

Eastman Kodak, the world's leader in photography at the time, was on the first *Fortune* 500 list and held on to its leadership through 2012 when it filed for bankruptcy.

The company was done in by the rise of digital photography, an innovation that a company engineer developed. The company passed on bringing it to market, seeing it as a threat to its flagship film-and-paper-based business.

Digital photography ultimately proved to be Kodak's undoing. It should have followed the "Cannibalize yourself before you are cannibalized" strategy. Instead, it failed to pivot and ultimately crashed and burned.

Abercrombie & Fitch's Fall from Grace

Fashion retailer Abercrombie & Fitch never made it to the *Fortune* 500, but it got close in 2007 at number 602. Founded in 1892 by David Abercrombie, the store sold outdoor sports equipment, and when Ezra Fitch acquired part ownership in 1902, his name was added to the company's banner.

Eventually, Fitch bought Abercrombie out and opened the twelve-story A&F department store on Madison Avenue in New York City, retaining its roots in sporting goods and adding women's clothing in 1910.

By 1939 it declared itself the "greatest sporting goods store in the world" and continued to expand through the 1950s and early 1960s, when sales began to plummet. Declaring bankruptcy in 1977, it was acquired by Oshman's Sporting Goods, which eventually sold it to Limited Brands, home of Victoria's Secret, in 1988. Limited Brands repositioned it as exclusively a fashion brand.

Mike Jeffries, who came in as president in 1992, foresaw the rise of the teen retail market and pivoted toward more youthful, casual looks. The brand was eventually spun off as a public company in 1996, then things got dicey.

Under Limited Brands, Abercrombie & Fitch presented customers with an edgy, racy image, following its sister brand Victoria's Secret. It found early favor with teens and grew to over one thousand stores. But over time, A&F pushed the envelope and became hypersexualized, alienating parents who were ultimately paying the bills.

Then, in a fateful 2006 *Salon* interview, CEO Jeffries alienated just about everyone else when he described his vision for the brand. "We go after the cool kids. We go after the attractive all-American kid with a great attitude and a lot of friends. A lot of people don't belong [in our clothes], and they can't belong. Are we exclusionary? Absolutely. Those companies that are in trouble are trying to target everybody: young, old, fat, skinny."

Just as the culture was moving toward more inclusivity, A&F was hanging on to its exclusionary image. "That's why we hire good-looking people in our stores. Because good-looking people attract other good-looking people, and we want to market to cool, good-looking people. We don't market to anyone other than that," he said.

Following a number of lawsuits alleging discriminatory hiring practices and sexual misconduct, as well as a Change.org petition demanding inclusivity, Jeffries left the company in 2014. It is now led by Fran Horowitz, who is working to rehabilitate the brand. But she has a long way to go.

It would have been much easier if A&F had pivoted early instead of pursuing Jeffries's course, which was destined to fail.

CREATING A CULTURE FOR FLEXIBILITY

Around 500 BC, the Greek philosopher Heraclitus said, "The only thing constant is change." That is even more true today with the pace of business change now running at warp speed. It requires businesses to be ready, willing, and able to flex as market conditions change—or as Robert Jordan wrote in *The Fires of Heaven*, "The oak fought the wind and was broken; the willow bent when it must and survived."

In the forest, we can easily distinguish between the oak and willow, but it is not so easy in business. Research led by Professor Dennis Herhausen set out to develop a field guide to tell hardened business "oaks" from flexible "willows."

The results, originally published in the *British Journal of Management,* compiled data from ninety-eight different studies covering twenty-seven thousand firms, to provide a meta-analysis of the "enablers, inhibitors, and triggers" of strategic flexibility.

Strategic flexibility was defined variously as

- a firm's ability to respond to various demands from dynamic competitive environments;

- the capability of the firm to proact or respond quickly to changing competitive conditions and thereby develop or maintain a competitive advantage; and

- the ability to adapt to environmental changes, to change game plans, to precipitate intentional changes, and to continuously respond to unanticipated changes.

The researchers' premise that was proven in the research is that strategic flexibility is required for businesses to "remain competitively vital, in order to strategically flourish over time." The study goes on to reveal antecedents or precursors for strategic flexibility. Those include an entrepreneurial, marketing, and learning orientation—qualities that Ken instilled in his company—as well as a decentralized corporate structure and formal "routines [what Ken would call processes] to enable a firm to become flexible.

"Engaging in these firm-wide orientations demands the ability to engage in ambidextrous and polydextrous behaviours that allow these different 'plates' to be consistently and simultaneously spun," the authors write.

Interestingly, a decentralized organizational structure was found to have the highest impact on enabling strategic flexibility, more than any other factor, a structure that Ken firmly advocates.

The research also found that the firm's size or age in no way hinders strategic flexibility, so whether big or small, long-lived or new venture, strategic flexibility can be built into corporate culture.

At its core, strategic flexibility is a function of the organization's culture.

Ironically, a company's history of past successes tends to inhibit flexibility. So a company with a strong track record of success is less likely to be willing or able to change direction, even as the market shifts. Such is the case for Blockbuster, Kodak, Abercrombie & Fitch, and other notables that lost ranking on the *Fortune* 500 and S&P 500 lists.

FLEX WHEN YOU NEED TO FLEX

Determination and perseverance are essential qualities for the corporateneur. Yet those very qualities can make for rigidity when flexibility is needed.

"Allow for many paths to your goal. Do not fixate on one path, because then you are likely to give up when that path is blocked," said author and journalist Po Bronson. Instead, Ken says to fixate on the ultimate goal—creating a sustainable, profitable business—and be flexible in finding your way there.

Everyone who has worked with Ken knows he has a strong personality and is very determined about his goals. But he never let that determination get in the way of doing things differently when it was needed, nor did he blindly follow conventional wisdom that people in the industry said was the proven way to do business.

When the whole industry needed to flex, Ken spearheaded the charge when he offered dealers "selective exclusivity" in distribution, when "exclusive distribution" through just one dealer was the industry standard.

Ken didn't want to put all his eggs in one basket, so he flexed to offer dealers the opportunity to be one of a select few in their region to carry the Rohl product line. Dealers loved the idea of being members of a select group and enjoying the extra benefits and personal attention that came with membership. The selective-distribution model went on to become the industry norm, replacing exclusive distribution.

Ken made it a process to regularly gather input from those around him, including business partners and employees, to make sure his determination wasn't getting in the way of the company's progress.

"I kept everyone focused on the long-term strategies, goals, and processes. At the same time, I had to be flexible in my approach with individuals and encourage the free flow of information. Everyone has a point of view that comes from different experiences. I focused on relationship building to gain different perspectives."

Ken was never an "It's my way or the highway" kind of manager. Rather, he fixed everyone's sights on where they all were going—the goal—and let each employee help find the best way to get there by working together.

FLEXING TO WIN

Longtime associate Kevin Bixby describes himself as Ken's "hired hand," someone called upon over the years to help flex the company. He started working with Rohl as an intern while getting an MBA at the University of California, Irvine, and made regular house calls when specific projects needed his expertise.

Diversification projects—another term for flexing the business—are how Kevin describes the tasks he was assigned to, such as when the company had to pivot into digital marketing or when it acquired 50 percent ownership in the UK-based Perrin & Rowe faucet manufacturer in 2014.

Perrin & Rowe had been a longtime Rohl partner, providing authentically crafted luxury plumbing fixtures. It eventually became one of Rohl's best-selling brands. When Perrin & Rowe hit hard times and faced the threat it would have to close its factory, Ken stepped in to provide a leg up and keep the company going.

"Ken had been burned a couple of times in the past by suppliers deciding to pull the plug on a product line or the whole line, like when KWC decided to take over their own US distribution," Kevin recalls. "At the time, he said, 'I don't want to be dependent on the whims of some corporate guys who make decisions just like that which ultimately impacts our business.'"

Kevin helped Ken and the Rohl team evaluate the flex from being primarily a wholesale distributor of other companies' products to owning part of a manufacturing company. Such a paradigm shift came with risk, but they determined that the rewards far outweighed them.

Moderating the risk was the fact that Ken and the team knew the Perrin & Rowe company and its owners intimately. Ken also felt qualified to evaluate its manufacturing operations from his corporate experience, even though he planned to have no direct involvement with day-to-day operations after the deal.

"Ken has the ability to take a look at where he wants to go and strategically assess the risks and opportunities and predict the future as best as anyone can," Kevin shares.

"At the time, Ken felt that owning the process and having control over Perrin & Rowe would bring something new to our company and not leave us vulnerable to the vagaries of the manufacturer. It was a strategic move that took us in a different direction than we'd gone before, but it had a big benefit," he continues.

As it turns out, Rohl's pivot to owning part of Perrin & Rowe made the company an even more attractive acquisition candidate when Fortune Brands came calling.

FLEXIBILITY REQUIRES DIFFERENT POINTS OF VIEW

Kevin reflects that the corporate culture Ken fostered was a key advantage that made flexing the business possible through the years. "Ken was the kind of person who wasn't afraid to buck the status quo in his outlook or perspective on things. For that, he relied on getting a diversity of opinions," he explains.

To come up with the best solution, you have to get people in the room who don't just agree with you but have diverse opinions.

278

"He was always on top of things because he listened to other people. To come up with the best solution, you have to get people in the room who don't just agree with you but have diverse opinions, so you can look at all sides of things."

And helping the strong-willed and determined Ken be more flexible was the diversity of contacts and interests that he cultivated beyond business.

"Ken was active in the kitchen-and-bath industry association. He met with key accounts and suppliers. He also was involved with UCI graduate school, its basketball team, and did nonprofit work with the Irvine Barclay Theatre. And then he made business a family affair, too, and gave not just his sons but everyone in the company a chance to spread their wings and grow," Kevin reflects.

"Ken wanted to make sure that even though he is in business, he wasn't all business all the time. He knew how to balance the personal and business side of life."

As a corporateneur, you are at a junction that requires flexing, from the comfort and security of a corporate position into the possible discomfort and uncertainty of entrepreneurship.

While "Make a plan. Work the plan" is Ken's primary directive, he also advises the corporateneur to have contingency plans on hand if alternate paths are required. That was how he and Raghu Rai pivoted with Jio Health when the US healthcare market was effectively closed but Vietnam was open for business.

Determination balanced by flexibility will be needed as you move on in your corporateneur journey. And be ready to lean into the perspective of those who share your journey so that you don't get blindsided by your own fixed determination.

Ken's Key Takeaways ──────

- Business flexibility—the ability to anticipate market changes and adjust effectively to meet them—is one of the *key performance indicators* (KPIs) for a strong business that can endure.

- The length of time industry leaders stay on the *Fortune* 500 or S&P 500 lists is contracting as the business environment shifts so rapidly and businesses fail to flex.

- Research has found that the size and age of a company have no bearing on strategic flexibility. Further, strategic flexibility is supported when a company maintains an entrepreneurial, marketing, and learning orientation; has a decentralized structure; and has established processes in place that favor flexibility. On the other hand, past business successes tend to make a company less flexible and less able to respond effectively to market shifts.

- Corporateneurs, by their very nature, are determined individuals—which can result in less rather than more flexibility. That's why the corporateneur must foster a company culture that encourages flexibility to flourish.

- Gathering different points of view from those inside the company and also from business partners outside is critical to building a company able to flex. And developing interests beyond the business gives the corporateneur a wider perspective that makes for a more flexible business leader.

Your Corporateneur Road Map

1. Look at your industry and the companies that have failed or are failing because they lack flexibility. What lessons can you draw from their experience?

2. Do you often find yourself being inflexible and too determined to have it your way? When has inflexibility gotten you in trouble and worked against your best interests?

3. How open are you to listening when people tell you that you are on the wrong track?

CHAPTER 15

The Strategic Corporateneur

*"I may not have gone where I intended to go, but I
think I have ended up where I needed to be."*

—DOUGLAS ADAMS, *THE LONG DARK TEA-TIME OF THE SOUL*

pple topped the *Forbes* list of the world's most valuable brands in 2022, as it's done for the last several years. Called by marketing guru Seth Godin a "mythic brand," he says Apple gained that status by being more than just a company producing products and garnering sales and profits. A mythic brand like Apple has a transcendental quality that elevates it above the temporal plane.

"Mythological brands make a spiritual connection with the user, delivering something they can't find on their own … or at the very least, giving people a slate they can use to write their own spirituality on. People *use* a Dell. They *are* an Apple," he writes.

Apple—the company making products, sales, and profits—has plenty to crow about. In terms of total revenues, it ranked number three on the *Fortune* 500 list in 2021, behind only Walmart and Amazon. But as a brand, Apple rises above all others.

In August 2022, Apple achieved what Walmart and Amazon haven't. It scored the highest stock market valuation in the past forty years among companies on the S&P 500. Why? Because of its brand value.

APPLE'S UPS AND DOWNS

One might think Apple has followed a steady upward trajectory to achieve those goals, but it's had plenty of ups and downs since its founding in 1976 by Steve Jobs and Steve Wozniak. In less than ten years, Apple achieved mass-market success through its introduction of Apple II and Macintosh computers, the first to offer a graphical user interface.

But it took a lot of capital to get the company off the ground, so Jobs and Wozniak brought investors in early, who eventually ended up owning a majority share of the company. By the early '80s, the board pushed for professional management to be brought in, believing that Jobs was too young and temperamental to manage a company of its size. PepsiCo president John Sculley seemed to fit the bill, and he was tasked with running the company, letting Jobs focus on what he did best: being a visionary.

That didn't last long, and by 1985 Jobs was out of a job. He went on to found the computer company NeXT. But over time, neither Apple nor NeXT were doing well. Scully left Apple in 1993, and by 1997 Apple came close to bankruptcy. Seeing a way to get some of its old magic back, Apple acquired Job's NeXT company that year. Shortly after, Jobs returned to leading the company, and its transformation began in earnest.

Emblematic of his readiness to reinvent the company, Jobs changed his look. He wore corporate shirts and ties during his first stint running Apple, dressing up for the CEO role, but returned for his second wearing his signature black turtleneck—ready to do the real work. He had personally transformed, and now it was time to transform the company.

Jobs introduced the iPod in 2001, the iPhone in 2007, and the iPad in 2010—mainstay products that remain top sellers to this day. With Jobs passing away from pancreatic cancer in 2011, Tim Cook, one of Jobs's chief lieutenants, took the helm and has continued to follow with success after success.

Under Cook's leadership, the company is now in a wide range of businesses, including wearables (like the Apple Watch and AirPods) and services (such as advertising, AppleCare tech support, payment services through Apple Card and cashless Apple Pay, and cloud services). It also offers a broad spectrum of digital content, including music, games, entertainment, books, personal fitness, and more, through the Apple App Store. It also operates some five hundred brick-and-mortar Apple retail stores in twenty-five countries and has nabbed a partnership with Target to place 150 Apple shop-in-shops in its stores.

Cook's management style is in sharp contrast to the hands-on approach of Jobs. Before Jobs personally recruited him to join Apple in 1998, he had worked twelve years at IBM and earned an MBA from Duke University. Jobs, by contrast, dropped out of college after only one semester.

Cook's corporate experience serves him well at Apple, and he has taken the company to heights that Jobs never achieved. Before his death, Jobs warned Cook not to imagine what he would do when faced with a tough decision. "Just do what's right," Jobs advised him, and Cook seems to have taken that advice.

While Cook has changed many things about the company's day-to-day operations, one thing he has never changed is the strategic vision that Jobs defined and that carries the Apple brand to where it is today. It was epitomized in the famous "Think different" ad campaign the company first ran in 1997. While that campaign ended in 2002, its spirit remains and continues to drive the company and the brand forward.

> Here's to the crazy ones. The misfits. The rebels. The trouble-makers. The round pegs in the square holes. The ones who see things differently. They're not fond of rules. And they have no respect for the status quo. You can quote them, disagree with them, glorify or vilify them. About the only thing you can't do is ignore them.

> Because they change things. They push the human race forward. And while some may see them as the crazy ones,

we see genius. Because the people who are crazy enough to think they can change the world, are the ones who do.

Steve Jobs said this in a voiceover to a backdrop featuring pictures of Albert Einstein, Muhammad Ali, Pablo Picasso, Thomas Edison, Richard Branson, Martin Luther King Jr., Bob Dylan, and others who changed the world.

STRATEGY WITH A CAPITAL *S*

Harvard University professor Michael Porter is recognized as one of the world's leading authorities on strategy. His first book was devoted to the subject—*Competitive Strategy*. He said, "The essence of strategy is choosing what not to do," and added, "Sound strategy starts with having the right goal."

At its most basic, business strategy is understood as the plans, actions, and goals that outline how a business will compete in a particular market. This would be *strategy* with a small *s*, because as essential as plans are to strategy, they only reveal the actions or processes to be taken to achieve the goals. Yet, determining the goals for the organization is where Strategy must start, and that is another question entirely—*Strategy* with a capital *S*.

Writing in *Harvard Business Review* in an article titled "Demystifying Strategy: The What, Who, How and Why," Professor Michael Watkins explains, "A business strategy is a set of guiding principles that, when communicated and adopted in the organization, generates a desired pattern of decision-making."

Implementing the *how* of the business strategy—turning the dream into reality—requires three other perspectives: the *what, who,* and *why*.

- *Mission* is about *what* will be achieved. The mission identifies what is to be accomplished and is broken down into specific goals and performance metrics.

- The *value network* is about *who* creates the value and *who* receives the value the organization will deliver. The value network includes suppliers, customers, employees, and investors that together create value and consume value, and today customers can become cocreators of value as well.

- *Vision* is *why* people in the organization should feel motivated to perform at a high level. Visioning is a critical role of the corporateneur, through which the leader inspires people in the value network to work in and through the company.

Watkins concludes, "Together, the mission, network, vision, and strategy define the strategic direction for the business. They provide the what, who, why, and how necessary to powerfully align action in complex organizations."

In other words, business Strategy, with a capital *S*, requires mission and vision before leaders decide the steps needed to accomplish the goals—the *how* strategy.

And as Michael Porter reminds us, "The best CEOs I know are teachers, and at the core of what they teach is strategy," so communication within and among the company's value network is critical to accomplishing the business strategy.

START WITH THE *WHY*

When Ken first saw the pullout faucet that launched his corporateneur journey, he identified a market position that was uniquely differentiated—dual-function faucets that both supply water and direct spray—and he focused strategy on achieving dominance in a niche market (the luxury market).

These are two of the three generic competitive strategies that Michael Porter identified—differentiated and focused on a niche—and the same two Apple followed. Both companies rejected Porter's other generic strategy, low-price leadership.

And also like Apple, Ken's value-creation strategy required uniquely defining the company mission (the *what*) and vision (the *why*) before implementing downstream strategies to develop the value network, organizational structure, and operational processes.

"Strategy is upstream from process and organization. It encompasses the overall mission and vision of the company," Ken says. "These are the broader brushstrokes that will bring everything and everybody together to make a sustainable company."

Ken admires the work of Simon Sinek, author of *Start with Why*, published in 2009. Sinek's book wasn't around to influence Ken during his company's formative years, but Sinek put words to the strategies that he intuitively followed when founding his business.

Sinek's basic premise is that people don't buy the products or services that you sell. They buy the reason *why* your company does what it does. He gives Apple as a prime example. "Apple is just a computer company. They have the same access to the same talent, the same agencies, the same consultants, and the same media. But why is it that they seem to have something different?"

He explains that unlike Dell, HP, and other computer companies that communicate only the specific *what* and *how* of their products—"We make great computers. They're beautifully designed, simple to use, and user-friendly. Want to buy one?"—Apple works from *why*.

Apple starts with its vision and mission. Sinek explains, "We [at Apple] believe in challenging the status quo. We believe in thinking differently. The way we challenge the status quo is by making our products beautifully designed, simple to use, and user-friendly. We just happen to make great computers. Want to buy one?"

And by communicating the *why* first and then moving on to the *what* and *how*, Apple gets people to line up to buy the next iPhone. And by starting with the company's *why*, Apple can easily expand into new product lines by taking the same challenge-the-status-quo approach.

Other computer companies are equally qualified to make the same technology products, and they do. But they sell only the *what* and *how*, which limits their potential.

On the other hand, Apple communicates its *why* first and proves it with the products it sells. Making more money than any other computer company is simply a reward for being different and doing things differently.

The goal is to sell to people who believe what you believe.

"The goal is not just to sell to people who need what you have. The goal is to sell to people who believe what you believe," he said. And that is also the way to hire people and get suppliers and business partners to work with you. They have to believe in the mission and the vision, and then they will jump through hoops, climb mountains, and swim oceans to accomplish it.

"It's all grounded in the biology of our brain," Sinek explained. "The neocortex is responsible for our rational, analytical thought and language. It corresponds to the *what* and *how* level. It can process vast amounts of data and information. But underneath the neocortex is the limbic brain responsible for our feelings, like trust and loyalty. It's also responsible for decision-making and controlling behavior, but it has no language capacity. It's where gut decisions come from."

Other computer companies stop short at the neocortex brain level, never going deeper into the feeling, decision-making part of the brain as Apple does.

STRATEGY IS RATIONAL, GETTING PEOPLE TO EXECUTE IT TAKES FEELINGS

Business strategy is a rational pursuit and is part of our science thread in the corporateneur circle of success. But getting people to execute it, bringing partners along to support it, and getting customers to buy it takes feelings, which is part of our art thread.

That's why Ken made it a first priority to define for his company its vision, mission, and promises, encoding it in the company's credo card.

"My strategy was always to manage by objectives, and the number one objective was to honor our vision, mission, and promises," Ken says. "From there, we executed the overarching strategy with specific processes defined by goals, action plans, and timetables. My primary responsibility was to write them down and share them out."

In other words, he was doing what Michael Porter said the best CEOs do: teaching strategy.

As a corporateneur—whether you're selling computers, plumbing fixtures, or any product or service—the business strategy must start with why your company exists: its mission and vision. After that, you are ready to proceed to the next level of *what* and how you are going to bring that business strategy to life and into the market.

Ken's Key Takeaways ────────

- Apple has reached the status of a mythic brand by using its "Think different" vision and mission to guide business strategy.

- Business strategy is understood as the plans, actions, and goals that define how a business will compete in the market. That is *strategy* with a small *s*.

- *Strategy* with a capital *S* is the set of principles that guides decision-making from which business plans, actions, and goals originate.

- *Strategy* with a capital *S* requires more than business plans, goals, and actions. It also must be powered by mission and vision that are communicated to the business's value network, which creates the value that consumers purchase.

- Apple is a company that starts with an overarching mission and values, uses them to guide product development as proof of the mission and values, and communicates the *why* of the brand first before the product specifics. Its competitors stop at the product specifics.

- *Strategy* with a capital *S* is upstream from *strategy* with a small *s*, which includes plans, operations, and processes.

- Strategy must combine rational business decision-making with the *why* of the brand, where feelings of trust and loyalty are engendered. People don't buy what the company does; they buy *why* you do what you do. They buy based upon feelings.

Your Corporateneur Road Map

1. What's the *why* driving you to create a company?

2. What emotions will your company engender in its employees, partners, and customers? What do you want them to feel from their interaction with your company?

3. Define your mission and values.

4. In what ways are you thinking differently than the competitors in your market?

CHAPTER 16

The Innovative Corporateneur

"After us they'll fly in hot-air balloons, coat styles will change, perhaps they'll discover a sixth sense and cultivate it, but life will remain the same."

—ANTON CHEKHOV

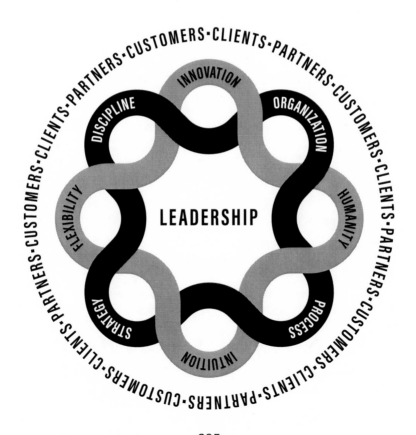

S teve Jobs condensed the secret of Apple's success into two words, incorrect grammar and all: *Think different.* That is the North Star for every corporateneur. Think differently about the market, the business model, and the products and processes involved in planning, launching, and running your business.

In other words, innovate. The more innovative your new venture is, the more likely it is to disrupt the status quo and ultimately be successful. Of course, innovation doesn't come without its fair share of risk. But then, taking risks is part of the corporateneur's job description.

Innovation came naturally to Steve Jobs because before he was the innovative CEO of Apple; he was an inventor. *Innovation* and *invention* are two words that are often used interchangeably, but there are important differences between them.

Inventing something is creating something entirely new, and filing a patent is its milestone. For example, Steve Jobs is listed as the primary or coinventor on nearly 250 patents, though not all of them made it to market.

Innovation, on the other hand, implies a new "use" for an idea or method that changes behavior or interactions. An invention may or may not be an innovation. Only an estimated 2 to 10 percent of all patents make enough money to maintain their protection.

An invention may have a patent sitting on the shelf, but it's not an innovation unless it is brought to market, then adopted by consumers. For example, Thomas Edison holds a record 1,093 patents, but he is primarily remembered for a handful of marketable inventive innovations, including the light bulb and electric utility system, recorded sound, motion pictures, and the alkaline storage battery.

An invention is something new, while an innovation may be an evolutionary change to existing processes, uses, or functions. And businesses can be innovative without inventing anything other than a different way to do things. The concept of a research-and-development function in business was an innovation of Thomas Edison, not an invention.

On the invention-innovation scale, as innovative as Apple is, it would lean toward the invention side, while Amazon is firmly on the innovation end of the scale.

AMAZON DIDN'T INVENT IT BUT INNOVATED IT TO WORLDWIDE DOMINANCE

Amazon's Jeff Bezos didn't invent the world wide web; Swiss professor Tim Berners-Lee did when he set up the first public website using http (hypertext transfer protocol) communications in 1991.

Bezos didn't invent e-commerce either. Online shopping was pioneered by UK entrepreneur Michael Aldrich in 1979, even before the internet. He used a dial-up modem to connect business users to a real-time multiuser computer processing system that enabled them to conduct business transactions using a modified television.

The concept was adapted by Charles Stack in 1992 for his Book Stacks Unlimited company, in a dial-up bulletin board format, and moved to the internet as Books.com in 1994. So Jeff Bezos can't claim to have invented the online bookstore either.

Rather, he was the innovative perfector of online retail, starting with books and expanding into selling everything else. Plus, he also innovated by selling services that grew out of Amazon's internal capabilities, such as cloud-computing AWS, logistics, and delivery.

Like Steve Jobs, Bezos was always interested in computers, but unlike Jobs, he graduated from college, majoring in computer science at Princeton University. And Bezos started his career as a hedge fund manager, working for investment firm D. E. Shaw, unlike Jobs who founded Apple right after quitting college.

But after four years on the job, Bezos got antsy. Intrigued by the potential of the internet for online shopping, he drew up a list of twenty possible products to sell online and picked books, perhaps following Stack's Books.com lead. So in 1994, at thirty years old, he made the leap from the corporate world to entrepreneurship. He became a corporateneur.

After moving from New York City to Seattle, Bezos set up shop in his garage and began selling books online in 1995. Within its first months of operation, the company was selling books in all fifty states and in forty-five different countries. With the business concept and model proven, he took Amazon public in May of 1997.

Bezos laid out Amazon's mission, vision, and promise—commitments the company has never deviated from—in his first stockholder letter in the 1997 annual report. He articulated a vision not just of the company but the potential of the internet and e-commerce that few could see at the time:

> This is Day 1 for the Internet and, if we execute well, for Amazon.com. Today, online commerce saves customers money and precious time. Tomorrow, through personalization, online commerce will accelerate the very process of discovery. Amazon.com uses the internet to create real value for its customers.

He defined the company's Day 1 goal: "Our goal is to move quickly to solidify our position while we begin to pursue the online commerce opportunities in other areas."

Thus, from the first day, becoming the online "everything store" was the aim. Selling books was just the test of concept.

Always Day 1

At the time he wrote that letter, it was virtually Day 1 for online retail, but Bezos also used the term metaphorically, because for him every day is Day 1. And to remind people of that, the company's headquarters building is named "Day 1."

He explained why the Day 1 concept was so important to him in his 2016 shareholder letter. "Day 2 is stasis. Followed by irrelevance. Followed by excruciating, painful decline. Followed by death. And that is why it is always Day 1."

Companies that succumb to Day 2 status lose focus on their mission. Day 2 companies put the process ahead of the mission, rather than use process as the means to fulfill the mission.

"Good process serves you so you can serve the customers," Bezos wrote. "But if you're not watchful, the process can become the thing. You stop looking at outcomes and just make sure you're doing the process right. Do we own the process, or does the process own us? In a Day 2 company, you might find it's the second."

Day 2 companies lean away from external trends rather than lean into them. "The outside world can push you into Day 2 if you won't or can't embrace powerful trends quickly. If you fight them, you're probably fighting the future. Embrace them and you have a tailwind."

And Day 2 companies are too slow at decision-making, giving Day 1 companies the first-mover advantage.

"Day 2 companies make high-quality decisions, but they make high-quality decisions slowly. To keep the energy and dynamism of Day 1, you have to make high-quality, high-velocity decisions," he wrote, adding that most decisions are reversible, two-way doors. "If you are good at course correcting, being wrong may be less costly than you think, whereas being slow is going to be expensive for sure."

Long-Term Vision

On Day 1 of Amazon, the company operated in fast-growth mode at the expense of profits. It took until 2001 for the company to make its first quarterly profit and until 2003 to accrue an annual profit. So early on, Bezos faced an uphill battle with shareholders to get them to buy into his vision.

He addressed that in his 1997 shareholder letter by explaining that it's all about the long term. "Because of our emphasis on the long term, we may make decisions and weigh tradeoffs differently than some companies," he wrote.

Here he hinted at the oft-cited "fail fast, fail often" culture of Amazon, with Bezos saying the company will relentlessly learn from its successes and failures. It will make bold rather than timid investment decisions, "jettison those that do not provide acceptable returns," and "step up our investment in those that work best."

He added, "Some of these investments will pay off, others will not, and we will have learned another valuable lesson in either case."

Achieving long-term profitability required the company to scale fast, and to do that, he committed to continuous, ongoing innovation to find what works and quickly lean into those innovations that show the most promise.

Customer Obsession

Bezos's obsessive commitment to the customer is a takeaway for every corporateneur. "We set out to offer customers something they simply could not get any other way," he wrote back in 1997.

In his 2016 letter, he provided more detail. "There are many ways to center a business. You can be competitor focused, you can be product focused, you can be technology focused, you can be business model focused. But in my view, obsessive customer focus is by far the most protective of Day 1 vitality."

He continued:

> There are many advantages to a customer-centric approach, but here's the big one: customers are always beautifully, wonderfully dissatisfied, even when they report being happy and business is great. Even when they don't yet know it, customers want something better, and your desire to delight customers will drive you to invent on their behalf. No customer ever asked Amazon to create the Prime membership program, but it sure turns out they wanted it, and I could give you many such examples.

He added, "A remarkable customer experience starts with heart, intuition, curiosity, play, guts, taste." And these qualities can lead the corporateneur to innovate on behalf of and to the benefit of the customers.

Innovate by Working Backwards

Continuous, ongoing innovation is what made Amazon great. Bezos used a three-prong strategy to achieve that by doing the following:

- Keep being Day 1 focused.

- "Fail fast, fail often" to quickly identify innovation opportunities that can yield long-term profitability.

- Obsess relentlessly over customers, their needs and desires.

That innovation strategy was translated into an innovation process called "working backwards." The concept is simple: "Work backwards from the customers, rather than starting with an idea for a product and trying to bolt the customers onto it," explained former

Amazon executive Ian McAllister. The concept was further explained in a book by the same name, *Working Backwards*, by authors Colin Bryar and Bill Carr.

McAllister said any new Amazon initiative had to start with the team leader presenting an imagined press release announcing the finished product, rather than a long, drawn-out PowerPoint presentation, as is common in Day 2 companies. In effect, the press release becomes the innovation proposal and plan.

In only one or two pages, the customer problem is defined, telling how current solutions fail and how the new offering will solve for those failures. It's a quick and simple process in keeping with the company's Day 1 commitment to fast decision-making.

"If the benefits listed don't sound very interesting or exciting to customers, then perhaps they're not (and shouldn't be built)." Should the idea as described in the internal press release show promise, the team continues to develop it further by iterating the press release, not actually developing the product or service until the proposal is green-lighted.

In writing the internal press release, everything is simplified, described as being written in simple "Oprah speak," rather than in "geek speak," so the customer can easily understand the features and benefits, McAllister advised.

If the project goes forward, the internal press release becomes the plan that keeps the development team on track so the project doesn't slow down due to scope creep. And in another time-saving move, a drafted press release for the launch is already in the bag.

All the upfront work happens around the internal press release. By putting the ends (the customer benefit) before the means (the company innovation), this process pushes the team to view the proposal from the customer's point of view, not the company's. Putting the company first can too easily sideline valuable innovations.

Innovation Is Everyone's Responsibility

On Amazon's website, there is a list of sixteen leadership principles that describe what the company expects from its employees. Essentially it's an employees' code of conduct and an HR hiring guide rolled into one. Many of its leadership principles point to the need for an innovation orientation, including the ability to invent and simplify, learn and be curious, be biased for action, and deliver results.

It concludes, "We must begin each day with a determination to make better, do better, and be better for our customers, our employees, our partners, and the world at large. And we must end each day knowing we can do even more tomorrow."

That, in a nutshell, describes innovation as the day-in, day-out driving force for everyone at Amazon.com.

INNOVATION AT ANY SCALE

Amazon epitomizes innovation at scale, but no matter how big or how small, every corporateneur needs to develop an innovation mindset and a process that supports it, not just on Day 1 but every day thereafter.

Ken set the course for innovation from Day 1 at Rohl when he opened an entirely new category in the plumbing market, previously dominated by generic mass-market brands and offerings. He pioneered by introducing authentic luxury faucets and kitchen experiences to discerning homeowners.

When he found that kitchen-and-bath dealers couldn't get their sales forces excited to push its luxury plumbing offerings—luxury kitchen appliances got the lion's share of their attention due to appliances' higher price tag and commission—Ken innovated by positioning the faucet-and-sink combination package as a "water appliance."

He backed it up with research that found people use their kitchen water appliance more than their stove and refrigerator appliances combined, on a daily basis, thus justifying a greater investment in quality for the most essential kitchen appliance.

Ken further promoted the luxury message by innovating its in-store displays. Unlike the standard one-size-fits-all displays used by other brands, Rohl's were customized to each dealer's specifications and featured real wood and rich furniture-quality finishes, in keeping with their luxury image. That allowed each Rohl dealer to show a unique, hand-selected collection to its customers in a display that coordinated with the dealer's image rather than conflicted with it.

And Ken kept innovating by identifying new products that offered new features and benefits to the luxury customer. He and his team kept their nose to the ground to discover solutions to water-use problems that customers might not even have realized they had but that Rohl could solve.

For example, the company was way ahead of the industry in offering water-saving features, water filtration systems, and built-in protections against hot-water scalding. They anticipated future water conservation, purity trends, and antiscalding regulations and were ahead of the curve.

"To be innovative, you have to be curious, creative, and open to stepping outside the known," Ken says. And it is necessary to create a corporate culture that supports curiosity, creativity, and stepping beyond the boundaries. To do that, he practiced the "teach, don't tell" method.

He knew that people learn the most by watching others doing it and doing it repeatedly. Ken was innovator-in-chief and demonstrated an innovation mindset and action orientation every day. He showed others how it is done and encouraged them to follow his lead.

In meetings, he always asked for alternative approaches, even demanded it from those around the table. It's also a leadership principle at Amazon. "Leaders are obligated to respectfully challenge decisions when they disagree, even when doing so is uncomfortable or exhausting," the company's leadership principles state.

Great leaders, whether Jeff Bezos or Ken Rohl, welcome challenges and don't shrink from them because only by challenging the status quo, conventional wisdom, or groupthink, can game-changing innovation be discovered.

And both Bezos (on a grand scale) and Ken (in a smaller company) understand that innovation inevitably involves the potential for mistakes. "Failure and invention are inseparable twins," Bezos said.

Only by trying and sometimes stumbling can learning happen. And whether the learning comes from failure or success, all learning is invaluable to advance the company.

PROCESS FOR INNOVATION

The management consulting firm McKinsey & Company conducted a study among 2,500 executives across more than three hundred companies worldwide to discover what separated the innovation leaders from laggards. The results aimed to help big companies become high-performance innovators.

"Since innovation is a complex, company-wide endeavor, it requires a set of crosscutting practices and processes to structure, organize and encourage it," the McKinsey authors Marc de Jong,

Nathan Marston, and Erik Roth wrote. "Well-established companies, by and large, are better executors than innovators and most succeed less through game-changing creativity than by optimizing their existing businesses."

Because it is easier to design an innovation mindset into a company at the outset than to change a rigid, inflexible organization into an innovative one, the takeaways from that study are particularly relevant for the corporateneur.

The McKinsey research found eight attributes associated with companies that excel in innovation. The first four help companies set and prioritize the conditions that allow innovation to thrive in the organization. The next four help companies organize and deliver innovation repeatedly, to contribute "meaningfully" to overall performance.

Creating Conditions for Innovation

- **Aspire.** A far-reaching vision for the company acts as a catalyst to energize people in the organization to innovate. Bezos did this through his Day 1 approach. Ken did it by defining the company's mission, vision, and promises to customers. In a nutshell, he defined the creed by which the company operated and reflected its Day 1 customer-obsessive focus:

    Its mission: "To be the supplier of choice." It realizes that mission through "selective distribution, consistent trade and consumer communications, innovative products, a passionate commitment to customer service and consistent attention to meeting unmet needs of the marketplace." This baked innovation into the very fiber of the company from Day 1. Innovation was in everyone's job description and their responsibility.

And its promises: to uphold trust through courteous, efficient, ethical behavior and practices that respect the customers' interest and to always keep the door open for customer input and suggestions.

The open-door policy, in particular, gave the company a much broader perspective to drive innovation beyond what those inside the company alone could imagine. The customers were invited to be cocreators of innovation from Day 1.

- **Choose.** "In our experience, many companies run into difficulty less from a scarcity of new ideas than from the struggle to determine which ideas to support and scale," McKinsey authors wrote. This hearkens back to Michael Porter's statement about strategy: "The essence of strategy is choosing what not to do."

  The researchers found companies tend to favor safe, short-term, and incremental projects. And they may spread themselves "too thin" on the safer choices, leaving more-risky but higher-potential projects languishing in the back room.

  "These tendencies get reinforced by a sluggish resource-reallocation process, sentencing innovation to a stagnating march of incrementalism," they explain. Or as Jeff Bezos would say, they are working in Day 2, not Day 1.

- **Discover.** Creative genius aside, innovative ideas are best discovered through a methodical and systematic process that combines the following:

  1. A customer problem that needs to be solved.

  2. A company capability or technology that enables a solution.

3. A business model that can generate revenue and profits from it.

"Nearly every successful innovation occurs at the intersection of these three elements. Companies that effectively collect, synthesize, and 'collide' them stand the highest probability of success," the authors wrote.

The insight/discovery process can be aided through consumer research, but the company may not have the capabilities or technology to solve, or is missing essential pieces of, the customer puzzle because of its established boundaries. In this case, strategic partnerships can be the "lifeblood of innovation."

Ken leaned heavily on his supplier and dealer networks as cocreators and partners for innovation to bring to the market. Those partners supplied insights and technical solutions that his company might have missed.

- **Evolve.** "Business model innovations—which change the economics of the value chain, diversify profit streams, and/or modify delivery models—have always been a vital part of a strong innovation portfolio," the authors wrote. Technological advancements have made this an even more urgent priority, as has the evolution of the service economy.

  A business model simply defines the value the company creates that customers will pay for. The McKinsey authors caution that innovating the business model is something that established companies are reluctant to do, opening the door for competitor disruption. It's far better for companies to "disrupt yourself before you are disrupted" through innovation.

  In the McKinsey report, Amazon is presented as a prime example of a company that excels at business model innovation.

It started as a pure-play online retailer, buying books wholesale and selling them retail, then it expanded to other products under the same wholesale-to-retail model.

That evolved into a marketplace business model, offering its platform to other companies to sell their products, pocketing fees for service. It's carried the services business model forward to cloud computing and managing logistics for its partners.

And it's innovated its business model further through subscription services into Prime and streaming entertainment, as well as expanding into physical retail with Amazon Go and its acquisition of Whole Foods.

Ken innovated Rohl's business model beyond its wholesale distribution model when he acquired half interest in the Perrin & Rowe kitchen sink manufacturing company. That step not only kept one of Rohl's major suppliers viable but also became an important factor in Fortune Brand's ultimate decision to acquire the company that Ken built.

Organize and Deliver Innovation

- **Accelerate.** Corporate bureaucratic policies can significantly inhibit innovation, slowing them down or getting them off track. Start-ups may have less embedded bureaucracy, but they still can be less than supportive of innovation endeavors.

    Designing internal systems that provide defined innovation pathways can keep innovation moving forward, especially since innovation projects engage cross-functional teams and may potentially take staff away from their day-to-day activities.

    Innovation projects need commitment all along the line, not just whatever attention is left over after all the other work is done.

Ken always pushed for alternative approaches and new ideas. His action orientation helped accelerate the business to go faster and farther.

- **Scale.** Early testing and market feedback is essential to finding the right scale to ensure that enough of the right resources are allocated to innovation projects. A "too little, too late" market introduction can result if the innovation project's potential is not accurately measured early.

  Ken was challenged when KWC, Rohl's major faucets supplier, pulled out of its distribution agreement, so he quickly moved to scale back the company since virtually 90 percent of its existing business was going to evaporate. But in an ironic twist of fate, when KWC closed the door, it opened an even bigger one for the Rohl company, as well as its other partners and customers.

  Ken turned to Italian manufacturer Nicolazzi, who supplied its bathroom faucets to fill the void in the kitchen. Nicolazzi has a line of kitchen faucets; they were designed as two-handled models appropriate for Europe but not the US, where single-handled kitchen faucets are preferred.

  Sitting together over dinner one evening, Ken shared the design need with Bruno Nicolazzi, who was the founder of the company and its design director. Bruno grabbed a cocktail napkin and drew a picture of the design Ken wanted. Then a day later, Bruno's team had a working prototype to show Ken.

  Bruno saw the potential to scale in the US market with Rohl and committed time, materials, and resources to make it happen in record time.

- **Extend.** As in the discover process above, reaching beyond the boundaries of one's own organization is helped through collaborative partnerships. The McKinsey authors describe this as an "ecosystem for innovation" that enables a company to "transcend its corporate and geographic boundaries," they wrote. "High-performing innovators work hard to develop ecosystems, increasing the likelihood that the best ideas and people will come their way."

Good ideas can come from anywhere. The stronger the corporateneur's network, the greater the potential to discover innovative opportunities beyond the company's capabilities, with reach and access to new markets.

Ken was always a great networker, and his leadership activities within the kitchen-and-bath industry extended his reach to a wide ecosystem of innovation.

- **Mobilize.** Innovation is where the company started, its Day 1. Innovation must be part of the company's every Day 1 after that, or inevitably it begins its Day 2 descent toward irrelevance and stagnation.

  "The best companies find ways to embed innovation into the fibers of their culture from the core to the periphery," the report stated. "They start back where we begin: with aspirations that forge tight connections among innovation, strategy and performance.

  "There's no proven formula for success, particularly when it comes to innovation," the report authors observed. However, innovation is a proven factor in any business's formula for success.

  The McKinsey authors call on large and small companies to "assimilate and apply these essentials in their own way, in accordance with their particular context, capabilities, organizational culture and appetite for risk."

  Ken used all these eight principles—aspire, choose, discover, evolve, accelerate, scale, extend, and mobilize—to continuously innovate in his company.

But perhaps Ken's most effective innovation strategy was the simplest: to keep his door open and to press everyone every day to challenge the systems, processes, and conventional wisdom to find ways to improve for the sake of the company's customers and partners. Through that strategy, the company found opportunities to grow.

Ken's Key Takeaways

- *Innovation* and *invention* are two words often used inter-changeably, but a company can be innovative without inventing anything. An innovation is an evolutionary change to existing processes, uses, or functions. A business can be innovative without inventing anything. Amazon, for example, is a highly innovative company but not necessarily an inventive one. Its primary innovation is extending the internet's processes, uses, and functions in new directions.

- An innovative company is poised for action and doesn't get bogged down in bureaucracy or become a slave to processes and procedures that inevitably sideline innovation. They have an innovation mindset—operate in Day 1 mode, not Day 2—and establish a culture and processes that support innovation.

- By focusing relentlessly and zealously on the needs and desires of customers, businesses can allow innovation to flourish. Even the most satisfied customers want more, and the truly consumer-centric company is always looking at ways to deliver more and better to the customer.

- Companies activate innovation by creating a far-reaching mission, vision, and promises to the customer. They aspire to do more for the customers. They are careful in choosing the right path to develop and don't sideline innovation too quickly; rather, they lean into it. They are always in the process of discovering new ways they can solve problems for customers and evolving as innovative opportunities arise.

- One of the best ways to discover innovation opportunities is to invite outsiders in to cocreate innovation, including customers, dealers, and business partners. And innovative businesses are always looking to bring in new partners to help execute innovative opportunities.

 Your Corporateneur Road Map

1. What innovation are you bringing to the market through your new venture? Is it innovative enough?

2. Are there other ways to innovate for your target customers beyond simply creating a new product or service? Are there opportunities for business model innovations?

3. What steps can you take to design an innovation orientation into your company? Use McKinsey's eight steps to drive innovation and create a plan and a to-do list for each of the following: aspire, choose, discover, evolve, accelerate, scale, extend, and mobilize.

CHAPTER 17

The Disciplined Corporateneur

*"The pessimist complains about the wind; the optimist
expects it to change; the realist adjusts the sails."*

—WILLIAM ARTHUR WARD

By any measure, Tom Brady is the most winning quarterback of all time. He holds the record for most regular season wins, 243, to the number two position held by both Brett Favre and Peyton Manning, tied at 186. He holds every major quarterback record that matters, like passing yards, completions, touchdown passes, and games started.

Brady also claims the most postseason wins, at thirty-five, more than double the number two Joe Montana claims, at sixteen. He has played in more Super Bowls than any player ever and won seven of his ten appearances, another record. And since Brady is still playing at the advanced age of forty-four, he will only continue to break records.

Despite being the oldest player in the NFL, his Tampa Bay Buccaneers coach Bruce Arians said, rather than slowing down, Brady is "throwing the ball better than he did two years ago."

On virtually every sporting GOAT (greatest of all time) list, Brady takes his place alongside Michael Jordan, Tiger Woods, Muhammad Ali, Michael Phelps, Serena Williams, Roger Federer, and Pelé, among others. "I wasn't born a prodigy, like a three-year-old the world bestowed greatness on," he said.

Unlike the other GOATS who seemingly emerged from the womb designed for greatness in their chosen sport, nothing early on hinted at Brady's greatness to come. He was only a good enough ball player in high school and college—he was the 199th pick in the NFL 2000 draft.

MIND OVER MATTER

However, Brady was determined to be the best quarterback that he could be, and in pursuing that goal, he became the best quarterback the game has ever seen. And he continues on, a decade after most football players have hung up their helmets and cleats.

New England Patriot's Bill Belichick, who coached Brady through twenty seasons, said, "He's not a great natural athlete. He wasn't all that good when we got him. He mechanically wasn't anywhere near where it eventually ended up."

Belichick credits Brady's overarching achievements to using mind over matter for peak performance. "When you're in a Super Bowl game and your team is three touchdowns down and the clock is running, mental toughness is what makes the differences at the end," he said.

Brady's superpower is self-discipline, which he detailed in his book *The TB12 Method: How to Do What You Love, Better and for Longer*, where he shared his diet, training, and body and mind fitness regime.

We can take Brady at his word when he said, "I was never really, in a way, the most talented. I lasted that long for a reason. I just try to continue to find ways to improve." He added, "If I don't really work at it … and if I don't play to my strengths, I'm a very average quarterback."

Brady has honed self-discipline into an art. In the spring of 2020, at "The Match" made-for-TV golf exhibition, where he was teamed with Phil Mickelson against Tiger Woods and Peyton Manning— Woods and Manning won by one hole—Brady spent time waiting to play in the parking lot running wind sprints. Charles Barkley happened upon the scene and asked him why he wasn't in the clubhouse like the other players, to which he replied, "I'm trying to win a Super Bowl."

One indisputable quality that Brady was born with was his competitive nature. "If you don't play to win, don't play at all," he said. Yet his fiercest competitive drive has always been directed against himself, not the other team. "It's never come easy for me. I don't think my mind allows me to rest ever," he said.

What separates winners from losers in football is what separates them in business. "Winners focus on winning. Losers focus on winners," he said. Winners have determination. They have a long-term goal, not just to win the next game but the next one and the one after that. And they have the discipline to work doggedly toward the goal.

"To anyone who is struggling early in the morning or late at night in pursuit of your dream, struggles that many will never see, keep going, because Will always finds a way," Brady assuredly said.

DISCIPLINE REQUIRED

Self-discipline is required to succeed in any endeavor—the ball field, in business, or anything else you set out to do.

Interestingly, being disciplined in body by exercising and eating a healthy diet is linked with being disciplined in mind. Multiple studies have proven the mind-body connection.

So while Tom Brady's stringent physical and dietary regimes are necessary for his performance on the playing field, they can also pay off in other areas of life. That's why Dana Cavalea—former director of strength, conditioning, and performance for the New York Yankees— has shifted his coaching career from the dugout to the business world and written a book, *Habits of a Champion Team: The Formula to Winning Big in Sports, Life and Business.*

Coach Cavalea says, "Discipline is a muscle. It can be built." And while exercising the discipline muscle, the corporateneur is also building muscle memory, where the brain creates neurological pathways that make specific tasks virtually automatic and so require no conscious effort. The same muscle memory that can improve throwing a football, riding a bike, playing a musical instrument, or dancing can also improve an executive's business performance.

To succeed in sports, life, and business takes a combination of mental, physical, and emotional strength and stamina. Developing in one area at the expense of the others may yield a measure of success, but it takes all three working together for an individual to achieve the highest probability of success.

Coach Cavalea has studied peak achievers in sports and business who outperform their peers and found they exhibit certain habits that predispose them for success. And like any habit, once learned, they become automatic. These habits become their personal process or formula for winning.

Make Time for Yourself

"All work and no play" not only makes Jack a dull boy, but it undermines anyone's ability to succeed. The human body can't function optimally without rest; likewise, the mind needs downtime to work most effectively. Getting off the grid is even more critical for the corporateneur, as they continually face new challenges where creative problem solving is required.

Putting in long working hours—their shoulders always to the grindstone—effectively grinds the corporateneur down. To build oneself up mentally and emotionally, time for rest and recovery is required.

It's the same with the physical body. When exercising, muscles are challenged almost to the breaking point, as essentially the muscle fibers are broken down. Then during sleep and the recovery period, the body strengthens the exercised muscles to be able to handle the extra load.

Ken always made it a priority to take time off so he could work better and smarter. That took discipline.

Ken rested and refreshed his mind by working his body in sports, often in team sports where he cross-trained his leadership and team-building skills. He also passionately pursued hobbies, like hot-air ballooning. As physically and mentally demanding as piloting a balloon one thousand feet in the air is, it also provided quiet time for contemplation and reflection. These were his "blue sky" periods.

Fly-fishing was another hobby that gave time for reflection, including hours spent in detailed work preparing lures and then the even more rewarding experience of standing knee-deep in the river.

Fly-fishing even provided Ken with an unexpected business payoff. Right after KWC pulled its business from Rohl, he was called on by John Green whose company had pullout faucets as a replacement. At the time, Ken had a bitter taste in his mouth after the KWC affair and thought to proceed in a different direction.

"My immediate response was 'I don't need another kitchen faucet—been there, done that.' I was about to dismiss the call, but remembered Green's factory was in New Zealand, which is the world's mecca for fly-fishing," Ken reflects. "So I decided to combine a little business with pleasure and visit the factory in New Zealand. That began a long-term relationship with Green."

Prioritize

Peak athletes are highly attuned to their body clock, when they perform at their prime and when they are off, in order to prioritize their daily schedule. However, Coach Cavalea observes that many business people run on a reactive schedule, allowing themselves to spend too much time putting out fires when they lack energy or are unable to focus. Sometimes it's better to let the fires burn.

"I function at my best between 5:00 a.m. and 2:00 p.m., so I work during those hours. But after that, there's no high-level thinking or work for me," he said. The corporateneur needs to become self-aware about when they are most creative, focused, and energized and structure their workday around those windows.

It takes discipline to say "No, not now" when business seems to demand immediate action. Al Rykus recalls a time when senior management and the entire customer service department were called into an early morning meeting because troubles had surfaced handling customer requests. The problem demanded an immediate fix. But as they started to dig in, they found the issues were more deep-seated than expected, and the meeting ran over into the company's official 9:00 a.m. start time.

"By ten o'clock, the phones were ringing off the hook," Al recalls. "Everyone was getting upset and wanted to answer the phones. But Ken said, 'Let those phones ring. We aren't working as a team, and until we do, we're not going to answer those phones. Worry about when those phones stop ringing. If we don't fix this now, they won't be calling us later.'"

During that meeting, the phone calls were a distraction from the real work that was needed. The temptation was to answer the calls—put out the fires—but the more important work got done by resisting that temptation.

Keep It Simple

"The best players, they keep it simple. They're very consistent people. They know their talent, and they become consistent in their training and their habits," Coach Cavalea said. Keeping it simple means establishing boundaries and not getting pulled away by distractions.

Occam's razor, also known as the law of parsimony or the law of economy, is the philosophical underpinning for simplifying life and business. It is a guide to problem solving proposed by the fourteenth-century Franciscan friar William of Ockham (who came from Occam, England, thus its name).

"Entities should not be multiplied beyond necessity," he wrote, meaning when presented with competing theories or explanations of why something happened, the simpler one with the fewest assumptions or contingencies is likely true.

The razor term was applied to Ockham's principle to signify the "shaving away" of extraneous material and assumptions. He also wrote, "It is vain to do with more what can be done with fewer."

In other words, the simplest explanation, the simplest solution, or the simplest way is usually the best, but things, people, and circumstances tend to complicate rather than simplify life.

It takes discipline to stay on track and take the narrow road. But keeping it simple makes prioritizing tasks and decisions easier. In business, Ken broke it down to three simple words: *vision*, *mission*, and *promises*. Business decisions were weighed against one of those three foundational principles. If a solution didn't reflect the company vision, further its mission, or honor its promises, it probably wasn't the right solution.

Throughout this book, we've shared many of Ken's Occam's razor simplifying principles for the corporateneur, like "Teach what you have to learn"; "Promises made, promises kept"; "Forget the many; be important to the few"; and "Business's three-legged stool: product, marketing, financials."

But to Ken's mind, none are more important than "Make a plan. Work the plan." It was a discipline he followed rigorously throughout his corporate and corporateneur careers and one that he taught to all those who worked with him.

WHEN THE FIRST PLAN DOESN'T WORK, MAKE ANOTHER

When Emily and Spencer Shapton decided to combine their talents, skills, and interests to launch a joint venture, they turned to Ken for guidance. With a degree in marketing, Emily followed a traditional corporate career path working with two major brands, one in fashion and the other in beauty. Spencer studied at the Culinary Institute of America and worked in restaurants before taking a corporate chef's job. They decided they had what it takes to launch a catering and event-planning business.

Ken agreed and became a sounding board as Emily wrote up the business plan and Spencer got the menus and recipes prepared. Then COVID hit, and their big plans had to be scaled back. But they held on, and after a year and a half of operations, doing in-home cooking and small-scale outdoor events, they began to get calls to do larger events as their reputation grew.

With confidence growing, they invested in a 1975 Airstream trailer to turn into their catering kitchen. A practical need drove the decision because cooking in different kitchens and maintaining multiple licenses was challenging. Having their own traveling licensed kitchen solved for that.

But refurbishing the Airstream required much work and stretched their already tight finances. "When I first proposed the idea of buying the Airstream trailer, I expected Ken to say it was crazy and talk us out of it, but he said, 'It sounds like a good plan,'" Emily relates.

In the meantime, they had become friends with the owner of a local resort lodge where they had catered some private events. Impressed with their work and professionalism, he came to Emily and Spencer first when he needed to replace the lodge's property manager. After much soul-searching and discussions with Ken, they jumped.

"We wouldn't have gotten this job managing the entire venue, if we hadn't had the experience of starting our own company and showing what we were able to accomplish," Emily shares. "We were able to show how we grew our business during such a rough time, how well we work together and how multifaceted we are. So we came full circle from corporate to corporateneur then back to corporate."

However, they still operate their own catering business, but only on the back burner, as they devote full time to the lodge. "We think of it more as diversifying what we do and how we do it," Spencer says.

"We are able to have the best of both worlds, a regular paycheck as we continue to remodel our Airstream and do some additional catering on the side. We don't do as much catering as we thought initially, but we are patient and it will come later as we build up staffing. Now this new experience managing the lodge is helping both of us grow and stretch," Emily adds.

Ken didn't hesitate to advise the couple to take the new opportunity because he also saw how the added experience would only contribute to their eventual corporateneur success when they return full time to their business.

"Ken is so pragmatic and practical. He has a very strong sense of what makes sense and what doesn't," Emily says. "Ken always said 'Play to your strengths,' and the lodge opportunity is only going to build our combined strengths."

BE STICKY

The best websites are said to be "sticky." They invite visitors to stay and look around and come back often.

Likewise, the most successful corporateneurs are sticky. They stick to the task at hand. They stick to their goals. They stick to the problem that must be solved. That takes discipline because everywhere they turn, something else crops up and demands their attention.

"Discipline is what keeps a business aligned with its values and executing its processes day in, day out," Ken says. To build that discipline, as in breaking a bad habit, start small and work from little successes to bigger successes.

"Start by writing a to-do list in the morning and reviewing it at the end of the day," Ken says. On day one, you might check off only a few things on the list, but the daily discipline of making and reviewing a to-do list will eventually turn into more tasks completed than left undone.

Ken lived and taught the practice to write down short-term goals for the day, midterm goals for the next quarter, and long-term goals five years down the road. Having a goal and, each day, taking little steps and occasional big leaps to achieve them is the best way to build the muscle of discipline.

"It takes discipline to do the work of keeping the business aligned and moving forward consistently. It takes discipline to follow proven processes. It takes discipline to communicate the plan to everyone and discipline to maintain yourself in good physical and mental condition," he asserts. "And that discipline will pay off with success."

Ken's Key Takeaways

- Discipline is a habit, and like any habit, it gets stronger by doing it.

- Success in business, as in sports, requires mental, physical, and emotional strength and resilience. The corporateneur needs to develop disciplined habits that build up all three factors. It means taking time for yourself to exercise and to unplug from business to refresh mentally and emotionally.

- The corporateneur must prioritize their time and not let distractions of the moment take them away from their short-term and long-term goals.

- Simplifying life and business requires discipline, but it also makes achieving goals easier to accomplish.

- Planning is an ongoing activity for the corporateneur, and as one follows the plan, discipline is required to constantly review it. Sometimes it needs to be revised and adjusted, and sometimes another plan may be required.

 ## Your Corporateneur Road Map

1. How disciplined are you in your personal life? How disciplined in your work life? Do you shortchange one in favor of the other? How can you be equally disciplined in both?

2. Do you easily get distracted by things that seem to demand immediate attention? Practice the skill of prioritizing, recogniz-

ing when something is really urgent and needs to be done now versus what can be put off.

3. Develop a habit of writing a daily to-do list and follow it.

The Humane Leader

*"Your love is like a hot-air balloon, rises me up without
breaking my promise to touch the sky."*

—FATHIMA SHAMLA

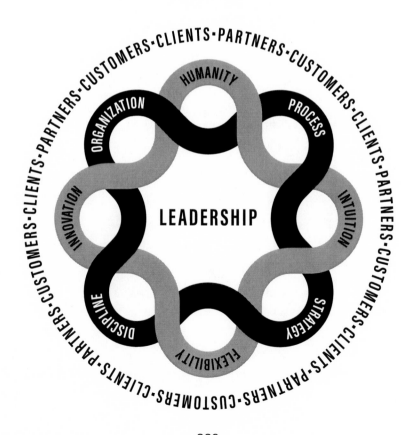

ohn D. Rockefeller, Cornelius Vanderbilt, J. P. Morgan, and Andrew Carnegie—the golden age industry titans—left a lasting philanthropic legacy. Rockefeller funded colleges, established a charitable foundation, and supported Christian missionaries. Vanderbilt endowed a Nashville university that eventually took his name. Morgan was a patron of the fine arts and made New York City's Metropolitan Museum of Fine Arts what it is today.

And Andrew Carnegie may hold the title of America's most influential philanthropist of all time. He built nearly three thousand public libraries, and though not a religious man, he gave 7,500 organs to churches. He also founded Carnegie Technical Schools, which became Carnegie Mellon University, and started numerous charitable foundations.

Despite all the good works these men did, they were widely reviled in their day and considered as unscrupulous, greedy, unfeeling, immoral, even evil. They weren't called robber barons for nothing, and their philanthropic works can be seen as penance for their wicked deeds.

While the reality of how these men acquired their great riches has passed from memory, Charles Dickens left an indelible impression of the kind of businessmen they were in his fictional portrait of Ebenezer Scrooge. In fact, pictures of the aged John D. Rockefeller, a man who was said to never smile, are spitting images of John Leech's portrayal of Scrooge in the debut publication of *A Christmas Carol. In Prose. Being a Ghost Story of Christmas.*

Dickens introduced Scrooge:

He was a tight-fisted hand at the grindstone, Scrooge! A squeezing, wrenching, grasping, scraping, clutching, covetous, old sinner! Hard and sharp as flint, from which no steel had ever struck out generous fire; secret, and self-contained, and solitary as an oyster.

The cold within him froze his old features, nipped his pointed nose, shriveled his cheek, stiffened his gait; made his eyes red, his thin lips blue; and spoke out shrewdly in his grating voice. A frosty rime was on his head, and on his eyebrows, and his wiry chin. He carried his own low temperature always about with him; he iced his office in the dog-days; and didn't thaw it one degree at Christmas.

Scrooge's backstory was revealed through the Ghost of Christmas Past and how he became the man we meet with the Ghost of Christmas Present. The only good thing anyone could say of Scrooge was "He was an excellent man of business." Then the Ghost of Christmas Future shows how Scrooge will end up if he continues on his present course—his karma. The novella has a happy ending, as Scrooge repents and is transformed.

"He became as good a friend, good a master, and as good a man, as the good old city knew, or any other good old city, town or borough, in the good old world," Dickens wrote. "Some people laughed to see the alteration in him, and he let them laugh. His own heart laughed: and that was quite good enough for him."

BAD PEOPLE MAKE BAD BOSSES

From Dickens's day to the present, there is no shortage of bad business people and bad bosses. The irony is bad people can be good at business, like Scrooge. But also like him, they are bad bosses, taking advantage of the people who work for them to make more money.

Money doesn't buy happiness, and inevitably those bad bosses suffer the most, or as Scrooge's nephew Fred said, "His wealth is of no use to him. He don't do any good with it … I am sorry for him. Who suffers by his ill whims! Himself, always."

While good people may be good or bad at business, being a good person is a prerequisite for being a good boss. Combine the two—a good person who is good at business—and you have an unbeatable combination. Truly great business leaders combine the art of dealing with people and the science of managing a business.

In business circles, a popular way to measure a person's people skills is the construct of emotional intelligence. As expressed in the *Frontiers in Psychology* journal, emotional intelligence is generally understood to be:

> The ability to perceive accurately, appraise, and express emotion; the ability to access and/or generate feelings when they facilitate thought; the ability to understand emotion and emotional knowledge; and the ability to regulate emotions to promote emotional and intellectual growth.

However, sociopaths and the even more sinister and potentially dangerous psychopaths can show high levels of emotional intelligence, only they use their EQ traits differently than normal people do. Officially there is not a definitive diagnosis for either in the *Diagnostic and Statistical Manual of Mental Disorders*. Rather, they are classified under "antisocial personality disorders," and they exist along a graduated scale with the sociopath being the lesser of two evils.

For example, both have a poor sense of right and wrong, though conscience seems to be totally lacking in psychopaths. Sociopaths may experience some guilt when doing wrong, but it doesn't stop them from doing it. Both also lack empathy, but psychopaths have even less regard for others and see other people merely as objects to use for their own benefit.

Sociopaths have less control over their own emotions and thus are less effective at manipulating others. Psychopaths, by contrast, are more "coldhearted" and calculating, which also makes them more dangerous. Some psychopaths may express their drive for power and control through violent acts, but hardly all.

Overall, an estimated 1–2 percent of the general population shows psychopathic tendencies. It's much higher among the prison population, where about 16 percent of all male prisoners were found to be psychopaths, according to psychologist Kent Kiehl and jurist Morris Hoffman.

However, the prevalence of individuals exhibiting clinically significant levels of psychopathic traits may be the same or even higher, up to 21 percent, in the C-suite, according to research by forensic psychologist Nathan Brooks, coauthor with Katarina Fritzon of the textbook *Corporate Psychopathy*. Brooks describes these individuals as "successful psychopaths."

Successful psychopaths are chameleons, using their high degree of emotional intelligence to get their way. They are also highly intelligent and so can be successful in their chosen careers.

British psychologist Eric Barker found the top career choices of psychopaths include CEO, attorney, media personality, and salesperson. He hypothesized that they are highly effective in "impression management" and can effectively hide their selfish tendencies.

An anonymous law enforcement official provided the following portrait of a successful psychopath, which also would describe the ideal CEO:

> He is a charismatic leader who inspires people to follow
> him. A strategic thinker who can master the details. A

tireless worker with incredible focus and problem-solving skills. Above all, he is an exceptional communicator. He can convey a vision to any audience, from Wall Street to the most junior employee.

The choice of the "he" pronoun is chosen explicitly because research also indicates psychopathic tendencies are far more prevalent among men than women.

The corporateneur should aspire to that description of the charismatic leader, but with an essential dose of humanity that the psychopathic CEO is missing.

HUMANITY IS THE ESSENTIAL QUALITY

There are two dictionary definitions of *humanity*, the first being "the quality or state of being human." Psychopaths exhibit that but none of the other, which is defined as showing "compassionate, sympathetic, or generous behavior or disposition; the quality or state of being *humane*." The definition of *humane* circles back to the other: one who exhibits "compassion, sympathy, or consideration for humans or animals."

Ken quips, "We're working to create corporateneurs, not saints"— but the corporateneur will achieve far greater success in business and life if they are more saint than sinner.

MAKING THE HUMAN CONNECTION

Transitioning from the corporate world to entrepreneurship— becoming a corporateneur—requires a paradigm shift in your approach to business, management, and leadership. You must shift from being more transactional in your approach to business to a more relational/relationship model.

Building strong and lasting relationships with your employees, business partners, and customers is critical to the success of the corporateneur. Transactions will come and go, but relationships last and will keep your venture sound and moving forward.

This paradigm shift takes adjustment because the corporate world is characteristically transactional. It runs on metrics, like revenue-and-profit growth, margins, ROI, cost per lead, conversion rates, customer lifetime value, and many others.

People climb the corporate ladder largely based on accomplishing specific goals and objectives, most especially if the individual's performance can be measured by one or more of those corporate metrics.

"The corporate world can be very cutthroat," Ken says. "The best ideas don't always win. The hardest workers don't always succeed. There's a lot of gamesmanship and politicking. It's highly structured, and you've got to conform. Everyone is a cog in the wheel of the business, and the wheel clicks along by transactions."

> **You're going to need to lean into solid relationships and build them over time. It can't be merely transactional; it must be relational.**

Starting out, the corporateneur hasn't got a "wheel" and has no transactions to move it forward. They've got a business idea, and to turn that idea into reality, they will need a supportive network of personal relationships to draw upon.

"When you start a small business, you're working with a small team. You've got to go out and build a customer base with no track record. You're going to need to lean into solid relationships and build them over time. It can't be merely transactional; it must be relational. It moves forward through the human connection," Ken says.

This is not to say that relationships aren't formed in corporations or that relationship businesses don't require transactions. But the underlying principles that transaction-oriented businesses and relationship ones run on are different. The corporateneur must put the transactional approach learned in the corporate environment aside and lean into developing a relationship model to power their business forward.

RELATIONAL VERSUS TRANSACTIONAL BUSINESS MODELS

Relational businesses focus on meaning and purpose. They connect on the human level, solving problems for their customers, business partners, and employees. Everyone who is part of the business or is touched by it, such as customers or business partners, has a stake in it.

A relationship business, just as in personal relationships, is a two-way street, where the ultimate goal is for all to succeed. Under a relationship business model, everyone succeeds—employees, business partners, and customers—or nobody succeeds.

Ken points to the difference between a corporate transactional orientation and a relational one in comparing KWC and Rohl. He built the Rohl business on relationships, introduced KWC pullout faucets to the market, and grew the business from nothing to being the leading brand in premium, luxury kitchen-plumbing fixtures.

KWC approached its business purely on a transactional level, and when they decided to take over distribution in the US market, they were following a business practice they had used in other markets.

"They had a corporate policy that got in front of common sense," Ken reflects. "We expected them to honor the work that we had done to build their relationships in the US market. They didn't understand that their business here would never have succeeded without the relationship foundation we built. But they simply were looking at transactions, and they'd get more margin by distributing their products themselves than through us."

"We were at cross-purposes," he continues. "They were following corporate dictates, and we were building lasting relationships with customers and our dealer network. That is what kept us going after we lost about 90 percent of our business in the stroke of a pen."

Your relationships are money in the bank for your business that can be drawn upon when things get rough. Transactional businesses operate like families living paycheck to paycheck with little or no cushion.

Transactional businesses might put plenty of profit aside, but they don't necessarily build good will or loyalty among their customers. A recent Nielsen study found that only 9 percent of Americans are brand loyalists who wouldn't think about switching to another brand, while 35 percent are always looking for a new brand and 55 percent will occasionally try another brand.

And transactional businesses gain no loyalty from their business partners or employees. When those business partners and employees don't get what they want, they are off like a shot to the next supplier, retailer, distributor, or employer.

However, relationship businesses have an insurance policy against customers, business partners, and employees jumping ship.

GOOD PEOPLE FORM GOOD RELATIONSHIPS

Forming good business relationships is just like forming any personal relationship. It takes a confluence of many factors, but in observing and working with Ken, there are eight qualities that contributed most to his success as a corporateneur, and they are qualities that aspiring corporateneurs should work on if lacking.

Trust

"Trust is the foundation of all relationships, and I have always made my word my bond," Ken says. "That's why I put so much emphasis on creating a company mission, vision, and promise in the earliest stages of forming a company. They serve, in effect, as the contract with your customers and must be upheld as if written in stone."

Ken's reputation for trustworthiness preceded him in his business dealings, which allowed him to make lasting business relationships on a handshake alone. "Trust in a brand and company is built over time. You do that by doing the right things consistently and persistently. Trust is soft capital that builds over time," Ken shares.

Curiosity

Curiosity is a superpower for new business founders. That's how you find white space in a market that your company can fill. Ken discovered KWC's pullout faucet at a European trade show and was drawn into its display, out of curiosity, because he'd never seen anything like it before. He took it back to his then boss at Elkay, who said nobody would pay $200 for a faucet when a perfectly good one is available for $50.

Ken instinctively saw the potential to open up an entirely new market for high-end, premium fixtures in the US market. But he needed to validate his assumptions and turned to his wife, Helene, whom he called Amber for the color of her hair. She was an experienced interior designer, serving the very luxury consumer segment he wanted to target.

Coming from the Midwest with solid middle-class values, Ken didn't live the "luxury lifestyle," though he'd traveled widely and enjoyed his share of luxury experiences over the years. He wasn't personally in touch with the luxury world of fashion, accessories, and auto and home furnishings, but Amber was.

She explained why consumers were willing to pay more for luxury brands. They were drawn to original design, craftsmanship, materials, provenance, and status signaling. She knew luxury kitchens were top on the list for affluent consumers in the home market and believed they would want a luxury kitchen faucet to match the quality of their appliances and cabinetry.

Ken listened and learned the "language of luxury" from Amber, and that carried the company forward to greater and greater success.

"God gives us two ears and one mouth to remind us that we should listen twice as much as we talk," Ken quips. That's why he kept his office door open and always sought different points of view from those around him. A telltale sign of curiosity is being a good listener. And it is also critical in sparking innovation.

Forthrightness

Forthrightness goes hand in hand with trust. People can't trust people or companies that aren't upfront, straightforward, and honest.

"You've got to be clear in what you want and communicate it clearly," Ken shares. "You've got to be clear about the goals, the corporate vision and mission, and what you expect from people to achieve it. You need to keep everyone focused so they are all speaking the same language."

And forthrightness means being decisive: "Let your 'yes' be 'yes' and your 'no' be 'no.'" It will be critical in decision-making. In your new venture, you'll be facing issues that you never anticipated, simply because you are doing something new. But you'll always have a guide if you use your goals, vision, mission, and promises as your North Star.

Self-Aware

We tend to associate introverted people as being more self-aware and intuitive because of the time they spend alone in contemplation. Extroverts, on the other hand, get their emotional substance by being with people. They are social to the extreme, and few would say they are contemplative.

Studies have shown extroverts are favored in business, with over 90 percent of business leaders identifying as extroverts, as compared with about 50 percent of the general population. And some 65 percent of senior managers believe introversion is a "barrier to leadership."

Ken would skew toward the extroverted side of the scale, yet he always carved out alone time to look inward. He was a dedicated journal keeper, where he recorded his thoughts and feelings and worked out problems on paper.

And that time gave him insight into his personal strengths and weaknesses so that he always played to his strengths and gathered around himself people who could make up for his weaknesses.

"Self-awareness is critical for the corporateneur, and it requires introspection. Your blind spots are your weaknesses, so aim to have twenty-twenty vision in self-awareness," he says.

Empathy

In business, it is as equally important to understand yourself as it is to understand others. Having empathy and compassion is a key element in all relationships. It is essential for management and business negotiations.

"You need to be able to understand the other's point of view, see things not just from your side of the table but from theirs," Ken says. "You've got to empathize and understand the other's pain and what they want, then figure out how to balance that with what you want. Everyone wants to be a winner, and it's your job to make that happen."

One way Ken showed empathy to employees who needed course correction was with the SKS principle: "Start doing. Keep doing. Stop doing." It provided staffers with positive reinforcement and encouragement while also softening the blow of being corrected or criticized.

Confident

Confident people speak with authority, carry themselves with authority, and give others confidence that they know what they are doing. As a corporateneur, you're moving from a corporate career where you know the rules into the entrepreneurial realm where there will be more unknowns than knowns. That can rattle one's self-confidence.

You must lean into your strengths and proceed along your path with the goals always out in front of you. There will be enough roadblocks along the way, so you can't afford to put any unnecessary ones in your way, like lacking self-confidence.

"Self-doubt is very common. It's part of the human condition," Ken shares. "But lack of confidence will get in your way, so if you are struggling with it, my advice is to 'fake it until you make it.' Remembering past victories, accumulating more of them as you build your enterprise, and always leaning into your strengths will help build greater self-confidence."

Generous

When starting a new business, you rarely can afford to be too generous with people's salaries, but generosity goes far beyond being generous with money. It's generosity of spirit and time. A generous person listens. They share time and are open with others, so others can be open with them.

Ken made a practice of keeping his office door open so people felt welcome to stop by and shoot the breeze. He wanted people in the company to grow in their work and succeed as a whole person. He gave them opportunities to try new jobs and expand their responsibilities. He took great pride when they succeeded.

"Traditional companies tend to measure everything in numbers on the ledger, reducing costs and increasing margins," Ken says. "While those numbers are always important when running a business, the corporateneur needs to broaden their scope. They must be dedicated to bringing more value to their customers and business partners. They also need to bring more value to the people working for them. A little time and attention can go a long way in making people working for you feel valued. The ROI on that is immeasurable."

People Person

All these qualities—trust, curiosity, forthrightness, self-awareness, empathy, confidence, and generosity—add up to being a person who people want to have a relationship with. All businesses, at their heart, are people businesses—created by people, for people, and delivered through people. Whatever the product or service offered, it's secondary to the company's people.

A people person wants everyone to win and uses their inner power and strength to help all achieve it.

SMELL THE ROSES

Ken admits he can be a workaholic. Even his hobbies—like ballooning, sailing, team sports, fly-fishing, and golf—have a work element, since it takes work to achieve any level of competency. He gives his wife, Amber, credit for helping him slow down and take time to "smell the roses."

She brought beauty into his life, not just in her person but in her soul. She was spiritually attuned and helped Ken tap his spiritual power. He always understood that having a positive attitude was critical to success in all aspects of life, including business, but Amber introduced him to the law of attraction, a philosophy that positive thoughts bring positive results and negative thoughts result in negative outcomes. Over the years, he saw it manifest in many relationships and experiences.

Whether it was Ken's innate positive outlook, the law of attraction, or mere destiny, he saw over and over again that good things happened around him, not just for himself and those closest to him but also flowing out in concentric circles. And when bad things happened, he always found the good hidden within.

Perhaps the greatest humanity lesson for all aspiring corporate-neurs goes back to a lesson from childhood: "Do unto others as you would have them do unto you."

Ken's Key Takeaways

- The corporateneur's business model should follow a relationship model rather than a transactional model to grow a sustainable, lasting business. A business based on trusted relationships with customers and business partners is a business made to last.

- Bad people can be good at business, but bad people don't have the people skills to create a relationship business.

- The corporateneur needs strong people skills to create a relationship business. Qualities such as being trustworthy, curious, a good listener, forthright, self-aware, empathetic, confident, and generous are necessary to form good relationships in business.

 ## Your Corporateneur Road Map

1. Taking on the responsibility of running your own business requires a heavy dose of humanity. Are you ready?

2. There are no pure introverts or extroverts. Everyone has a combination of both qualities, and no matter where on the introversion-extroversion scale you are, you can develop the weaker side. You should "fake it until you make it."

CHAPTER 19

The Corporateneur Leader

"Would you like to ride in my beautiful balloon?
Would you like to glide in my beautiful balloon?
We could float among the stars together, you and I
For we can fly, we can fly
Up, up and away
My beautiful, my beautiful balloon."

—JIMMY WEBB

347

The 5th Dimension sings about a balloon in their 1967 hit song. Seeing a hot-air balloon in the sky or riding in it to "glide among the stars" has a magical quality. We may know the science behind it—that hot air is lighter than cold air—yet it remains magical to behold.

So too is the quality of leadership that enables a business enterprise to soar. We can see it and its effects, but what it is and how a great leader works remains a mystery, though not for want of trying to unravel it.

Every year, thousands of books on leadership are written—Amazon lists over sixty thousand titles under *Business Management/Leadership*—and academics spend countless hours researching the subject and publishing papers.

Every academic business program teaches it, including some 250 MBA programs devoted exclusively to it, plus another hundred-plus online master's degree programs. In addition, North American corporations invested $165.3 billion in leadership training in 2020, according to TrainingIndustry.com.

Yet for all these efforts to make business leaders, McKinsey gives leadership-training programs a failing grade. They fail because such training is out of context, decoupled from real work, and underestimates the difficulty of changing people's mindsets and behavior. And leadership-training results also aren't measured effectively.

A Harvard Business School study concurs, finding that only 10 percent of corporate leadership-training programs are effective. The authors, Michael Beer et al., call it "The Great Training Robbery."

Despite all the attention that leadership is given and the valiant efforts employed to develop it, leadership remains a conundrum.

"Executive research on leadership behavior during the past half century has yielded many different behavior taxonomies and a lack of clear results about effective behaviors," wrote Gary Yukl, professor at the University of Albany. "It is important to recognize that observable leadership behaviors are not the same as skills, values, personality traits or roles. These other constructs can be useful for understanding effective leadership, but they differ in important ways from observable behaviors."

In other words, we have a lot of data and many theories about leadership, but some people just "have it" and some don't. It's called the great man theory. Apologies for it sounding sexist, but it was proposed by nineteenth-century historian and philosopher Thomas Carlyle.

The great man theory suggests that great leaders are born with certain traits that set them apart so that they ascend to roles of power and authority. Carlyle also theorized that great leaders arise when the need for them is greatest, implying some supernatural agency at work.

Today most academics in business management and social psychology reject the great man theory and state emphatically, "Leaders are made, not born." They back up their assumption with numerous studies that prove anyone can develop greater leadership traits, defined by behavioral scientist professor Paul Hersey as "working with and through others to achieve objectives." However, developing greater leadership traits isn't the same as being a great leader.

In Hersey and Ken Blanchard's book *Management of Organizational Behavior*, they conceived the concept of *situational leadership* to break apart and analyze specific leadership traits. Hersey trademarked his theories as the *situational leadership model*, which he taught not just to MBA students but to executives through the Center for Leadership Studies founded in 1969 and running strong today. The center claims to have trained fourteen million leaders in the situational leadership model and has been used by more than 70 percent of *Fortune* 500 companies.

Also in the late '60s and more than a decade after his passing, the company Dale Carnegie founded launched its own leadership-training program, and numerous other firms and academic institutions have followed suit with executive leadership-training.

There is no question that specific management-leadership skills can be taught. Ken would define them as the science of building, managing, and leading a business, including those aspects related to organization, process, strategy, and discipline.

However, the art of success in leading business—intuition, flexibility, innovation, humanity—is not so easily taught. Being gifted in the art of leadership is part and parcel of an individual's character, makeup, and mindset. This may explain the high failure rate of leadership-training programs that McKinsey and Harvard observed and why there remains a huge leadership gap in business.

In a recent study conducted by leadership consulting firm DDI, some 77 percent of organizations reported a lack of leadership talent, with 83 percent saying developing leaders at all levels of the corporation is a priority. However, only 11 percent of organizations reported having a "strong" or "very strong" leadership bench to move into increasingly responsible positions, according to DDI's 2021 Global Leadership Forecast.

If made-not-born proponents are right, then one would expect to see a significantly higher return on investment in leadership MBAs and executive-training programs.

LEADERS NEED SELF-AWARENESS

Emerging from what some might call the leadership-training boon-doggle are reputedly more scientific approaches to help people identify their specific personality strengths and weaknesses so they can develop their unique leadership talents. They include the widely used OCEAN theory of five key personality traits—openness to experience, conscientiousness, extroversion, agreeableness, and neuroticism.

The Gallup organization took a different approach based upon the work of educational psychologist Donald Clifton. Besides public-opinion polling, Gallup has a whole training, coaching, and consulting division based on the CliftonStrengths assessment, formerly known as the Clifton StrengthsFinder.

Some 28.4 million people have taken the hour-long Clifton-Strengths assessment, with the basic report giving a measure of one's top leadership talents within four domains: executing, influencing, relationship building, and strategic thinking. A more detailed report breaks down particular talents into thirty-four themes. For example, under *strategic thinking*, it measures analytic capability, ideation, and futuristic outlook, and under *influencing*, it assesses skills of activation, command, and communication.

All these personality assessment tools are well and good, and they certainly can be helpful to some people at certain points in their lives. But for the corporateneur of a certain age and who's put time in developing their careers, Ken wonders how helpful they can be.

"If you don't know who you are and you don't understand what your personal strengths and weaknesses are by the age of forty or so, you might not be cut out to start your own business," he says. "Self-awareness is a required superpower for the corporateneur."

CONTEXT IS KEY

The McKinsey leadership study underscores the critical component of context through which leadership is exercised. Specifically, "A brilliant leader in one situation does not necessarily perform well in another," the authors wrote. "Too many training initiatives we come across rest on the assumption that one size fits all … skills or style of leadership."

The authors continued:

> Focusing on context invariably means equipping leaders with a small number of competencies (two to three) that will make a significant difference in performance. Instead, what we find is a long list of leadership standards and a complex web of dozens of competencies. What managers and employees often see is an "alphabet soup" of recommendations.

In other words, trainees come out with a long to-do list. Recall Ken's story of Bob in Chapter 9, whom Ken taught how to make the leap from aiming to be the best player on the team to being the best coach, using the Eisenhower Grid model to identify precisely where he should focus his time and energy on business development. Ken is all for simplifying leadership competencies.

A brilliant leader in one situation does not necessarily perform well in another.

To do that, he focuses on the end goal of what the leader needs to achieve, rather than trying to fix what's missing in one's leadership toolbox. Rather than a top-down, fix-the-leader approach typical in leadership-training programs, Ken's process starts with the end in mind and works up to the means needed to achieve it.

"The corporateneur has three constituencies to lead: employees, business partners, and clients/customers. Each has a different context;

each has a different set of expectations and hoped-for results from their implicit agreement to be led," Ken says. "The end goal of leadership is to influence people to achieve specific goals. To do that, you need to help make your goals the individual's own. It shouldn't be so hard as long as you keep the context front and center."

Unlike in a corporate setting where the groups of people you lead—employees, business partners, and customers—are often pre-selected, the corporateneur establishing a new company gets to self-select the different groups to be led.

At the highest level, what will bring different people within your company's orbit are its mission, vision, values, and promises as communicated by the founder/leader who stands behind them and always lives up to them. Being a trustworthy leader is essential, so you've got to "talk the talk and walk the walk" every day and in every way.

Leadership requires good communication skills—talking the talk—but equally important is setting an example and showing others how to walk alongside you. Being a "stand-up guy or gal" best describes the leader's character—someone people can lean on, who has their back and who can be trusted to do the right thing when times are good or bad.

Leading Your Staff

A new company starts with a clean slate. The corporateneur gets to choose the players on their team. It is an opportunity to bring people alongside you who not only have the skill set needed but also believe in the greater purpose of the company you're creating. In hiring, you're not just filling a vacant slot. You want someone who will give all they've got to do what needs doing now and in the future. They've got to believe in the mission.

In hiring, Ken looked for specific competencies, but he also recognized that technical competencies and skill sets can be learned. The softer skills—like being a team player, stick-to-itiveness, and willingness to step up to new challenges—weighed more heavily than a candidate's specific skill set.

Throughout his career, he'd seen many exceptionally capable individuals fail because they didn't have the right personality, temperament, or just plain willingness to take on the full scope of responsibilities to get the whole job done, not just the technical piece of it.

If your employees stand behind the company's mission, values, and promises, they'll stand behind you and do whatever is required to fulfill the mission, values, and promises.

Leading Your Business Partners

The company mission, values, and promises will also be critically important in selecting your business partners. You want to ensure their mission and values align with yours so that your partners will support yours and vice versa.

For example, Rohl found its best partners, both suppliers and dealers, were smaller family-owned companies. In running a family business, Ken intimately knew the strengths of other family businesses, so they already had common ground.

He also found family businesses tended to have more at stake in working together—greater levels of commitment—than bigger corporations that look only at the bottom line. It allowed Rohl to develop closer relationships with business partners beyond just business.

But business was still priority number one, so Ken kept his partners' and his own company's business objectives top of mind as he aimed to lead all to greater mutual success. He put it together in a simple formula: Be different. Be profitable. Be easy.

Ken and his entire team were always looking for ways to be different from other suppliers' customers and other dealers' suppliers. They sought ways to help their suppliers and dealers make more money by working with Rohl, and they aimed to make Rohl the easy choice to work with among the field of competitors.

And another leadership principle Ken followed in developing business relationships was to "Be important to a few, not the many." Rohl was always a niche brand serving a niche market with products from a handpicked number of niche suppliers and selling through a carefully selected niche of retail dealers.

As Rohl's popularity with high-end homeowners and designers grew and dealer demand to stock its line increased, the company found it needed to curate its selection of stocking dealers, directing the smaller ones to regional distributors rather than trying to maintain individual dealer arrangements with each.

As the business grew, its ability to uphold its mission, value, and promises was threatened if it had too many small dealers. So tough decisions had to be made. Ultimately everyone benefited from the decision, and Rohl was able to maintain the goodwill and trust it had built up with those smaller redirected dealers. Business didn't suffer; it only continued to grow.

Leading Your Customers

Rohl's mission, vision, and promises were critical to drawing the right consumers to the company's brands as well.

"We never had a big budget for consumer advertising," Ken reflects. "But we kept visible in the shelter books, like *Architectural Digest* and *Metropolitan Home*, which higher-end customers, attuned to their homes and design, were most likely to read. We organized our placements and schedules so we could stagger and overlay our image across publications to create a 'mirage' effect and keep our budget in line.

"The same strategy was used when internet advertising and social media became more prominent. We always aimed to position our ads and posts to be important to the few who were going to matter to us," he continued.

Rohl also depended upon its dealers to influence the most high-potential/high-performing customers, so a good deal of its leadership was directed to influence the influencers through storytelling, education, and training.

The influence-the-influencer efforts helped the individual dealers and salespeople look like heroes to their customers because they carried and sold the top-of-the-line Rohl brand. It impressed the most discerning customers, and it reinforced the dealers' investment in Rohl.

Ken's Key Takeaways

- Part of the skill set required to lead your company can be taught. It's the science of leadership, including organization, process, strategy and discipline. The art of leadership, however, is not so easily acquired, including intuition, flexibility, innovation and humanity. If these soft skills are lacking, the corporateneur is at risk of failing in his or her most essential leadership role.

- Instead of taking a top-down, fix-the-leader approach in developing your leadership profile, use a bottom-up approach where you focus on the ends in mind, then work backward to the type of leadership you need to achieve those ends.

- The corporateneur leader has three different groups to lead, each requiring a different leadership model: employees, business partners and clients/customers. The corporateneur leader must be the influencer-in-chief across all three constituencies.

 ## Your Corporateneur Road Map

1. Self-awareness is a required superpower for the corporateneur. Do a thoughtful and honest SWOT analysis on your leadership qualities, then validate your assessment with people who know you well, such as your life partner, trusted co-workers, colleagues, and advisors.

2. Think back on the excellent leaders you saw in action and the outstanding leadership qualities they had. What can you learn, adapt and put into your leadership toolbox?

3. Do a situational assessment of times in your corporate career when you led a group, reflecting on your strengths and weaknesses at critical times in the process. What qualities and characteristics made for success? What would you do differently if you could do it over? How has your leadership style changed over the years?

Leaning into Your Corporateneur Strengths

"You've always had the power, my dear, you just had to learn it yourself."

—GLINDA IN *THE WIZARD OF OZ*

A hot-air balloon plays a pivotal role in the climactic final scene of the children's classic movie *The Wizard of Oz*. As the Wizard prepares to take Dorothy back to Kansas in his balloon, Toto jumps out of the basket, and Dorothy follows him, fearing he'd be left behind.

Of course, the inevitable happens, and the Wizard, who doesn't know how to operate the balloon, takes off leaving Dorothy and Toto behind. Suddenly the deus ex machina–like Glinda the Good Witch of the North appears and reveals that Dorothy always had the power to return, but she needed to go through trials and tests to learn it.

The movie and original book are a coming-of-age story, a traditional literary archetype also called a bildungsroman—from the

359

German *Bildung* (education) and *roman* (novel). The genre follows the protagonist-hero through a series of events and experiences that bring about personal transformation.

You, as a corporateneur, are on such a bildungsroman journey, which will try you and test you but ultimately transform you. No matter where you are on your life's journey, you have an adventure ahead.

In preparing this book, we've assumed you, our reader, are in the place that Ken found himself in middle age: successful as a midcareer professional but not seeing opportunities for growth if he continued on the corporate path. He wanted to test his mettle and find new meaning and purpose in his professional life. There was only one way to do that: get off the corporate career track and start a business.

The research shows that the most successful, sustainable businesses are started by founders in the same place and that it is a path that more midcareer professionals are taking. Psychologist Erik Erikson provides the underlying reason in his theory of psychosocial development.

In middle age, people desire to find more meaning in their lives. He theorizes that people between the ages of forty and sixty-five are at a time of life when they have a choice to slip into stagnation or rise above to "generativity"—leaving one's mark on the world.

Starting a business is an example of generativity. Individuals launch businesses to find more value in their lives and leave a legacy. It's a life stage when people feel most productive and capable to give back and make a lasting contribution. They are personally smarter, stronger, and more resilient. They've learned from past mistakes and have a greater capacity to learn and grow in the future.

B. C. Forbes, who founded his eponymous magazine in 1917 at the age of thirty-seven, understood the advantage age and maturity gave to company founders:

> For my part, I rather distrust men or concerns that rise up with the speed of rockets. Sudden rises are sometimes followed by equally sudden falls. I have most faith in the individual or enterprise that advances step by step. A mushroom can spring up in a day; an oak takes fifty years or more to reach maturity. Mushrooms don't last; oaks do.

If you've dreamed about starting a business but feel the opportunity has passed you or entrepreneurship is strictly a young person's game, think again. Now is the optimum time to take the next step.

NOW IT'S YOUR TURN

As you plan your exit strategy from corporate life to entrepreneurship—becoming a corporateneur—you bring many inherent advantages with you. You've learned a lot navigating the corporate world, honed your professional skills, filled your résumé with accomplishments and achievements, and made connections that will last. But as good a training ground as the corporate world is for the aspiring entrepreneur, nothing really prepares you for the challenges you'll face once you cut the cord.

Loss of a weekly paycheck aside, which is formidable since by midcareer you've acquired a lifestyle and financial responsibilities that may be at risk, you'll be challenged and tested at every turn. Hopefully, Ken's story and advice have prepared you for what you are about to undertake as you make your plan and work your plan.

At the same time, your journey will be your own, though with Ken's guidance and the lessons he's learned, you have some guideposts along the way so you don't have to learn it the hard way.

Ken has found new meaning in the later phase of life by mentoring young and not-so-young entrepreneurs. Everyone that he has interacted with and advised over the years has come away better for it, and that is the best legacy that any person can leave, in business or otherwise.

Facing the first day as you set out on your corporateneur journey, you'll need to be organized to manage your time, your most valuable resource, for the greatest return on investment. You'll need to plan each day, each week, each month, and so on, with as much rigor and diligence as you do in developing your initial business plan. You'll need discipline and a process to work your daily plan, taking incremental steps each day toward the realization of the goals in your business plan.

You'll also need multiple strategies to achieve your goals. According to the *Oxford Dictionary*, a strategy is nothing more than "a plan of action or policy designed to achieve a major or overall aim."

For the corporateneur, the plan of action is the processes carried out to achieve the major goals and overall aims of the business. Strategy needs to start with the overall mission and vision for the company and then work back to all the different ways and means the mission and vision are achieved.

But as you work your plan with strategy and processes, you also need flexibility to change course if you don't see the expected or needed results. Flexibility will also be needed if you discover your business plans achieve positive results beyond your imagining. In that case, it's time to double down on the highest-potential, highest-performing strategies and processes.

For all your planning and preparation, you will also need to tap your God-given intuition. It can be an early warning sign when things are going south and you need a reliable guide to finding true north. Reason and rational thought processes combined with facts, figures, and research can take you only so far. Intuition provides insights that a worksheet or mathematical formula never can. Innovation springs from the sixth sense of intuition.

Above all, bring your humanity to your new enterprise. Business is always personal. Businesses are built on relationships. And the foundation of all relationships—professional and personal—is the same: trust, forthrightness and honesty, empathy and generosity.

> **Business is always personal. Businesses are built on relationships.**

You can correct bad business decisions. Weak strategies can be adjusted. Broken processes can be fixed, and ineffective plans altered. But there's no coming back when the relationships on which your business depends are fractured.

Good people form good relationships wherever they go. And good things come to good people. And that is Ken's and my wish for you. Our goal was to help you realize your dreams of starting a business and, through that, realize your greater life's mission. Go out and make the most of your potential. Get ready to take off.

Ken's Life Lesson Learned ——

Your Future Starts Now

Forty years ago, I penned a poem titled "Starting Plan," expressing my belief that there must be something more beyond the corporate world of meetings, deadlines, and managing someone else's fortune. There must be more, new pursuits that "bring an essence to life beyond just changes."

That inspiration manifested itself into a ripple ... that became a wave ... that became a tsunami of a business that touched an industry, many lives, and most happily, my family.

Now I sit reflecting on the chapters of my corporateneur life and created *The Corporateneur Plan* to kindle your imagination with stories that motivate and that can shortcut your path to success.

The adage "Nothing happens until somebody sells something" underlies the truth of what drives every action in every walk of life.

By reading this book, you've triggered an openness to change, to achieve something more and find a fertile field for creative change.

Your dreams don't have to be glorious; in fact, I didn't really think much beyond my product niche and how it would be fun to show my enthusiasm for its uniqueness. Industry influencers shared my enthusiasm and helped make the product ubiquitous.

Yes, it was the pullout kitchen faucet and, by the way, followed by the farmhouse kitchen sink and "total immersion showerheads." My world was the kitchen and bath. Your world is the universe and an idea you can energize into something world class—or at least the class of the world you're serving.

Poetry, much like other creative outlets, inspires emotions that trigger the pursuit of romance, the contemplation of nature, and a host of thoughts that set us on new paths.

Robert Frost said it best:

Two roads diverged in a wood, and I—
I took the one less traveled by,
And that has made all the difference.

Best of luck as you set your course on making a difference. Fly away in your hot-air balloon. Just do it!

Rohl Family circa 2015: Mark Rohl, Lou Rohl, Amber Rohl, Ken Rohl, and Greg Rohl

BIBLIOGRAPHY

Agor, Weston. *The Logic of Intuitive Decision Making: A Research-Based Approach for Top Management*. Praeger, 1986.

Azoulay, Pierre, et al. "Age and High-Growth Entrepreneurship." *American Economic Review: Insights* 2, no. 1 (2020).

Bagby, D. Ray, and Leslie E. Palich. "Using Cognitive Theory to Explain Entrepreneurial Risk-Taking: Challenging Conventional Wisdom." *University of Illinois at Urbana-Champaign's Academy for Entrepreneurial Leadership Historical Research Reference in Entrepreneurship* (1995).

Barker, Eric. "Which Professions Have the Most Psychopaths? The Fewest?" *Barking Up the Wrong Tree*. September 14, 2015. https://bakadesuyo. com/2012/11/professions-most-fewest-psychopaths/.

Beer, Michael. "Who Is to Blame for 'The Great Training Robbery'?" *HBS Working Knowledge*. July 25, 2016. https://hbswk.hbs.edu/item/ whose-to-blame-for-the-great-training-robbery.

Brady, Tom. *The TB12 Method: How to Do What You Love, Better and for Longer*. Simon & Schuster, 2020.

Brinckmann, Jan, et al. "Should Entrepreneurs Plan or Just Storm the Castle? A Meta-Analysis on Contextual Factors Impacting the Business

Planning-Performance Relationship in Small Firms." *Journal of Business Venturing* 25 (2010).

Bryar, Colin, and Bill Carr. *Working Backwards: Insights, Stories, and Secrets From Inside Amazon.* St. Martin's Press, 2021.

Burke, Andrew E. et al. "Multiple Effects of Business Plans on New Ventures." *Journal of Management Studies* (March 5, 2009).

Carnegie, Dale. *How to Win Friends and Influence People.* Pocket Books, 1998.

Carroll, Ryder. *The Bullet Journal Method: Track the Past, Order the Present, Design the Future.* Zaltbommel, Netherlands: Van Haren Publishing, 2018.

Cavalea, Dana. *Habits of a Champion.* Dana Cavalea Companies, 2019.

Cialdini, Robert. *Influence: The Psychology of Persuasion*, Revised Edition. Revised, Harper Business, 2006.

Covey, Stephen. *The 7 Habits of Highly Effective People: 30th Anniversary Edition.* The Covey Habits Series. Anniversary, Simon & Schuster, 2020.

De Jong, Marc, et al. "The Eight Essentials of Innovation." *McKinsey Quarterly* (April 2015).

Di Fabio, Annamaria, and Maureen E. Kenny. "Promoting Well-Being: The Contribution of Emotional Intelligence." *Frontiers in Psychology* (August 17, 2016).

Drucker, Peter Ferdinand. *Concept of the Corporation.* John Day Co., 1972.

Erikson, Erik, and Joan Erikson. *The Life Cycle Completed.* Extended Version, W. W. Norton and Company, 1998.

Feser, Claudio, et al. "Decoding Leadership: What Really Matters." McKinsey & Company, February 22, 2019, https://www.mckinsey.com/featured-insights/leadership/decoding-leadership-what-really-matters.

Fritzon, Katarina, et al. *Corporate Psychopathy: Investigating Destructive Personalities in the Workplace.* Palgrave Macmillan, 2020.

Gast, Arne, et al. "Purpose: Shifting from Why to How." *McKinsey Quarterly,* April 22, 2020.

Gladwell, Malcolm. *Blink: The Power of Thinking without Thinking.* Annotated, Back Bay Books, 2007.

"Global Leadership Forecast 2021." DDI, https://www.ddiworld.com/global-leadership-forecast-2021.

Godin, Seth. *Purple Cow: Transform Your Business by Being Remarkable.* Gardners Books, 2004.

Hatten, Timothy S. *Small Business Management: Entrepreneurship and Beyond.* 6th ed. Cengage Learning, 2015.

Herhausen, Dennis, et al. "Re‐examining Strategic Flexibility: A Meta‐ Analysis of Its Antecedents, Consequences and Contingencies." *British Journal of Management* 32, no. 2 (June 25, 2020).

Hersey, Paul, et al. *Management of Organizational Behavior: Leading Human Resources.* Pearson, 2013.

Iyengar, Sheena S., and Mark R. Lepper. "When Choice Is Demotivating: Can One Desire Too Much of a Good Thing?" *Journal of Personality and Social Psychology* 79, no. 6 (2000).

Johnson, Mark W. et al. "Reinventing Your Business Model." *Harvard Business Review*, December, 2008.

Kahneman, Daniel. *Thinking, Fast and Slow*. Farrar, Straus, and Giroux, 2013.

Keen, Andrew. "Po Bronson on the Crisis of Creativity in American Business." *Harvard Business Review*, August 20, 2010.

Klein, Gary. *Sources of Power: How People Make Decisions*. 20th Anniversary ed. The MIT Press, 2017.

Kotler, Philip, and Kevin Lane Keller. *Marketing Management*. 15th ed. Pearson, 2016.

Kotler, Philip, et al. "Ending the War between Sales and Marketing." *Harvard Business Review*, July 20, 2017.

Kotler, Philip, et al. *Marketing 4.0: Moving from Traditional to Digital*. Wiley, 2016.

Kotler, Philip, et al. *Marketing 5.0: Technology for Humanity*. Wiley, 2021.

Kotler, Philip. "How to Develop a Marketing Strategy." The Marketing Strategist. YouTube, March 21, 2021. https://www.youtube.com/watch?v=ghFwpoH71NM.

Kotler, Philip. "Marketing and Value Creation." *Journal of Creating Value* 6, no. 1 (May 2020), SAGE Publications.

"Philip Kotler on Marketing's Higher Purpose." Kellogg Insight, May 11, 2019.

"Philip Kotler on Why the Four Ps Are Safe!" LeadersIn. YouTube, October 22, 2015. https://www.youtube.com/watch?v=X4T-a4AKMjQ.

"Philip Kotler: Marketing Strategy." London Business Forum. YouTube, September 5, 2008. https://www.youtube.com/watch?v=bilOOPuAvTY.

Martins, Luis L. et al. "Unlocking the Hidden Value of Concepts: A Cognitive Approach to Business Model Innovation." *Strategic Entrepreneurship Journal* 9 (2015).

Nielsen. "Build Trust to Build Trial: Trustworthy Channels Can Help." Nielsen, July 21, 2022. https://www.nielsen.com/insights/2022/build-trust-to-build-trial-trustworthy-channels-can-help.

Ohanian, Lee. "What Makes America Great? Entrepreneurship." *American Exceptionalism in a New Era*. Edited by Thomas W. Gilligan. Hoover Institution Press, 2018.

Porter, Michael. *Competitive Strategy: Techniques for Analyzing Industries and Competitors*. Illustrated. Free Press, 1998.

Robbins, Stephen, and Timothy Judge. *Organizational Behavior*. 19th ed. Pearson, 2022.

Rowan, Roy. *The Intuitive Manager*. Little, Brown and Company, 1986.

Sarasvathy, Saras D. "Q&A: Darden Professor Cracks the Code of How Great Entrepreneurs Think." Darden Ideas to Action. https://ideas.darden.virginia.edu/darden-professor-cracks-the-code-of-how-great-entrepreneurs-think.

Shepherd, Dean A., and Johan Wiklund. "Successes and Failures at Research on Business Failure and Learning from It." *Foundations and Trends in Entrepreneurship* 2, no. 5 (2006).

Simon, Herbert. *Models of My Life*. The MIT Press, 1996.

Sinek, Simon. *Start with Why: How Great Leaders Inspire Everyone to Take Action*. Reprint. Portfolio, 2011.

Sloan, Alfred. *My Years with General Motors*. Reissue. Currency, 1990.

"University of Toronto Study Finds Extroverts Enjoy Advantages in the Workplace." *University of Toronto News.* Accessed November 2, 2022. https://www.utoronto.ca/news/u-t-study-finds-extroverts-enjoy-advantages-workplace.

Watkin, Michael D. "Demystifying Strategy: The What, Who, How and Why." *Harvard Business Review*, September 10, 2007.

Wennberg, Karl. "Managing High-Growth Firms: A Literature Review." *International Workshop on "Management and Leadership Skills in High-Growth Firms."* Warsaw, May 6, 2013.

Yukl, Gary, et al. *Leadership in Organizations.* Pearson India Education Services Pvt. Limited, 2018.

ABOUT THE
AUTHORS

ABOUT KEN ROHL

K en Rohl is a corporateneur whose sixty-year business career is founded in Midwest roots, a liberal arts education, and strong family ties, and has included corporate management, building a family business, co-founding an omnichannel healthcare start-up, and nonprofit leadership positions with a local university and performing arts theater.

ABOUT PAMELA N. DANZIGER

S peaker, author, and market researcher Pamela N. Danziger is internationally recognized for her expertise on the world's most influential consumers: the American Affluent. She founded research firm Unity Marketing in 1992 and is a principal in The American Marketing Group consultancy.

She received the Global Luxury Award for top luxury industry achievers presented at the Global Luxury Forum in 2007 and was named to *Luxury Daily's* Luxury Women to Watch in 2013. She is a contributing columnist to *The Robin Report* and a senior contributor on Forbes.com.

Prolific writer and blogger, she's authored eleven books, including *Meet the HENRYs: The Millennials that Matter Most to Luxury Brands* and *Shops That POP! 7 Steps to Extraordinary Retail Success.*

Pam holds a B.A. in English Literature from Pennsylvania State University and an M.L.S. from the University of Maryland.

ABOUT GREG ROHL

reg Rohl is a writer, speaker, and consultant sharing the lessons learned from over thirty years successfully marketing luxury solutions in a commodity market. He is the founder of The Rohl Model, a learning and guidance service he shares with his brother Lou.